Best Practices in Management Accounting

Best Practices in Management Accounting

Edited by

Greg N. Gregoriou
Professor of Finance, State University of New York (Plattsburgh)
EDHEC Business School Research Associate, Nice, France

and

Nigel Finch
Senior Lecturer, The University of Sydney Business School

First published 2012 by
PALGRAVE MACMILLAN

Palgrave Macmillan in the UK is an imprint of Macmillan Publishers Limited,
registered in England, company number 785998, of Houndmills, Basingstoke,
Hampshire RG21 6XS.

Palgrave Macmillan in the US is a division of St Martin's Press LLC,
175 Fifth Avenue, New York, NY 10010.

Palgrave Macmillan is the global academic imprint of the above companies
and has companies and representatives throughout the world.

Palgrave® and Macmillan® are registered trademarks in the United States,
the United Kingdom, Europe and other countries.

ISBN 978–0–230–35836–2

This book is printed on paper suitable for recycling and made from fully
managed and sustained forest sources. Logging, pulping and manufacturing
processes are expected to conform to the environmental regulations of the
country of origin.

A catalogue record for this book is available from the British Library.

A catalog record for this book is available from the Library of Congress.

10 9 8 7 6 5 4 3 2 1
21 20 19 18 17 16 15 14 13 12

Printed and bound in the United States of America

Contents

Part III Intangibles and Non-Financial Performance Measures

Part IV Public Sector Management

List of Tables

List of Figures

Preface

The nature of business is change and evolution. Change in the way a firm interacts with its customers, suppliers, employees, and other external stakeholders, and evolution in the way that strategy unfolds due to technology, competition, regulation, markets and changing demographics. To study business is to breathe in this dynamic mix and hold it. To practise management is to breathe out and infuse the firm with new life, new ideas and new ways to help it reach its goals.

'What gets measured, gets managed' is one quote often attributed to the late Peter Drucker, author, business adviser and scholar. The measurement–management nexus is at the heart of management accounting as a science supporting managerial decision making. Given the rapidly changing and evolving landscape businesses exist within, the challenge for many firms is to identify what measurements are relevant at any point in time and what priorities should be taken in executing any management initiatives.

Since the 1970s, an ever-growing body of research and knowledge has accumulated to assist firms with the challenge of measuring or evaluating business performance and framing management initiatives as a response to steering strategy rather than just managing costs.

History has identified many successful firms and some common features among contemporary leaders are the performance measurement and management systems that lie at the heart of their business, and the ways in which tactics are driven and adapted to maximise not only stakeholder value but also concurrent goals, such as economic and environmental sustainability.

Today, this new management accounting paradigm is seen not only in multinational corporations, but also in small business, government agencies and the not-for-profit sector.

The objective of this book is not to provide an all-encompassing and definitive treatment of management accounting. Many books have been written by academics, practitioners and commentators that delve deeply into detail about cost accounting and management reporting systems. Instead, this book provides the reader with an accessible and practical introduction to the core issues and best practices in performance measurement and management by using case studies, commentary and analysis from international experts with experience in public, private and government sectors.

We hope this book will be read by business professionals who are focusing on developing greater awareness and expertise in performance measurement and management, and by business students looking to build a deeper expertise and speciality. We have sought to balance the need for detail with ease of understanding while covering a diverse range of business types and applications. We hope you will not only learn vital lessons from this book but also successfully apply this learning to the benefit of the organisations you own or manage as you lead through change and evolution.

Greg N. Gregoriou
Nigel Finch

Acknowledgements

We would like to thank Lisa von Fircks at Palgrave Macmillan for guiding us through the process. We would also like to thank Siew-Ching Lim for the excellent work in editing this manuscript. Thanks also for the anonymous referees who assisted in the selection of articles for this book and to each of the authors for their generous contribution of time, knowledge and expertise. While all care has been taken, neither the publisher nor the editors are responsible for the accuracy of each chapter written by the individual contributors.

Editor Biographies

Greg N. Gregoriou has published 42 books, 60 refereed publications in peer-reviewed journals, and 20 book chapters since his arrival at SUNY (Plattsburgh) in August 2003. Professor Gregoriou's books have been published by McGraw-Hill, John Wiley & Sons, Elsevier-Butterworth/Heinemann, Taylor and Francis/CRC Press, Palgrave Macmillan and Risk Books. His articles have appeared in the *Review of Asset Pricing Studies, Journal of Portfolio Management, Journal of Futures Markets, European Journal of Operational Research, Annals of Operations Research, Computers and Operations Research,* etc. He has also been quoted several times in the *New York Times* and the *Financial Times* of London. Professor Gregoriou is hedge fund editor and editorial board member for the *Journal of Derivatives and Hedge Funds,* as well as editorial board member for the *Journal of Wealth Management, the Journal of Risk Management in Financial Institutions, Market Integrity, IEB International Journal of Finance,* and the *Brazilian Business Review.* Professor Gregoriou's interests focus on hedge funds, funds of funds, and CTAs. He is an EDHEC Research Associate in Nice, France.

Nigel Finch has published more than 100 scholarly articles in the areas of accounting and financial decision making since commencing his academic career in 2005. Dr Finch is rated among the top 250 business authors in the world according to the Social Science Research Network (SSRN) and he is actively engaged in management education and business advisory in Australia and Asia. Dr Finch is the joint founding editor of the *Journal of Applied Research in Accounting and Finance,* editorial board member for *Journal of Intellectual Capital, Managerial Finance* and *Market Integrity* and co-author of *Fundamentals of Corporate Finance* (Pearson Education). Dr Finch is a senior lecturer in accounting at the University of Sydney Business School and a Visiting Fellow at Macquarie Graduate School of Management, Australia. His professional qualifications include membership of CPA Australia and the Institute of Chartered Accountants in Australia.

Contributor Biographies

Max L. Baker is a Lecturer in Accounting at the University of Sydney Business School. Prior to joining academia, Max worked at PricewaterhouseCoopers and Macquarie Bank. His research explores corporate social responsibility practices and includes active participation in conferences such as the Australasian Conference on Social and Environmental Accounting Research and the Accounting and Finance Association of Australia and New Zealand (AFAANZ/IAAER) Conference. Max has published widely in prestigious publications including the *Social and Environmental Accountability Journal* and the *Accounting, Auditing & Accountability Journal*.

Angel Barajas is Associate Professor of Financial Management at the Department of Accountancy and Finance, University of Vigo, Spain. He is visiting lecturer at the Instituto de Empresa Business School, where he teaches Managerial Accounting for Sport in the Masters in Sport Management course, and a researcher with the Spanish Economic Observatory for Sport (Observatorio Económico del Deporte). Angel's professional experience includes stints as internal auditor and consultant for PYMES, as member of the Board of a Press Distribution Company and as advisor to the Celta de Vigo General Manager.

Noah P. Barsky is a Professor at the Villanova University School of Business (USA). He was formerly a visiting professor for INSEAD MBA (Europe) and visiting research scholar at the University of Melbourne (Australia). His research and teaching focus on performance measurement, business planning, risk assessment and contemporary financial reporting issues. Dr Barsky delivers executive programs, management training and educational seminars for various business organisations and professional associations. His professional experience includes practice in the fields of accounting and finance as an analyst, auditor and business consultant.

Monica Bartolini is Assistant Professor of Management Accounting at the University of Bologna, lecturing in Financial Accounting and Management Accounting at the Alma Graduate School. In 2000–2001, she was Visiting Scholar at the Lean Enterprise Research Centre at Cardiff Business School, participating in the LEMA (Lean Management Accounting) Research Program and in '3DayCar', a research initiative collectively sponsored by the UK Engineering and Physical Sciences Research Council and 22 automotive companies. Her research focuses on strategic cost management, lean accounting, management control systems and international accounting standards.

David A. Brown is an Associate Professor in Management Accounting at the University of Technology, Sydney. His expertise is in the design and use of accounting and other management control systems. David has been involved in collaborative research projects with a number of Australia's largest companies in the sectors of banking, professional services, mining, energy and consumer products.

Mandy Man-sum Cheng is an Associate Professor at the Australian School of Business, University of New South Wales, where she teaches management accounting at undergraduate, postgraduate and MBA levels. Mandy's research focuses on behavioural accounting, with particular expertise in performance measurement systems, capital investment analysis and business negotiations. She has published extensively in prominent research journals, and is actively involved in the accounting research community.

Suresh Cuganesan is Director of the Centre for Enterprise Performance and Professor in Accounting at Swinburne University, Melbourne, as well as Visiting Professor at the Macquarie Graduate School of Management. Before his academic career, Suresh worked in the areas of management consulting and institutional banking, where he led research, strategy analysis, business development and large-scale project leadership. His research interests include strategic costing, business performance and intellectual capital measurement and management, and the design of management control systems. He is a member of the editorial boards of leading national and international academic journals, and has been awarded Australian Research Council funding for research.

Julie Foreman has taught for 11 years at undergraduate and postgraduate levels in various accounting and finance subjects, but primarily within management accounting and strategic cost management. Prior to her academic career, she has had extensive industry experience, the most recent of which was with Telstra. She has consulted widely in several areas, including funds management, financial products and costing. Her research interests are in strategic performance measurement and corporate governance. Her PhD thesis was in the area of sport governance and examined links between governance and performance.

Toomas Haldma is a Professor of Accounting and Dean of the Faculty of Economics and Business Administration at the University of Tartu, Estonia. His teaching activities as well as his research interests centre on the areas of management accounting, performance measurement and management, and management control in business and public sector organisations, in which he has published internationally and nationally. He has also served as a member of the supervisory board and as a consultant to various Estonian companies and public organisations.

Zahirul Hoque is currently a Professor of Accounting at the Faculty of Law and Management, La Trobe University, where he also served as Associate Dean (Research). His research interests include governance and performance management, public sector reforms, accounting for not-for-profit organisations, management accounting, qualitative case study research and critical discourse analysis. He was formerly Professor of Accounting at Deakin University, Professor and Head of the School of Business at Charles Darwin University) and Visiting Professor at Babson College. The author of numerous accounting texts, he is also the founding Editor-in-Chief of the *Journal of Accounting & Organizational Change*. He serves on the editorial boards of several journals including *Accounting, Auditing & Accountability Journal*, *British Accounting Review* and *AIUB Journal of Business and Economics*.

Jayanthi Kumarasiri is a lecturer at the Faculty of Business and Enterprise, Swinburne University, where she teaches financial and management accounting at both undergraduate and postgraduate levels. Before joining Swinburne, Jayanthi was a lecturer at the Department of Accountancy, the University of Sri Jayewardenepura, Sri Lanka. She is currently reading for her doctorate.

Kertu Lääts is a Lecturer in the Department of Accounting at the University of Tartu, Estonia, where she teaches management accounting, cost accounting and financial analyses. Her research interests include management accounting change perspectives, the influence of information technology on management accounting and control and management accounting practices in Eastern Europe.

Pankaj M. Madhani is currently Assistant Professor at ICFAI Business School, Ahmadabad, India. He holds an MBA degree from Northern Illinois University and an MS in Computer Science from Illinois Institute of Technology, Chicago. With over 23 years' experience in the corporate sector and academia, he has published seven books in the areas of finance, strategy and ERP as well as numerous research papers in peer-reviewed national and international journals. His areas of interest include finance, technology in business and strategic management.

Teemu Malmi is a Professor at the Aalto University School of Economics, Finland. His teaching and research focus on managerial control systems, strategy implementation and cost and profitability accounting. Teemu is the editor of the *Finnish Journal of Business Economics* and serves on the editorial board of *Management Accounting Research, European Accounting Review* and *Abacus*.

Garry Marchant is Deputy Vice-Chancellor and Provost at Bond University. He was formerly Dean of Business, Technology and Sustainable Development at Bond University and Deputy Dean of Economics and Commerce at the University of Melbourne. He has also served on the faculties of the University of Connecticut, the University of Texas at Austin, the University of New South Wales and INSEAD (Europe). Professor Marchant has held positions with the Reserve Bank of Australia and Woolworth's (Australia) Ltd. His expertise lies within the areas of performance measurement and evaluation, strategy implementation, cost management and the use of accounting information for strategic decision-making. He was formerly a KPMG Research Fellow and recipient of a KPMG Research Grant, and is currently the recipient of both ARC Discovery and Linkage grants.

Klaus Möller is Chair of Management Accounting and Control at Georg-August-Universität Göttingen. Since 2004, he has been a guest lecturer at the University of Innsbruck, the European Business School and the Technical University, Munich. He has consulted on numerous industry projects for the Federal Ministry of Education and Research, the Federal Network Agency for Electricity, Gas, Telecommunications, Post and Railway, the Federal Institute for Occupational Safety and Health and the German Research Foundation. Professor Möller's research papers have received numerous accolades.

Evelyne Poincelot is an Associate Professor of Finance at the University of Burgundy's Department of Business Administration and Director of the Bachelor's Degree in Management. She holds a PhD in Management Sciences from the University of Burgundy, where she also completed her tenure dissertation. Her research expertise is in the area of Organisational and Corporate Finance.

Jim Rooney is a lecturer in Accounting at the University of Sydney Business School. Prior to his appointment, Jim had over 20 years' work experience in substantive and diverse financial services roles including outsourcing relationship management; mortgage operations; process improvement; risk management and change management. He was responsible for business unit leadership for service delivery entities ranging in size and service delivery scope of up to 600 personnel (local and offshore) and up to A$100 million annual revenue. He specialises in accounting research on management control of inter-organisational relationships and NFP organisations, as well as credit risk management.

Riccardo Silvi is Professor of Strategic Cost Accounting and Director of the Masters Programme in Accounting, Finance and Control at ALMA Graduate School, University of Bologna. He has been a visiting scholar at the University of Sydney and Babson College. He was formerly a co-director of the LEMA (lean management accounting) research program at the Lean Enterprise Research Center, Cardiff Business School. Riccardo's research focuses on strategic cost management and strategic management accounting and he has published widely in numerous prominent academic journals and books.

Franco Visani is Assistant Professor in Business Administration at the Faculty of Economics of Forlì, University of Bologna and also teaches at the MBA level in several Italian business schools. He was formerly a visiting scholar at the Innovative Manufacturing Research Centre in Cardiff, UK in 2006. His research interests focus on strategic cost management, supply chain management and lean accounting.

Gregory Wegmann is an Associate Professor of Management Accounting at the University of Burgundy's Department of Business Administration. He holds a PhD in 'Management Sciences' from the University of Paris 1, Panthéon-Sorbonne and completed a tenure dissertation at the University of Nice. From 2009 to 2011, Gregory was based at the French Consulate in Shanghai as Consul for Education. His research focuses on innovations in management accounting tools.

Overview of Chapters

1 The Rhetoric and Reality of Budget Participation

In recent years, many companies have adopted budgeting programmes that appear to shift decision control to employees. While firms may easily espouse participation, it is important to determine whether they have substantively shifted from hierarchical control towards greater employee empowerment. This chapter uses social network analysis to examine the structure of ties amongst managers involved in corporate budgeting at an apparel manufacturer. Results show how a process described as participatory can actually serve to reinforce traditional hierarchical control. The integrated data set provides a foundation for enriching academic and practitioner understanding of budget participation: namely, management communication and control systems are playing an increasingly important role in corporate strategy and accountability. This study demonstrates that senior management must be aware of the social structure underlying the firm's formal hierarchy. This research identifies important considerations regarding the tension inherent in balancing empowerment and control in the modern network organisation. Simply adopting 'best practices' does not ensure that a firm will meet its communication and performance goals. This case enhances the contemporary debate about whether empowerment and participation are being substantively adopted by organisations, or if such myths have become institutionalised as nicer-sounding ways to reinforce the hierarchical control of top management.

2 Inter-Organisational Relationships as a Complex Adaptive System

This chapter examines current accounting research on the evolution of management control mechanisms over the life of an inter-organisational relationship. With outsourcing being the most prevalent example, the organisational forms and complexity of the arrangements between otherwise independent entities continue to evolve in theory and practice. Following calls to investigate the use of controls within inter-organisational relationships, material progress has been made in understanding a number of the influences behind Management Control System (MCS) design. However, with the continued evolution of inter-organisational practice, the static analytical approach adopted in the existing accounting literature has been challenged, drawing attention to the dynamic nature of these relationships. We survey the accounting literature leading to increasing adoption of System Theory perspectives, tracing key drivers for increased consideration of this dynamic perspective in response to criticisms of the extant research literature. Thus the underlying insights of the chapter are that:

- The accounting literature has increasingly recognised the complex and dynamic nature of inter-organisational relationships, consistent with the supply chain literature;
- Recent theory development is starting to move away from a static perspective dominating prior accounting literature, highlighting the role and complexities of management control problems in driving change in inter-organisational control design;
- Systems Theory has the potential to support greater understanding of these dynamics:
  - Management control design co-evolves with the immediate environment within which the inter-organisational relationship operates;
  - There appear to be multiple path dependencies when analysing the evolution of management control in an inter-organisational relationship.

3 Management Accounting in a Lean Environment

The Lean Management philosophy is based on the idea that companies should set their strategies according to what customers really value, systematically banishing waste both within the firm and along the supply chain.

Many companies, when implementing Lean Management, complain that traditional Management Accounting Systems are unable to support these kinds of projects. At best, they are perceived as bureaucratic tasks, and at worst, they are considered a key constraint on both the acceptance and success of lean projects.

The failure of these traditional Management Accounting tools and techniques has led to management consultancies developing a range of Lean Accounting approaches that are nevertheless not entirely satisfactory either. In particular, they do not support analysis of the expected results of lean projects, which are crucial in obtaining top management commitment. Moreover, they still focus on the short term and on cost dimensions while neglecting the value creation potential of lean projects.

Thus, this chapter develops an innovative Lean Accounting model based on the Strategic Cost Management framework, more aligned to the specific needs of lean environments. In detail, this model is based on two main goals: (1) exploring the lean performance potential at the planning and commitment stages of a lean transformation; and (2) controlling lean management effects in terms of cost reduction and value creation, at the implementation and consolidation stages of an ongoing lean process.

4 What *Really* Happens with Performance Management Systems

Businesses invest considerable financial and human capital in performance measurement systems. About a decade ago, a holistic performance management framework to systematically examine the management control systems, tools and techniques used by organisations was outlined. This chapter applies that framework to consider how core management processes work together to enable or hinder *performance management* in large companies by analysing written descriptions prepared by senior and frontline managers about the performance management systems, processes, tools and techniques being used at their employers.

Although the elements and processes described in a typical performance management framework were pervasive, there was a great deal of diversity in their nature, use and timing. The findings show isolated use or particular processes, great deviation from expectations of performance management use, and a clear gap between the rhetoric of performance management and the actual use of these systems in practice. Further, performance management systems were frequently found to be misaligned with corporate and individual goals. Rewards were often not based on performance evaluations, or evaluations were not based on targets. Such breakdowns can impair strategy execution, as elements of performance management framework are not appropriately connected or because processes operate differently in practice than designed.

5 Recent Developments in Management Control Depiction

This chapter examines current research on the classification of management control mechanisms applicable to inter-organisational relationships, of which outsourcing is one incarnation. The underlying principles are, firstly, that the accounting literature has begun to recognise the dynamic nature of inter-organisational relationships and the potential benefits of a multidisciplinary path. Secondly, there has been a recent increase in the development of multidisciplinary theory-building efforts in response. Finally, the increasing sophistication of the emerging management control literature has the potential to shed light on the dynamics and diversity of inter-organisational relationships. This chapter explores the strengths and weaknesses of alternative representations of management control on our understanding of post-contract management control in an inter-organisational setting.

6 Corporate Social Responsibility and Sustainability Reporting

This chapter focuses on sustainability and extended reporting frameworks and investigates the motivation by organisations to adopt such frameworks. Starting with a definition of corporate social responsibility (CSR) and sustainability, the chapter provides a brief overview of the historical development of the concepts of sustainability by focusing on understanding stakeholders and their importance as a motivator for organisations to adopt sustainability reporting frameworks.

This chapter also provides a background to the development of new reporting frameworks and focuses on the development of one particular framework, the Global Reporting Initiative (GRI).

The key motivation for adopters of sustainability reporting frameworks is to attempt to communicate, to a wide variety of stakeholders, the firm's performance in achieving long-run corporate benefits, such as improved financial performance, increased competitive advantage, profit maximisation and the long-term success of the firm.

7 Management Accounting Practices for Sustainability

The issue of ecological sustainability is widely recognised as one of the major challenges faced in contemporary societies. A widely accepted view among many professionals and the general public is that companies – key players in the modern global economy – are responsible for addressing the threat to ecological sustainability. Governments and regulatory bodies across the world are also tightening rules and regulations to exert pressure on companies to become socially responsible. They are therefore compelled to look for strategies which enable them to run their businesses in a socially and environmentally sustainable manner while also delivering sound economic returns.

There is potential for management accounting to play a significant role in driving organisations towards both environmental and economic stability. This chapter reviews research investigating the performance benefits of using management accounting techniques to integrate environmental considerations into the business decision-making process. It discusses leading examples of companies which use advanced management accounting techniques such as capital budgeting, performance measurements and incentives to manage and execute environmental strategy. It also presents emerging evidence on how companies are approaching the challenge of managing carbon emissions and responding to climate change.

8   An Integrated Package of Environmental Management Control Systems

This chapter explores how an integrated package of management control systems can be designed and used to manage a variety of environmental issues. While the proliferation of external sustainability reports is perhaps the most visible accounting response to environmental issues, accounting may also serve an internal function for management as a means of defining environmental objectives and performance measures. Research suggests that accounting motivates environmentally responsible decision-making and improves awareness and individual conduct in environmental activities. However, little attention has been paid to understanding how management accounting can operate as an integrated element of a wider set of management controls in relation to environmental issues. This chapter presents a case study of a large Australian energy company, considered to be an exemplar of 'best practice'. The findings suggest that a comprehensive approach to managing environmental issues can be achieved through a well-developed package of management control systems. Moreover, the partnership between regulators and the organisation can enable 'responsive regulating' and self-regulation, making the task of both environmental regulators and organisations easier.

9 Efficiency Measurement for Supplier Selection and Control: A Data Envelopment Analysis Approach

In management accounting, several techniques are used for supplier evaluation and selection. Of these techniques, Total Cost of Ownership (TCO) is probably the best known, regardless of the fact that it is uncommonly applied. TCO is complex: its application requires the buying firm to determine (usually by doing an ABC analysis) the costs related to the acquisition, possession and use or service of a product. Additionally, the data requirements and situation-specific applications are major drawbacks of the technique. We identify Data Envelopment Analysis (DEA) as a management tool to overcome the shortcomings of TCO, and to help executives to improve the efficiency of their supplier selection and control. The results show that DEA is far easier and less expensive to apply, but it is only partially capable of supplying the results given in a TCO analysis. Although DEA can rank suppliers, it cannot provide specific information about the differences in their performance.

10 Intangible Assets: Value Drivers for Competitive Advantage

In the current business environment of globalisation and a demanding competitive paradigm, it is essential from a strategic management perspective to focus on the financial dimension of value associated with intangible assets to create sustainable long-term advantages. Some of the organisational assets valued by the market but overlooked by current accounting practices are intangibles. This chapter underlines the significance of intangible assets in the knowledge economy and presents a resource-based view perspective of intangible assets. Recognition and characteristics of various components of intangible assets are also highlighted. The chapter further presents the key issues pertaining to the management of intangible assets, focusing on identification and measurement practices for the measurement of intangible assets and identifies value drivers for intangible assets.

11 Strategic Performance Measurement Systems and Managerial Judgements

Strategic performance measurement systems such as the Balanced Scorecard have become increasingly popular among both public and commercial enterprises, but how useful are these systems in assisting executives to make business decisions? This chapter reviews and synthesises recent research from the behavioural management accounting discipline on the effects of strategic performance measurement systems on managerial judgements. In particular, this chapter focuses on common cognitive biases and challenges faced by managers when using these systems to evaluate managerial performance and to inform their strategic choices. It also provides suggestions on how decision biases can be overcome.

12 Non-Financial Indicators and Strategic Management Accounting

In this chapter, we present the Strategic Management Accounting concept and how it affects the evolution of management accounting. We explain that Anglo-Saxon instruments like the Balanced Scorecard and non-financial indicators are well-known in European countries, and the objective of Strategic Management Accounting tools is to articulate the relationship between planning and control decisions and non-financial metrics. In the USA contractual theories constitute the background of the Strategic Management Accounting stream and the Balanced Scorecard model. This chapter explains that in some firms in Northern Europe there are some specific Balanced Scorecards called 'Intellectual Capital Scorecards', which have been designed in the framework of knowledge-based theories.

The chapter also describes the results of a survey conducted in France that aims to test the usefulness of non-financial indicators in driving a firm's objectives. It demonstrates that French managers associate non-financial indicators with strategic objectives and concludes that the Balanced Scorecard is a useful tool to drive their company.

13 Management Tools for Evaluating Performance and Value Creation in Sports Organisations

The sports business is a multi-faceted one. It can be studied from many perspectives such as team competition (leagues), individual sports (tournaments), sports events and public promotion. It offers different products such as the competition, the spectacle, the image or a media platform, and creates intangible benefits. These specific features require management tools. This chapter presents different initiatives in which some managerial tools were used, and the best practices in management used by Sport England assist in understanding how to apply them.

The strategy map will be useful in the configuration of the Balanced Scorecard. The necessary adaptation of the Balanced Scorecard and some key performance indicators for sports business are proposed.

14 Measuring Performance in Government and Non-Profit Organisations: The Role of the Balanced Scorecard

Recent performance measurement literature advocates 'newer' forms of performance measurement system development, such as the Balanced Scorecard for government and non-profit organisations, that are oriented towards longer-term strategies and outcomes. This chapter outlines the development of Balanced Scorecards in government and non-profit organisations using some field study and empirical examples, mainly from Australia. The chapter concludes with some policy implications for public sector and non-profit sector worldwide.

15 Performance Measurement in the Public Sector: Evaluating Performance Measurement and Reporting in Health

Research on public sector performance measurement has highlighted its deficiencies. Over-reliance on financial measures and excessive non-financial metrics are just two of the problems identified. Concerns have also been raised within the field of practice. Some government agencies have started to shift from typical outcomes and outputs frameworks, while public sector agencies have engaged in innovative ways of measuring their performance and impact. This chapter draws on the authors' prior research to present and discusses leading examples of how organisations in the public sector can measure their productivity, effectiveness and efficiency, and significantly enhance the design and use of performance measurement systems.

16 The Balanced Scorecard as a Performance Management Tool for Museums

The recent accounting reforms in the public sector have paved the way for a more performance-oriented approach in the management of public sector organisations. This chapter examines the impact of the design and implementation of the Balanced Scorecard concept on the development of performance measurement and management of museums, focusing on a central state museum as a case study.

Part I
Budgeting and Control Systems

1
The Rhetoric and Reality of Budget Participation

Noah P. Barsky

1.1 Introduction

In recent years, the business literature has heralded the rise of the team-based, network-centered adaptive organisation as a response to dynamic competitive market forces and emerging technology. Corporate budgeting presents a salient context in which to study managerial networks because it is a routine, widely used, high-profile process that incorporates and impacts all organisational functions. Participatory or 'bottom-up' budgeting is an example of a mechanism adopted by firms to promote employee empowerment and cross-functional interaction. Firms adopt participatory budgeting programs to 'empower' employees by allowing the workforce to set performance targets and allocate resources, as documented as long as 50 years ago (Argyris, 1952).

When evaluating the evidence, it is imperative to recognise that management's decisions are not only driven by rationality and efficiency aims, but are also reflective of the firm's socio-political culture (Covaleski and Dirsmith, 1988). In many cases, firms adopt certain practices to gain legitimacy and conform with the norms of the business environment. That is, certain processes and programmes gain footholds not because they facilitate efficiency and meet the demands of the workplace, but rather because 'rationalised myths in the institutional environment' (i.e., management fads) exert pressure on organisations to develop the structures that reflect broader institutions. The adoption of common practices may offers the appearance of legitimacy to constituencies.

In the case of bottom-up budgeting and other participative processes, an important question about firms that have adopted these programs is whether the goal is to improve productivity and performance or to make some attempt to *appear* to conform with well-publicised trends

3

towards employee empowerment initiatives. Access to such data can 'pierce the veil' of formal workplace protocols to examine systematically how information actually flows among managers.

The primary espoused objective of budgeting is to create a detailed plan that guides managers in the acquisition and use of an organisation's resources in pursuit of business strategy. Most companies engage in at least an annual budgeting exercise in which managers attempt to forecast the firm's business prospects for the next fiscal year. Budgets often require multiple rounds of review, revision and negotiation across multiple levels in companies. When the plans and projected results are acceptable to senior management and the company's owners, the resulting budget is adopted to guide the next year's operations and serves as a basis for performance evaluation.

Budgeting is expected to provide many benefits to a company. It is a high-profile activity because it affects virtually all operating areas and support functions within the organisation. Consequently, every manager in a firm is affected in some way by budgets. Given this pervasive influence, budgeting offers several important benefits.

Budgeting formalises ideas and forecasts about the company's future operations. Budgets help firms to allocate capital in pursuit of its business strategy. They often highlight scarce resources and assist managers in directing these resources to the most financially rewarding activities and performance benchmarks for eventual results. Budgets help companies to coordinate and align the activities of departments and units.

Although a critical tool for effective business decision-making, budgeting frequently presents challenges. Many managers and employees view budgeting negatively, frequently associating it with excessive pressure related to unrealistic goals, unreasonable restrictions, authoritarian decision-making and subjectivity. Since budgets represent a financial plan, users can frequently fixate on target financial numbers rather than on business processes. Successful budgeting demands the substantive participation of all managers; otherwise, budgets can undermine employee initiative by discouraging new developments and actions that are omitted from the budget.

According to social network theory from the organisational sociology literature, central positions within the organisation's 'underlying' social structure provide unique access to critical information. Such access often translates into power and influence for the individuals occupying these positions in the network. For example, when information is centralised in the finance function, accountants can act as information brokers and gatekeepers that reinforce traditional 'monitoring' roles.

One common implementation difficulty that companies encounter is the ease with which the language of empowerment may be adopted without substantively transferring control and substantive influence to front-line management. In such cases, employees may be involved in the mechanical aspects of the process, but often feel as though their input was not substantively considered or incorporated into the budget.

While business press is replete with findings that suggest that participation should benefit a firm, this study demonstrates some frictions associated with participative processes in action in organisations. Specifically, the results show that 'capturing the language' of participation while maintaining a traditional 'command and control' emphasis can impair management credibility and undermine the effectiveness of processes such as participative budgeting (Jablonsky and Keating, 1998).

Many companies use participative budgeting to 'empower' employees. In recent years, many firms have adopted programs that elicit greater employee participation. Questions remain about whether top management substantively transfers decision control to rank and file employees. This study examines the structure of ties among managers in a budgeting process that was claimed to be participatory. The results show that while formal guidelines may require many managers to work on the budgeting process, influence can remain highly centralised.

Budgeting serves as a hallmark of the way that firms adapt (or appear to adapt) to the broader initiative towards employee empowerment. In this case, the surface rhetoric of bottom-up budgeting and employee involvement differs from the reality of top-down management control. Adopting participative processes without substantive commitment can be detrimental to employee morale and management credibility.

1.1.1 The role of decision rights in the definition of participation

This chapter also contributes to the broader literature on budget participation. In terms of participation, Vroom and Yetton (1973) provide a continuum to describe the varying levels of participation. At one endpoint, management may employ some autocratic control. At the other extreme, employees may be fully empowered to allocate resources. Between these points, a host of interactive processes exist which involve some input from employees and some exercise of authority by top management.

Decision rights can be defined as the final authority to direct outcomes in the budgeting process. Along a continuum, decision rights in participative budgeting can be categorised in three general conditions.

First, at one end of the continuum, top management may retain all rights and direct a purely top-down budget. Second, management may involve employees in a proposal or negotiation-based process, yet retain ultimate decision power. Third, at the other end of the continuum, management may fully vest decision rights into the hands of front-line managers and employees.

1.2   Budgetary influence and involvement

Figure 1.1 illustrates budget roles along two dimensions: influence and involvement. Influence, along the vertical axis, represents the extent to which an individual or group plays a role in determining budgetary *outcomes* (i.e., allocations). Involvement, along the horizontal axis, represents the extent to which an individual or group spends time and effort formulating budgets. Each employee or employee group could be scored from low to high along each dimension. For purposes of analysis, scores may be self-assigned or assigned by others in the workplace. Pairing the scores along the dimensions of influence and involvement places an individual or group into one of the four quadrants (or budgetary roles) depicted in the diagram, numbered in a left to right, top to bottom fashion.

Quadrant I includes inviduals who are characterised as *power brokers*: parties with relatively high degrees of influence, yet seemingly low levels

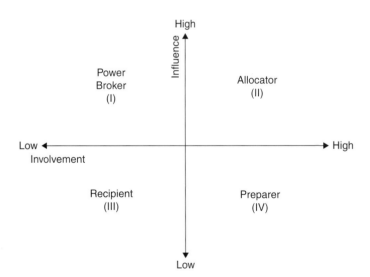

Figure 1.1   Budgetary influence and involvement roles

of involvement or time actively spent on the budgetary process. Those in this group often have strong political influence or 'behind-the-scenes' guidance on decision-making. Quadrant II is reserved for *allocators*, people who are highly visible in the budgeting process and who exert great influence. In many organisations, the Chief Financial Officer (CFO) often falls into the highest position of this quadrant.

Quadrant III captures parties with relatively low levels of influence and involvement. These people can best be characterised as budget *recipients*. In many organisations, this quadrant includes the greatest number of employees – namely those who receive budgetary allocations, yet spend little time crafting budgets and have little voice in apportionments. Such parties often include front-line employees, particularly those with no supervisory responsibilities or spending discretion.

Finally, Quadrant IV, represents *preparers* of budgets, those individuals who contribute significant amounts of time, yet who do not significantly affect final budgeting decisions. Parties in this category may include corporate accountants and bookkeepers. In some dysfunctional organisations, parties in this quadrant are better characterised as *pseudo-participants* – those who operate with an expectation of influence on outcomes, yet in the final analysis realise that the considerable time spent preparing budgetary reports yielded little effect on final decisions.

By plotting individual coordinate pairs on the diagram, great insights into perceptions of the nature of the budgeting process can easily be drawn. For example, a clustering of points on an upward diagonal, with most falling in Quadrants II and III (allocators and recipients) is more likely to be reflective of a well-functioning organisation with high levels of trust and certainty. Alternatively, a cloud of points on the downward sloping diagonal, with most falling in Quadrants I and IV (power brokers and preparers) is more likely to be reflective of organisational dysfunction and workplace dissatisfaction.

1.3 Case example: APCO

Apparel Company (APCO) is a leading brand-name designer and manufacturer of athletic performance and fashion clothing with annual sales of roughly $500 million. The company is publicly listed and ranks in the top five of its Standard Industrial Classification (SIC) code in terms of market share. The US-based company outsources production to the Far East and Latin America. At APCO, the budgeting process involves many managers, lasts several months and appears to elicit bottom-up participation. According to company executives, the primary goal of the process was to eliminate hierarchy and better integrate the network of managers. In the new budgeting process, the front-line and general managers should be most central and influential in outcomes.

Hence APCO's budgeting process de-emphasises capital budgeting (asset acquisition) and focuses on developing an operating expense budget to meet sales goals. The centralisation of services and employees at one North American location allows for a one-period, parsimonious research design that incorporates *all* of the managers who participate in the annual budgeting process. In a historical context, this study was conducted in an important year for APCO's budgeting process. For fashion and apparel designers, success and market growth can occur rapidly and quickly transform the organisation from a 'niche' manufacturer to a major, large-scale international enterprise. For nearly 20 years, the company existed as a limited scale entrepreneurial venture. The company issued an initial public stock offering in the early 1990s which radically changed the size and scope of APCO's operations. In an effort to match company capabilities with global market demands, the firm underwent a rapid period of 'professionalisation' of its workforce. These changes primarily consisted of the hiring of professional accountants, production planners and a corporate marketing team.

In an effort to stabilise and formalise processes such as budgeting, the CEO (and company founder) invested in the financial education of functional managers. The goal was to develop an integrated workforce in which employees would readily share bases of functional knowledge to achieve corporate performance goals. Budgeting was seen as a 'flag-ship' process which could be used to impart strategic and financial goals, facilitate cross-functional communication, and enable the appropriate allocation of resources.

The finance group was directed to 'financially educate' functional managers over a period of years through the extensive year-round use of profitability reports. During the budgeting process, financial managers aided the operational managers in the basic techniques of how to use budget spreadsheets. Company management believed that, by the year of this study, the front-line managers had gained a satisfactory level of financial understanding and experience to independently develop operating budgets based on their business knowledge. The financial managers were expected to act as coordinators and to serve as a support function, as needed.

Budgeting is a high-profile activity at APCO. The company holds a half-day budgeting process 'kick-off' meeting every September to 'establish the responsibilities and timing' for the development of the following year's budget. At the meeting, the top financial managers provide templates and guidelines for preparing operating budgets. All managers participating in the process are required to be in attendance. The memo (in a 24 point font) encourages employees to 'Take Ownership. Be Proactive. This is your budget. You will develop it and ultimately be measured by it'.

At APCO, while the budget memos tell employees that 'this is your budget; take ownership', control still rests with top management. The employees with the highest influence ratings were senior executives and financial managers (i.e., the controller) central to the budgeting process. Superficially, APCO appears to have a strong participatory orientation. An in-depth examination shows that the realities of the budgeting process were actually quite different. The process calls for a series of formal interactions between line managers and company executives. Strategic Business Unit (SBU) managers are responsible for developing detailed operating budgets. The finance department is responsible for coordinating the budgeting process and preparing a complete consolidated budget. Senior managers are responsible for reviewing their SBU managers' budgets. Lastly, executive management is responsible for approving a Consolidated Corporate Budget that is consistent with APCO's strategic plan and goals.

Clearly, the language in the memos and discussions with managers indicates that the budgeting process at APCO is intended to be bottom-up and participatory in nature. The design calls for a budget driven by the operating managers with executive oversight and final approval. In terms of the managerial network, one would expect general and front-line operating managers to be most central. Relying *solely* on company documents would lead one to conclude that APCO has a highly participatory process. Social network data help to examine the underlying structure to identify ties among managers.

APCO provides an appropriate context in which to study the network of ties among managers in a corporate budgeting process for two primary reasons. First, although APCO is a global corporation, the management group is relatively limited in number and located in one central facility. Network studies require that data be collected from all members of a group. Such a task would become quite unwieldy in a larger company with thousands of managers across the globe. Second, corporate budgeting at APCO is essentially the development of the operating budget. Thus, capital budgeting issues that impact multiple periods and may confound a research design are not present.

1.3.1 Data collection

Data were collected in three phases. First, management provided open access to individuals and company documents. Managers across functions were interviewed and documentation about the budgeting process was reviewed. These data were used to identify the managers involved in the budgeting process and to refine the questionnaire.

Second, managers completed a questionnaire that asked about demographics, perceptions about budgeting and workplace contacts. The questionnaire was reviewed by managers and a second network researcher for clarity purposes before it was distributed. In the second phase of data collection, the participants completed the research questionnaire. Network data were collected through 'name-generator' type questions: participants were asked to list the names of persons who (1) provide inputs or receive outputs of their routine work; (2) with whom they regularly talk about work-related activities; and (3) co-workers whom they consider to be friends or social associates.

In the second phase of the questionnaire, a two-stage process asked participants to provide perceptions of other managers' relative influence, using a seven-point scale. Participants first consolidated responses to the name-generator questions into one non-redundant list. The participants then rated the relative budgetary influence of each member of their personal workplace network. Also, after listing workplace contacts, participants then listed who they perceived to be the most influential managers (regardless of whether they were in contact with those individuals) and rated those persons' influence.

Last, participants also self-rated their own budgetary influence relative to others.

In the third phase, eight managers participated in semi-structured follow-up interviews. These interviews allow the researcher to interpret the questionnaire results more fully. The extent to which the finance function serves to either reinforce the corporate hierarchy or to promote mutual trust and team-based communication is an important element of the organisational context that affects the use of control systems, such as budgeting. These data and interview responses enrich the structural data.

1.4   Data analysis

The first step in analysing network data is to convert name-generator questionnaire responses to a data matrix that lists each participant in a column and a row. Each participant's responses were coded as binary variables (i.e., presence of relationship with others) and entered into the appropriate row (Scott, 2004). Since each member cannot identify him- or herself as a contact, the diagonal in the matrix appears as a line of zeros.

The next step in the analysis is to consider whether the research question addresses individual or group level questions. For example, one may study why certain members are (not) likely to associate with another particular member. In this case, the underlying pattern of ties among the members as a group is of interest.

There are a wide range of metrics and analyses that are possible using software, such as UCINET 6.0 software (Borgatti *et al.*, 2010). The most common analyses are to draw a map of the group's ties and to generate centrality metrics. The map offers a visual representation of the network data. The mapping function construct the most feasible geometric shape and clustering of members, based on the relationship data in the matrix. These relationships can also be represented through centrality scores that can be derived mathematically to represent each member relative position in the network.

1.4.1 Formal and emergent organisational structure

The Formal Hierarchy. The organisation chart for APCO is presented in Figure 1.2. This figure has been adapted from company documents. The position titles, without managers' names, are shown to illustrate how APCO divides employees along functions. The organisation chart shows that the company is comprised of seven primary functional areas. The Chief Executive Officer (CEO) founded APCO nearly three decades ago and remains the company's majority shareholder. According to several top managers, the CEO is actively involved in crafting corporate strategy and entrepreneurial vision.

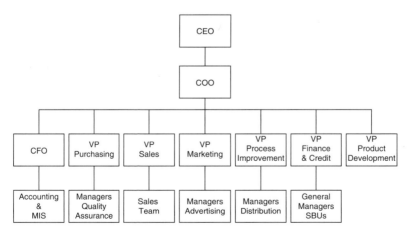

Figure 1.2 APCO's formal hierarchy – corporate organisation chart

The next prominent member of the senior management team is the Chief Operating Officer (COO). The COO is the corporate president and directs the company's senior management team. Each vice-president then manages directors and general managers in each functional area. Operations are divided into four primary strategic business units related to the company's product lines.

Each strategic business unit is responsible for product design, inventory planning and contracting with suppliers and customers. According to one SBU general manager, the critical success factors for APCO products are 'price, fashion and exposure'. To achieve these objectives, each SBU is supported by functional areas such as marketing, sales, finance and distribution. In terms of the budgeting process, the organisation chart provides a framework for understanding how APCO intends budgeting to be 'bottom-up'. Essentially, the budgeting process is designed to invert the hierarchical pyramid. After top management outlines the corporate sales goals, each functional area is required to develop an operating budget to facilitate those objectives. The process is designed to have employees determine what costs are necessary in each department.

The process is designed to 'roll up' each manager's operating budget into functional budgets and, ultimately, into the consolidated corporate budget. During the budgeting process, the finance department is responsible for preparing its own expense budget and providing technical support to the other functional areas. All decision-making authority with respect to the budget resides within the hierarchical chain of command. That is, any questions about a particular manager's budget are expected to be reconciled with that person's immediate supervisor. The chart provides the basis for visualising how various departmental managers are expected to interact. Social network analysis will be employed to show the actual patterns of managers' routine interactions. The formal hierarchy offers a benchmark by which the nature of structural data may be interpreted.

Network Data. The questionnaire provides two primary data outputs: a graph that illustrates APCO's underlying social structure and centrality data for each manager. The map depicting the network of ties among APCO managers is presented in Figure 1.3.

As Figure 1.3 shows, the social network of managers at APCO appears to be closely clustered. Additional data analysis shows that the greatest distance from any manager to any other manager in APCO's network is three connections. This means that to connect any manager to another

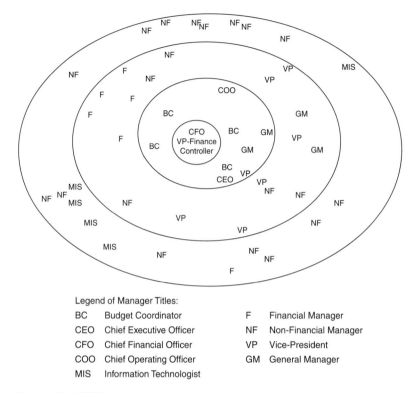

Legend of Manager Titles:

BC	Budget Coordinator	F	Financial Manager
CEO	Chief Executive Officer	NF	Non-Financial Manager
CFO	Chief Financial Officer	VP	Vice-President
COO	Chief Operating Officer	GM	General Manager
MIS	Information Technologist		

Figure 1.3   APCO's social network map

in this data set, we need to find no more than three ties. This maximum distance rating is small considering the number of managers (51) in the network. The close clustering of the managers is consistent with interview responses which indicate that politics (i.e., isolated factions) are relatively non-existent at APCO. These managers also commented that high levels of communication across functions are common at APCO.

The specific pattern of relationships and the positioning of particular managers provide the basis for understanding the nature of the network of APCO managers. Note that the graph does not show isolated clusters of managers. Rather, the data points appear in a pattern of concentric rings. The graph depicts what is commonly referred to as a 'core–periphery' structure. As the name implies, the network is characterised by a cluster of a few highly central managers surrounded by concentric groups of less central managers. The mean self-ratings of influence and influence ratings assigned by others were correlated at a statistically significant level, suggesting that participants were in fair agreement with others' overall assessment of their influence. The results revealed that that rank, centrality and membership in the finance function are important to being perceived as influential in the budgeting process. The importance of these statistical results is that they are *contrary* to the ostensible aims of the process – to shift influence from high-ranking finance officers to front line managers.

Given that we see that centrality is highly correlated with perceived influence at APCO, the next stage of the analysis is to examine which members are central and why those members are most central. A close examination of the network shows that the most central inner group is comprised of the three top financial managers – the Vice President of Finance (treasurer), the Chief Financial Officer (CFO) and the corporate controller. The next ring features the budget coordinators: the CEO and COO. The non-financial managers, general managers and a few vice-presidents are not in the inner rings. The Management Information Systems (MIS) professionals are clustered in the lower-left.

In terms of the budgeting process, this network is quite revealing about the actual interactions among APCO managers. The finance function plays a highly central role in the network. The quantitative data indicate that centrality was the strongest singular predictor of budgetary influence. The budgeting process was designed, however, to have operating managers play the most significant role. The network graph suggests that influence on the budgeting process is driven by a set of individuals other than the operating managers. Some low-level finance managers (i.e., budget coordinators and senior accountants) are more central than some members of the senior management team.

An interesting observation drawn from these data is how the emergent reality of the social structure differs from the desired state. The process was designed to have functional managers in central positions. The goal of the process was to have the functional managers responsible for their respective unit's budget. In terms of the social structure, management expected operating managers to be at the hub with top management and financial managers along the periphery. The language of the budget memo clearly states that decision power should rest in the hands of the functional managers (i.e., 'This is your budget. Take ownership.'). Nonetheless, the difference between the desired state and the emergent network is quite stark. The graph shows that the communication flows as a group did not evolve as planned. This difference is particularly important considering the high levels of influence of the central (finance) managers. These results raise natural questions regarding the difference that emerged.

Several alternative explanations are possible. Three of the strongest possibilities are discussed below.

First, operating managers may have felt uncomfortable with the language of accounting and may have relied on finance managers for support. Many operating managers may lack the background to handle technical accounting procedures or may be intimidated by (or uninterested in) communicating in terms of the language of finance. However, the interview data will show that APCO managers actually felt quite comfortable and capable of preparing financial budgets that relate to business goals.

Further, participants rated their own influence and involvement. Across levels of the organisation, managers were actively involved in the process, investing 80 hours of time, on average. A review of these data reveals an interesting pattern. When comparing each participant's Likert-scale self-ratings of influence and involvement, the results show that 43 per cent of the participants rated their influence lower than their involvement; 43 per cent of the participants rated their influence equal to their involvement; and only 14 per cent of the participants rated their influence higher than their involvement. These results and the interview comments illuminate the apparent mismatch between high/low levels of employee influence and involvement and help to explain why the central core of managers seems to be so influential at APCO.

Second, operating managers may have been reluctant or uncomfortable interacting across functions. Hence finance may have acted as a conduit or intermediary between the operational functions. Senior management believes that the complex nature of the competitive environment demands cross-functional interaction to meet strategic goals. Thus the process was designed to encourage such interactions. However, in some organisations functional managers may limit or avoid such interactions if the allocation of scarce resources is at stake. The interview data show that the functional managers are quite aware of their strategic interdependence and were quite willing and comfortable with such interactions as a necessary means to achieve corporate goals.

Third, finance may play a central role in the budgeting process if the overall perceived role of finance is to support the command and control function of top management, as opposed to promoting cross-functional interaction. To the extent that top management maintains a strong commanding managerial role (and finance reflects such an operating philosophy), such organisations are highly likely to have finance play a central role in the allocation of resources and setting of performance goals. Hence understanding the underlying culture at APCO is important in interpreting the results.

1.4.2   Interviews with APCO managers

Interviews with managers at APCO indicate that asking employees to spend time on the budgeting process and not incorporating their input may have a detrimental effect on senior management's credibility. Many managers questioned whether the budgeting process at APCO was simply form over substance. This 'pseudo-participation' undermined the credibility of the budget process and impaired employees' perceptions of top management. Many employees commented that a top-down process would be preferred over a process that asks employees to spend several working weeks on an activity that had little impact on outcomes.

The interviewees suggested that senior management and top financial managers played the most significant role in the budgeting process. One general manager said:

> [APCO's budgeting process is] bottom-up until it reaches senior management. You work to achieve an end ... [then, budgets] get handed in and get kicked right back to you saying [here's the number and the allocation] ... Let's just say from Day 1 ... we [the SBU] got a Travel budget of a $1 million ... that will be broken up [these ways]...figure out where it falls within your group. It would be better to say ... this division is going to be allocated these dollars ... make it fit ... you know your business better than anybody.

Another top manager remarked that managers believed in the process:

> We felt very good about the process from the bottom-up point of view. [Finance] gave people historical information as best [Finance] could ... we felt pretty good that [managers] spent the time pulling together their budgets. [Managers] were going through an inventory, sales and cost of sales budget in detail. They really tried ... tried to get their numbers down on paper and make it work ... It could have been a wonderful process, I feel really proud of [the managers] out there. They really bought into it and did the work. They had to budget salaries and a lot of detail and they did it ... The managers really took the time and had the respect for the process. And these are busy guys, but they took the time out to make sure that they did it as best they thought.

This manager continued that the planned budgeting process really never occurred:

> I think it meant something to the SBU Managers. What ultimately happened was the budget was rolled together. Of course, you don't like your first level results. Of course, you ask for too much.
>
> Instead, senior management ... didn't get together ... they didn't meet the deadlines. They were the ones who weren't getting together with their direct reports (SBU and cost center managers) ...
>
> And before you knew it, the budget that was put together on a detailed basis was gone ... It was all thrown to the wayside ... it fell apart ... all of a sudden the budget just became some top-down high level number ... the only thing that we had was some massaged number that [went] into the cost center reports.
>
> [The] goal of the budget process was to make the budget be legit ... how 'bout that? Actually, come to an agreement. That's where it fell apart when it went to a higher level.

The manager commented that the events damaged the credibility of the process:

> 'So, months and months of work and respect for the budget process was lost. Until mid-October when it was down at the first line management level ... It was a process we could all be proud of ... and by the time it was finished, we didn't even want to talk about it.
>
> We didn't care at that point. You should have never had us go through, 2½ months of serious work putting together a budget if it didn't really mean anything to [top management] in the first place.

When asked about networks and communication, one manager commented that the budgeting process initially helped functional managers to better understand finance, and helped the financial managers better understand the business. Employees quickly realised the outcomes were directed and determined by senior management.

> 'I think that process is what APCO can change the attitude about ... [At first] we [different functions] became friends, we wanted to help each other. I think [the budgeting] process help turn the corner ... all kinds of communication started. [For example,] Marketing had no idea of accruals ... none of those concepts were familiar. [The budgeting process] helped things change.

> [For the budgeting process to have credibility in the future]
> Management has to put their money where their mouth is ... when
> they say you have to meet deadlines. They got up at the kickoff ...
> and said that [senior management] supports this process, deadlines,
> etc ... [senior management] actually have to understand that that
> applies to them as well.

These comments shed light on why the central core of managers is so influential at APCO. These findings show that companies should consider the implications of participative budgeting. Overall, these qualitative data enhance the interpretation of the quantitative results. These interviews with managers enable the development of a comprehensive perspective about APCO's budgeting process. This perspective is necessary to address questions which remain about why a company which designs a bottom-up process, in the end, seems to revert to traditional top-down management.

For example, why did top management seem to abandon the input of the front-line managers? Did senior management act in a duplicitous or strategic fashion? What elements of APCO's competitive environment might have influenced top management to act in such a way? Discussions with senior management revealed that they claimed that were not fully aware of the impact of their actions. That is, senior management felt that it did not act in a duplicitous or insincere fashion. Rather, senior management asserted that they were ignorant of the effects of actions on employee perceptions and commitment.

1.5   Conclusions

Regardless of what point along the continuum top management chooses, the results of this chapter suggest that management's language should reflect the delineation of decision rights. Friction developed at APCO when management retained decision rights, although they had declared that ownership rights resided in the hands of front-line managers. Further research is necessary to elaborate points along this continuum. While the results in this chapter do not suggest which approach is best, the findings do shed light on communication factors that may enable or inhibit budgeting success. Designing systems that balance control with empowerment looms as one of management's greatest challenges on the path to strategic success (Simons, 1995). The findings of this project were of value to APCO's executives and should be applicable to others. These results could aid managers in balancing the competing tensions of budget participation, a process that pits employee empowerment against organisational control. This balance can be key to uniting (dividing) employees towards (from) corporate goals.

Management communication and control systems are playing an increasingly important role in corporate strategy and accountability. Firms are trying to design unique ways to balance empowerment and control. Simply adopting 'best practices' does not ensure that a firm will meet its communication and performance goals. This study demonstrates that senior management must be aware of the workplace social structure underlying the firm's formal hierarchy. This research identifies important considerations regarding the tension inherent in balancing empowerment and control in the modern network organisation. Careful executive oversight can amplify whether empowerment and participation are being substantively adopted by organisations, or if such myths have become institutionalised as pleasant-sounding ways to reinforce the hierarchical control.

References

Argyris, C. (1952). *The Impact of People on Budgets*. The Controllership Foundation, New York.
Borgatti, S. P., Everett, M. G. and Freeman, L. C. (2010). UCINET 6.0. Columbia, SC: Analytic Technologies.
Covaleski, M. A. and Dirsmith, M. W. (1988). 'The Use of Budgetary Symbols in The Political Arena: A Historically Informed Field Study', *Accounting, Organizations and Society* 13, 1–24.
Jablonsky, S. F. and Keating, P. J. (1998). *Changing Roles of Financial Management*, Financial Executives Research Foundation, Morristown, NJ.
Scott, J. (2004). *Social Network Analysis*, Sage Publications, New York.
Simons, R. (1995). *Levers of Control*, Harvard Business Press, Boston, MA.
Vroom, V. H. and Yetton, P. W. (1973). *Leadership and Decision-Making*, University of Pittsburgh Press, Pittsburgh.

2
Inter-Organisational Relationships as a Complex Adaptive System

Jim Rooney

2.1 Overview

Accounting literature on control of inter-organisational relationships is largely focused on developing control archetypes and exploring contingency relationships between characteristics of the transaction environment and management controls. To date, however, findings are inconclusive if not contradictory (Caglio and Ditillo, 2008), suggesting that richness of the underlying control phenomena is yet to be adequately uncovered. Further, the relationship between transaction environment and controls is often seen as static and linear (Caglio and Ditillo, 2008) with resulting calls to examine 'dynamic relationships between variables over time' (Dekker, 2008, p. 938).

Adding to the complexity of the domain, controls have been found to change not only in response to inter-organisational factors but also to intra-organisational influences (see Mouritsen *et al.*, 2001 for an early example). Expressed in terms germane to the supply chain practitioner, there is a material level of frustration with the ineffectiveness of management control that can 'stem from the inability to recognise that there are differences between these two aspects of the SN management and apply them strategically' (Choi *et al.*, 2001, p. 354). In exploring the dynamics of inter-organisational relationships, it is apparent that the performance of an inter-organisational relationship depends on timely control interventions either to deterministically reduce the scope of independent action for agents or allow for the emergence of autonomous behaviour as circumstances provide.

As a point of departure from much of the prior literature, this chapter takes a lead from Thrane (2007) in the accounting literature and recent work in the supply chain literature (see Li *et al.*, 2009) to examine management control in inter-organisational relationships from a systems perspective. This lens is potentially useful in examining dynamic concepts of control that encompass relations of reciprocity between accounting, the inter-organisational relationship and the (external and internal) organisational environments of relationship partners. In particular, there is evidence in favour of a Complex Adaptive System (CAS) perspective (see Schneider and Somers, 2006) reflecting the degree to which Complexity Theory applies to the inter-organisational context.

Adoption of a CAS perspective also responds to calls by academics and practitioners in the supply chain and management control literature to address the complex range of problems faced by managers in such inter-organisational relationships (Caglio and Ditillo, 2008; Choi and Krause, 2006; Li *et al.*, 2009). It is consistent with Chenhall (2003) as a means of addressing concerns about model under-specification, a common criticism of contingency-based approaches.

The chapter starts by outlining prior accounting literature on inter-organisational management control. It includes a review of accounting literature addressing characteristics of the transaction environment. It will compare and contrast alternative approaches in both the accounting and supply chain literature. *Inter alia*, constructs associated with related theoretical perspectives, including cooperation, coordination, appropriation and dependency, will be discussed. It also brings together aspects of Systems Theory germane to inter-organisational relationships. At an applied level, the chapter includes discussion on identification of management control problems and the development of diagnostic support tools that may help safeguard outsourcing and other inter-organisational relationships. Finally, the chapter provides guidance for future exploration on the systems nature of inter-organisational control.

2.2 Overview of current theory and practice

Consistent with organisational (Schneider and Somers, 2006) and supply chain (Holweg and Pil, 2008) literature, among others focused on such arrangements, management control research has recognised the need to explore the form and dynamics of inter-organisational relationships. To date, the academic literature has largely focused on explaining the alignment or fit between control and transaction attributes (for a detailed review, see Caglio and Ditillo, 2008).

Despite the extensiveness of this literature, there has been mixed progress to date, characterised as an inconclusiveness [that] is even more severe if we consider that the findings proposed by contributors are in some cases contradictory' (Caglio and Ditillo, 2008, p. 874). More broadly, empirical research on management control has been observed as producing 'unclear findings and conflicting results' (Sandelin, 2008, p. 325). This suggests that relations between transaction environment, attributes and control are more complex than has been described to date. Supporting this, other research has sought to identify the intra-organisational influences that operate along inter-organisational exchange factors in influencing management control (see Cuganesan, 2006 as a recent example).

In recognition of this complexity, more recent studies have begun to adopt alternative perspectives to uncover the richness of inter-organisational management control. Sandelin (2008), using Open Systems Theory, for example, looks for possibilities of alternate management control configurations to achieve an equivalent functional requirement outcome (known as equifinality), while Thrane (2007, p. 256) attempts to introduce 'a more complex system understanding [that] views the system as being in continual flux and change'. Alternate theoretical lens have been applied in the supply chain literature to understand the dynamics of supply chains, a recent example being a comparison of Resource-Based-View (RBV), CAS and Adaptive Structuration Theory (AST) in Holwig and Pils (2008). Overall however, the literature is deficient, with limited insight of the interplay between emergent inter-organisational control problems and evolution of control design (Caglio and Ditillo, 2008). More specifically, there is limited understanding of the processes that lead to change in the design of management controls (v. d. Meer-Kooistra and Scapens, 2008).

To further aid our analysis, we need to explore inter-organisational relationships using more than one theoretical lens. This allows more detailed understanding of the emergence of order associated with co-evolution of controls and environment over time. Such an approach responds to calls in the supply chain and management control literature to address the complex range of problems faced by managers in such inter-organisational relationships (Choi and Krause, 2006; Li *et al.*, 2009). The simultaneous use of multiple theories to explore complex phenomena is also consistent with Chenhall (2003) as a means of addressing concerns about model misspecification, a common criticism of contingency-based models in particular. This approach may help address related concerns about construct definition and measurement (see Auzair and Langfield-Smith, 2005; Gerdin and Greve, 2008).

In the following sections, we examine the emergence of control problems as the catalyst for change in the mix of management controls.

The control mechanisms described in Dekker (2004) are also highlighted. As identified in Caglio and Ditillo (2008) this control description is non-deterministic and does not denote ideal types. In addition, Dekker (2004) is cited in the inter-organisational literature and is broadly consistent with a number of recent control typologies such as that of Malmi and Brown (2008). These control problems and mechanisms are identified with techniques described in the management accounting or organisation literature; for example, accounting concepts (such as budgets, standard operating procedures) in the case of formal controls (Dekker, 2008) and constructs from sociology or organisation literature (such as trust, embeddedness and organisational norms) in the case of informal controls (Dekker, 2008). Given that the typology and mechanisms are detailed in Caglio and Ditillo (2008) and Dekker (2004) respectively, they are not described in detail here.

To adequately explore the dynamics associated with the emergence of control problems and the interplay with evolving control design, a framework that recognises the complexity and dynamism of interactions within an inter-organisational relationship is required (Thrane, 2007). An overview of this perspective and, in particular, the resultant mapping of control changes are outlined in the next sections.

2.3   Adoption of a systems approach

Arguably identified as a founder of Systems Theory, von Bertalanffy demonstrated that it can apply to physical, biological and sociological entities; basically 'phenomena of any kind' (von Bertalanffy, 1950, p. 304). Applied to organisations, general Systems Theory focuses on the entire organisation and considers the primary system objective to be sustainability of existence. In broad terms, a system accomplishes this through adaptation following constant interaction with its environment.

In recognising the recursive nature of Systems Theory, Otley and Berry (1980) highlight both the need and theoretical ability to study bounded systems in order to progress understanding of the complex process of organisational management and control. While this entails an inherent risk that material components and interactions are omitted (Gray, 1992), a core concern of Systems Theory and practice is to identify the effect of such omissions on intellectual enquiry (Boulding, 1956). Further, the use of Systems Theory or, at least, analysis (Gray, 2002) 'allows a conceptualisation of change in systems with blurred boundaries, which is not linear, is dynamic, unstable and multi-dimensional' (Thrane, 2007, p. 249). The intent is 'to develop and study non-linear dynamical systems models of organisational change and development' (Van de Ven and Poole, 1995, p. 535). Given the advances in Systems Theory, it is not surprising that there are limits to its use. For example, Thayer (1972) criticises Systems Theory as promoting hierarchy to a point of impersonalisation among operating subsystems. He also contends that the requirement that systems grow to avert entropy results in huge organisations that eventually work at odds with the environment, thereby resulting in destructive outcomes. Devine (1985) considers General Systems Theory too general for purposes of developing accounting standards. He considered it's applicability to understanding the role of accounting in organisations, concluding that open or closed classifications are not useful in accounting discussions. However, the argument was focused on organisational scope, structure and political attributes rather than the role accounting plays in the development and presentation of information to decision-makers.

In an open systems model, a possible performance criterion could be the absence of control problems, incorporating the achievement of contractual performance targets. In particular, the emergence of control problem is defined as a disruption to equilibrium states consistent with a three-phase typology describing actor interactions. As defined in Heiskanen *et al.* (2008), the three alternate phases are 'acceptance, equivocation, rejection'. Acceptance of manifestation of a control problem conforming to the Caglio and Ditillo (2008) framework by actors in an inter-organisational relationship would signal emergence of disequilibrium. A disequilibrium state, in turn, would require the evolution of a control mechanism to force a return to equilibrium or a conscious decision to allow equilibrium to emerge. This approach builds on the definition of 'episodic' provided in Weick and Quinn (1999, p. 365) that 'occur during periods of divergence when organisations are moving away from their equilibrium conditions'.

A contingency view of performance may be applied using the classification scheme of Gresov and Drazin (1997) with a high degree of conflict in functional demands and unconstrained structural options applicable to an individual firm. For a firm buying outsourcing services, these functional demands relate to outsourcing goals such as reduction in operational costs and avoidance of future IT investment. This view recognises that performance can vary between firms and be sub-optimal even where the function–structure combinations of an individual inter-organisational relationship are considered to be 'successful'.

Further, functional equivalence can be defined in terms of the maintenance of an equilibrium state in achieving agreed functional demands specific to an inter-organisational relationship. Over time, functional demands can evolve to include or substitute for other demands such as an increased level of customer service. How an inter-organisational relationship responds to evolution in functional demands with different function-structure configurations is a focus of this chapter. The existence of different management control configurations in achieving equifinality (i.e., equilibrium achieved using different control configurations or mix) and homeostasis (i.e., a return to equilibrium) would provide tentative evidence for an open systems perspective of inter-organisational controls. This principle can explain why equivalent business outcomes are achieved using different combinations of organisational structures, functions and controls when the same business contingencies apply (Gresov and Drazin, 1997).

Contrary to this focus on equilibrium, recent multidisciplinary exploration of inter-organisational relationships in the supply chain literature suggests that it may be more appropriate to analyse such arrangements in the absence of equilibrium. Systems operating in a state of continual flux are more indicative of a Complex Adaptive System. They exhibit complex agent behaviours underlying interactions that flux in terms of control behaviours rather than equilibrium states. This may provide insights into balancing control and the emergence of self-organising behaviour in a complex supply network (Surana *et al.*, 2005). Li *et al.* (2009) suggest that recognition of the systems nature of supply networks is based on the need to understand the complex and evolving interplay between its structural-function configuration and environment-collaborative fit.

Consistent with organisational (Schneider and Somers, 2006) and supply chain (Holweg and Pil, 2008) literature, management control research has arguably started to acknowledge the need to explore the forms of trade-off between control and transaction attributes within inter-organisational relationships (for a detailed review see Caglio and Ditillo, 2008). In order to explore this trade-off, we use an agent-based or 'bottom-up approach' to help with understanding of the processes likely to drive emerging patterns of inter-organisational behaviour (Surana *et al.*, 2005).

As the unit of analysis for this chapter, outsourcing relationships are a form of supply network in terms of value creation based on substantive knowledge flows. As such, they involve interaction between the three generally accepted CAS foci of internal mechanism, external environment and co-evolution (Choi *et al.*, 2001). Within these elements, the presence of meaningful agents, the emergence of structured collective behaviour and an operating environment that includes intra-organisational as well as industry or market mechanisms qualifies the research sites explored in this chapter within an accepted form of a CAS (Surana *et al.*, 2005). This approach also recognises that the nature of complex systems may blur the boundaries between firms, making separation of intra- and inter-organisational performance unproductive (Thrane and Hald, 2006). Given the ample precedents for this stance in the systems and accounting literature (see Gray (1992) for a brief discussion in a sustainability context), this aspect of the analysis is not discussed further.

To utilise the CAS framework (Li *et al.*, 2009), an inter-organisational system would need to demonstrate the emergence of more than one system state in resolving emerging control problems, emphasising a holistic epistemology associated with general systems theory (von Bertalanffy, 1950). Such a result would support a self-organising rather than deterministic mode of enquiry, with the prospect of multiple context-specific system states. In other words, a Complex Adaptive System.

Given the above issues with General Systems and Open Systems theory cited above, the chapter will focus on examining inter-organisational relationships using a CAS perspective. This focus will allow a more detailed examination of the emergence of patterns associated with co-evolution of control mechanisms and environment over the term of an inter-organisational relationship (Holweg and Pil, 2008).

2.4   Complex Adaptive Systems

As mentioned earlier, a CAS perspective is considered potentially useful in seeking to examine a dynamic concept of control that encompasses relations of reciprocity between accounting, the inter-organisational relationship and the (external and internal) organisational environments of relationship partners. This approach also supports exploration of control systems through more than a single perspective.

Accordingly, the remainder of this chapter will explore two key aspects of dynamics pertinent to the management control of inter-organisational relationships. The first aspect is to the co-evolution of control mechanisms during the post-contractual phase of an outsourcing relationship. The intent is to highlight such phenomena at the level of Buyer–Supplier agent interaction, incorporating the immediate environment in which the control mechanisms operate. The second aspect is to discuss current explanations for the existence of multiple control designs in response to functionally similar control problems (Gresov and Drazin, 1997). Thrane (2007, p. 256) highlights three patterns of change within a complex system: 'bifurcation, oscillation, and schizophrenia'. Given that the focus of this chapter is the patterns of change in management control design rather than patterns of complex system change, this aspect of the inter-organisational context is not explored further.

By taking into account the perspectives of actors, this approach builds on prior work on buyer/supplier/transaction characteristics described in Anderson and Dekker (2003), Reuer *et al.* (2006) and Dekker (2004, 2008). It also provides improved understanding of the dynamics of control problem emergence based on the interaction of actors within an inter-organisational collaboration. In analysing control problems and the co-evolution of control mechanisms and the inter-organisational business environment, exploration of the complexity and potential evolution of management control pathways is more likely. This includes aspects of emergence and path dependence in control design (Gerdin and Greve, 2008).

To facilitate analysis, a single source of system perturbation is more prevalent from a practitioner viewpoint namely, forms of management control problems arguably the problem typology described in Caglio and Ditillo (2008) in order to tie current theoretical constructs with practice. *Inter alia*, it may provide greater understanding of alternate paths of control design in response to the emergence of these problems. Recognition of system disruption or perturbation in the sense defined by Thrane (2007) is based on acceptance by both entities in an inter-organisational relationship that a control problem conforming to the typology described by Caglio and Ditillo (2008) has emerged and the perturbation is recognised by focal actors in the inter-organisational relationship as an underlying cause. A perturbation requires evolution of a control mechanism to mitigate its impact or a decision to allow a new state to emerge with this interaction capable of being two-way, broadly consistent with the accounting-as-actant perspective of inter-organisational relationships (Thrane and Hald, 2006). This approach is consistent with Caglio and Ditillo (2008), given their recognition that explanations of observed behaviour provided by the theories driving their typology 'may be incomplete'.

To be consistent with the CAS world (Li *et al.*, 2009), the inter-organisational system needs to demonstrate the emergence of more than one system state in resolving emerging control problems, in contrast to the Open Systems Theory adopted by Sandelin (2007). Such a result would support a self-organising rather than deterministic mode of enquiry, with the prospect of multiple context-specific system states. In contrast to an open system, there would be no equilibrium state and the absence of equifinality, with the system in flux with its environment.

Consideration of a complex adaptive system framework provides illumination of a range of evolutionary influences on the inter-organisational arrangement. While the effect of landscape fit on control problems appears to have a major effect in the evolution of new post-contractual functional demands, control mechanisms also evolve in response to influences that were driven by both inter- and intra-organisational processes. The combination of control problem/control evolution, business environment evolution and ongoing landscape fit result in path dependencies consistent with the three foci of CAS research, namely internal mechanisms (i.e., control mechanisms), environment (i.e., the micro-operations ecology of home loan lending) and co-evolution (i.e., mechanisms and micro-operation environment evolving simultaneously, at times influencing each other).

In the post-contractual operation of the inter-organisational relationship, management controls aim to achieve a balance of inter-organisational performance against competing functional demands. Recognisable in the form of inadequate performance against one or more of these demands, evolution in control design is required. This is recognisable predominantly as a change in the mix of control mechanisms. This path divergence appears to be driven to a considerable extent by the respective relationship preferences attached to individual control mechanisms from the early stage of the relationship, as well as organisational structure.

Rooney and Cuganesan (2010) found that, in addition to the influence of inter-organisational control problems, management control mechanisms may also evolve in line with shifts in the environment within which the exchange partners operated. This has concomitant implications for the inter-organisational and intra-firm dynamics (Kauffman, 1993). Hence evolution in control problems and mechanisms responds at least partly to changes in consumer demand and industry competitors (McCarthy, 2004). The influence of the inter-organisational environment was found to be less applicable at a macro or economy-wide level as all buyer firms operated within the same industry and national economy, emphasising that evolution at a micro-operation ecology level that 'specifies the demand, the supply, the price, the lead-time and the competitors for each individual firm' (Li *et al.*, 2009, p. 842) appears to influence control evolution.

Earlier evidence of the co-evolution outlined above exists in the accounting literature, albeit not always described using a CAS perspective. For example, Cuganesan and Lee (2006), in an actor–network study of an online procurement network, found that changes in management control design influence the attributes of the outsourcing transaction, parties and experiences and that the influence is bi-directional.

2.5 Conclusions

The aim of this chapter was to describe recent developments in achieving a deeper understanding of the interaction between management control mix and the environment in which inter-organisational relationship are sited. In particular, it examined system characteristics that represent the fundamental dynamic nature of such a relationship. *Inter alia*, it summarises recent accounting literature exploring the evolution of control patterns within inter-organisational relationships. The resulting research provides insight on how controls co-evolve with the business environment within which exchange partners operate. The key benefits and gaps in the systems perspective were also reviewed.

This chapter explored the domain of the ongoing management control of inter-organisational alliances based on the recognition of its properties as a CAS. Li *et al.* (2009) suggest that recognition of the systems nature of supply networks is based on the need to understand the complex and evolving interplay between its internal mechanisms and the environment within which it operates. The chapter emphasises four key differences from the static models favoured in the accounting literature, based on terminology in Boulding (1956) as cited by Thrane (2007), namely the presence of a multi-centred contestable inter-organisational space (i.e., problems, controls and environment); a focus on context-driven patterns of change; porous organisational boundaries affected by ongoing interactions between intra- and inter-organisational actors (including the environment); and the emergent nature of control.

Exploration of these differences is required in order address current gaps in the academic and practitioner literature listed Section 2.2. This perspective is compared and contrasted with the open systems approach following a preliminary review of selected accounting and supply chain literature pertinent to the inter-organisational unit of analysis studied here. The chapter builds on a systems perspective of inter-organisational relationships that goes beyond the static view prevalent in these accounting literatures.

Implications for accounting theory

Examination of inter-organisational alliances on the basis of a Complex Adaptive System framework is consistent with recent supply chain literature (Li *et al.*, 2009) and, while not widespread, has been considered recently in the accounting literature (Thrane, 2007). In addition, the use of Complexity Theory and its adaptive systems incarnation as a framework for descriptive analysis has, arguably, accepted precedents in the accounting and organisational science literature (Gray, 1992).

The key implication for accounting theory is that evidence in favour of the presence of non-cyclical disruption and the emergence of change due to positive rather than exclusively negative interaction between firms operating within an inter-organisational alliance supports deeper understanding of the dynamic nature of such relationships. It focuses attention on the nature of the interaction rather than the search for equilibrium states. Differentiation based on these properties is consistent with Schneider and Somers (2006, p. 353), adapted from Katz and Kahn (1978).

Implications for practice

A focus on the components within a system and greater understanding of the interactions of these components and the environment (in this case, the industry) in which they operate has the potential to improve knowledge of ongoing outsourced operations. Given the mixed success of outsourcing arrangements over many decades, it appears to be a phenomenon that appears to be poorly understood in practice.

References

Anderson, S. and Dekker, H. (2005). 'Management Control for Market Transactions: The Relation Between Transaction Characteristics, Incomplete Contract Design and Subsequent Performance', *Management Science* 51 (12), 1734–52.

Auzair, S. Md. and Langfield-Smith, K. (2005). The Effect of Service Process Type, Business Strategy and Life-Cycle Stage on Bureaucratic MCS in Service Organizations', *Management Accounting Research*, 16, 399–421.

von Bertalanffy, L. (1950). General System Theory: A New Approach to Unity of Science, 1. Problems of General System Theory', *Human Biology*, 23 (4), 30–311.

Boulding, K. E. (1956). 'General Systems Theory: The Skeleton of Science', *Management Science*, 2 (3), 197–208.

Caglio, A. and Ditillo, A. (2008). 'A Review and Discussion of Management Control in Inter-firm Relationships: Achievements and Future Directions', *Accounting, Organizations and Society*, 33 (7–8), 865–98.

Chenhall, R. H. (2003). 'Management Control Systems Design within its Organizational Context: Findings from Contingency-based Research and Directions for the Future', *Accounting, Organizations and Society*, 28 (2–3), 127–68.

Choi, T., Dooley, K. and Rungtusanatham, M. (2001). 'Supply Networks and Complex Adaptive Systems: Control versus Emergence', *Journal of Operations Management*, 19 (3), 351–66.

Choi, T.Y. and Krause, D.R. (2006). The Supply Base and its Complexity: Implications for Transaction Costs, Risks, Responsiveness, and Innovation', *Journal of Operations Management* 24, 637–52.

Cuganesan, S. (2006). 'The Role of Functional Specialists in Shaping Controls within Supply Networks', *Accounting, Auditing and Accountability Journal*, 19 (4), 465–92.

Cuganesan, S. and Lee, R. (2006). 'Intra-Organisational Influences in Procurement Network Controls: The Impacts of Information Technology', *Management Accounting Research*, 17, 141–70.

Dekker, H.C. (2004). 'Control of Inter-Organizational Relationships: Evidence on Appropriation Concerns and Coordination Requirements', *Accounting, Organizations & Society*, 29, 27–49.

Dekker, H. C. (2008). 'Partner Selection and Governance Design in Inter-organisational Relationships', *Accounting, Organizations and Society*, 33 (7), 915–41.

Devine, C. T. (1985). *Studies in Accounting Research #22-III*, Sarasota, FL, American Accounting Association.

Gerdin, J. and Greve, J. (2008). The Appropriateness of Statistical Methods for Testing Contingency Hypotheses in Management Accounting Research', *Accounting, Organizations & Society*, 33, 995–1009.

Gray, R. (1992). 'Accounting and Environmentalism: An Exploration of the Challenge of Gently Accounting for Accountability', *Transparency and Sustainability, Accounting Organisations and Society*, 17 (5), 399–425.

Gray, R. (2002). 'Messiness, Systems and Sustainability: Towards a More Social and Environmental Accounting and Finance', *British Accounting Review*, 34, 357–86.

Gresov, C. and Drazin, R. (1997). 'Equifinality: Functional Equivalence in Organization Design', *Academy of Management Review*, 22, 403–28.

Hakansson, H. and Lind, K. (2007). 'Accounting in Interorganisational Settings', in C. S. Chapman, A. G. Hopwood and M. D. Shields (Eds), *Handbook of Management Accounting Research*, vol. 2, Elsevier, Amsterdam, The Netherlands, 885–902.

Holweg, M. and Pil, F. K. (2008). 'Theoretical Perspectives on the Coordination of Supply Chains', *Journal of Operations Management* 26, 389–406.

Katz, D. and Kahn, R. L. (1978). *The Social Psychology of Organizations*, 2nd edn, New York, Wiley.

Kauffman, S. A. (1993). *The Origins of Order: Self-Organization and Selection in Evolution*, New York, Oxford University Press.

Lia, G., Yanga, H., Suna, L., Jib, P. and Fenga, L. (2010). 'The Evolutionary Complexity of Complex Adaptive Supply Networks: A Simulation and Case Study', *International Journal of Production Economics*, 124 (2), 310–30.

McCarthy, I. P. (2004). 'Manufacturing Strategy: Understanding the Fitness Landscape', *International Journal of Operations & Production Management*, 24 (2), 124–50.

Malmi, T. and Brown, D. A. (2008). 'Management Control Systems as a Package – Opportunities, Challenges and Research Directions', *Management Accounting Research*, 19, 287–300.

v. d. Meer-Kooistra, J. and Scapens, R. W. (2008). 'The Governance of Lateral Relations between and Within Organisations', *Management Accounting Research*, doi:10.1016/j.mar.2008.08.001.

Mouritsen, J., Hansen, A. and Hansen, C. O. (2001). 'Inter-Organizational Controls and Organizational Competencies: Episodes around Target Cost Management/Functional Analysis and Open Book Accounting', *Management Accounting Research*, 12 (2), 221–44.

Otley, D. T. and Berry, A. J. (1980). 'Control, Organisation and Accounting', *Accounting Organisations & Society*, 5, 231–44.

Reuer, J. L. and Arino A. (2002). 'Contractual Renegotiations in Strategic Alliances', *Journal of Management*, 28 (1), 47–68.

Rooney, J. and Cuganesan, S. (2009). 'Contractual and Accounting Controls in Outsourcing Agreements – Evidence from the Australian Home Loan Industry', *Australian Accounting Review*, 49 (19), 2.

Sandelin, M. (2008). 'Operation of Management Control Practices as a Package – A Case Study on Control System Variety in a Growth Firm Context, Management', *Accounting Research*, 19, 324–43.

Schneider, M. and Somers, M. (2006). 'Organizations as Complex Adaptive Systems: Implications of Complexity Theory for Leadership Research', *The Leadership Quarterly*, 17, 351–65.

Surana, A., Kumara, S., Greaves, M. and Raghavan, U. N. (2005). 'Supply Chain Networks: A Complex Adaptive Systems Perspective', *International Journal of Production Research*, 43 (20), 4235–65.

Thayer, F. (1972). General System(s) Theory: The Promise that Could not be Kept', *The Academy of Management Journal*, 15 (4), 481–93.

Thrane, S. (2007). 'The Complexity of Management Accounting Change: Bifurcation and Oscillation in Schizophrenic Interorganisational Systems', *Management Accounting Research*, 248–72.

Thrane, S. and Hald, K. S. (2006). 'The Emergence of Boundaries and Accounting in Supply Fields: The Dynamics of Integration and Fragmentation', *Management Accounting Research*, 17, 288–314.

Van de Ven, H. A. and Poole, M. S. (1995). 'Explaining Development and Change in Organisations', *Academy of Management Review*, 20, 510–40.

Weick, K. E. and Quinn, R. E. (1999). 'Organizational Change and Development', *Annual Review of Psychology*, 361–86, http://www.questia.com/PM.qst?a=o&d= 5001249962 (accessed 27 October 2010).

3
Management Accounting in a Lean Environment

Riccardo Silvi, Monica Bartolini and Franco Visani

3.1 Introduction

Lean production methods were pioneered by Toyota in Japan (Toyota Production System). Thereafter, Lean Thinking (Ohno, 1988; Womack *et al.*, 1990; Womack and Jones, 1996) distilled the essence of the lean approach into some key principles and extended them beyond automotive production to any company or organisation, in any industry, in any country, thanks to its positive effects on process improvement, productivity, waste reduction, quality management etc.

Management Accounting Systems (MAS) (Anthony, 1965; Merchant, 1985; Simons, 1995) can play a significant role in the success of Lean Management (LM) initiatives. First, they can be considered the 'transmission belt' between their proponents and top management, reporting the relevance and potential impact of a lean project in financial terms. Indeed, top management commitment is essential for success. Moreover, MAS can also be crucial during project implementation – also when LM is already in place – measuring and controlling results, suggesting modifications etc.

Despite this potential role, the real contribution of MAS in supporting the development and implementation of LM projects has been the subject of numerous criticisms (Maskell, 2000; Grasso, 2006; Jusko, 2007). For instance, traditional MAS – based on standard costs and variance analyses – can lead to incorrect behaviours, contrary to the goals pursued by LM (Kroll, 2004). Indeed, standard costs are often defined at a 'medium', 'normal' or 'historical' level of efficiency and are only occasionally revised. As a consequence, they can include significant waste (Maskell, 2006). This situation clearly conflicts with the principle of continuous improvement, typical of LM.

33

On the basis of these criticisms, those involved in the development and implementation of LM often consider MAS at best a useless bureaucratic task and at worst an obstacle to the project's success. Two different approaches have been developed to solve the aforementioned problems. The first asserts the need to remove any financial measures from the operational control tools and should be conducted on the basis of technical and operational measures alone (Johnson, 2006).

The second approach, namely Lean Accounting (LA) (Maskell and Baggaley, 2003; Kennedy and Huntzinger, 2005), instead proposes some new tools specifically developed for lean environments. According to these, LA should be based on a three-level reporting system:

- the single work cell level, where only operational indicators are defined according to LM targets;
- the value stream level, where operational indicators are coupled with a Profit and Loss Statement (called Value Stream Costing), based on the value stream's direct costs and with very few allocations of indirect costs;
- the strategy level, where strategic lean-based Key Performance Indicators are defined, together with a map of the linkages between the different strategic targets (Kennedy and Brewer, 2005).

Despite the fact that LA brings concrete issues to the fore and offers some interesting solutions, this approach leaves numerous gaps and unsolved problems (Van der Merwe and Thomson, 2007). In further detail:

- it does not supply any tools to forecast the results expected from lean initiatives;
- it refers only to the cost element and not to the capability of generating value for the customer (McNair, 1994; McNair et al., 2001a,b; Ostrenga and Probst, 1992), simply considering LM as a set of tools to improve efficiency but not to enhance effectiveness;
- it supplies a standardised solution, without considering the company's specific characteristics such as size, industry, business model, the level of development of lean initiatives etc.;
- it does not deal with the cost of unused capacity.

These gaps bring to light interesting research areas that will be explored in this chapter, which develops an innovative LA model based on the

Strategic Cost Management (SCM) framework (Shank and Govindarajan, 1989), more aligned to the specific needs of lean environments. In detail, this model is based on two main targets: (1) exploring the lean profit potential, at the planning and commitment stages of a lean transformation; and (2) controlling lean management effects, in terms of cost reduction and value creation, in the implementation and consolidation stages of an ongoing lean process.

In particular, the following section describes the weaknesses of traditional MAS, while Section 3.3 illustrates the LA approaches developed by literature and their limitations. Section 3.4 presents an innovative LA model, and finally Section 3.5 concludes, reporting the most relevant issues for any MAS in a lean environment.

3.2 Criticisms of traditional accounting systems in a lean environment

In order to comprehend why traditional MAS fails in supporting lean initiatives, it is important to start from the key principles of the Lean Management philosophy.

In order to go lean, companies must understand their customers and what they really value. For a company to focus on these needs it must first define its own value streams (all the activities that are needed to provide a particular product or service) and, thereafter, the value streams of its wider supply chain. To satisfy customers, companies need to subsequently eliminate – or at least reduce – the wasteful activities in their value stream, since their customers do not wish to be encumbered with the payment of these.

In sum, the five lean principles are:

1. *Specify* what does and does not create *value* from the customer's perspective and not just from the perspective of the company or the individual functions and departments;
2. *Identify* all the steps necessary to design, order and produce the product across the *whole value stream* to highlight non-value adding activities;
3. Make those actions that create value *flow* without interruptions, detours, back-flows, waiting or scrap;
4. Make only what is *pulled* by the customer;
5. Strive for *perfection* by continually removing successive layers of waste as they are uncovered.

These principles are fundamental to the elimination of waste in addition to adding more value both to the customer and to the members of the entire value chain.

Considering these principles should make it easier to understand the reasons why traditional MAS are not effective in supporting the development and implementation of LM projects (Maskell, 2000; Grasso, 2006; Jusko, 2007). Many authors have even pointed out the risk of failure of lean projects due to the use of misleading information from traditional MAS (Maskell and Baggaley, 2003; Kennedy and Huntziger, 2005; Jusko, 2007). The main reasons follow.

3.2.1   Standard costing and variance analysis: do they support waste reduction?

The first consideration relates to the typical standard costs and variance analyses that can lead to incorrect behaviours contrary to the goals pursued by LM (Kroll, 2004). Indeed, standard costs are often very distant from the 'ideal' level of efficiency, since they are only occasionally revised. They can consequently include significant waste (Maskell, 2006) and be in conflict with the key lean principle of perfection.

Furthermore, variance analyses developed on the basis of traditional standard costs can promote behaviours that are opposite to those LM aims to attain, particularly when linked to management evaluation systems (De Luzio, 2006). For example, to improve Purchase Price Variance, a purchasing manager could decide to increase the purchase volume to obtain volume discounts. He could also choose the lowest-priced supplier, neglecting other attributes such as quality and delivery time, even though the savings do not bridge the quality gap.

Moreover, in evaluating manufacturing efficiency, the adoption of absorption variance (i.e., the rate of production overheads absorbed by the actual production level) can easily lead to overproduction.

The same negative effect could be generated by traditional Cost Accounting Systems (Johnson and Kaplan, 1987) due to the allocation of indirect production costs and overheads based on the number of units produced or hours worked. This method encourages overproduction and an inventory increase (Kennedy and Huntzinger, 2005).

3.2.2   Inventories: asset vs. waste

Traditional MAS consider inventory as an asset, value generated by the company that increases profits. In contrast, LM adopts a Just-in-Time approach and banishes inventories – due to overproduction (Goldratt,

1990) – since they reduce flexibility and create constraints, particularly when markets are unstable and competition is aggressive.

3.2.3   Management accounting systems: are they lean?

Finally, another significant criticism of traditional MAS is that they themselves are generally not 'lean'. Moreover, the reports are very frequently based on financial measures, which may be too complex to help improve efficiency and effectiveness (Johnson, 2006).

In sum, the entire traditional MAS approach is based on a top-down culture, where 'managers are the knowledge holder and workers are supposed to act, not to think' (Grasso, 2006). They nevertheless largely prevail due to their short-term and financial focus and as a consequence of insufficient information systems.

3.3   Lean accounting approaches developed by theory

The criticisms of traditional MAS described in the previous section have produced two types of reactions.

The first, previously reported by Johnson (2006), suggests that Management Accounting should disregard the shop floor environment. In the eyes of the accounting department, the shop floor level is seen as a 'black box' and since Operations management does not require financial measures, it develops its own set of control tools.

This approach presents some potentially dangerous limitations. As a first limitation, empirical evidence demonstrates the increasing difficulties that top management have in controlling 'finance' as company complexity increases and the number of businesses, markets, plants etc. grows. This condition necessarily requires greater support from the information system comprising financial variables.

A second limitation is the need for top management commitment to any lean transformation, usually driven by operations and logistics personnel. Since top management is particularly sensitive to the financial language, involvement in Management Accounting can provide insight into the impact that any lean programmes have on performance. This is essential to obtain commitment.

Based on these concerns, a number of other authors have supported the development of some lean versions of MAS, namely Lean Accounting (Maskell and Baggaley, 2003; Kennedy and Brewer, 2005; Kennedy and Huntzinger, 2005), specifically designed for companies applying LM. These alternative approaches have the following common characteristics.

3.3.1 Focus on the value stream

An LA system emphasises the value stream as the single cost object. A value stream includes all the steps necessary to design, order and produce any value-adding attributes of products and services in the eyes of the customer (MacInnes, 2002).

Value Stream Costing (VSC) requires the identification of revenues and costs directly related to value streams, since in a lean organisation most of these are value stream driven. This consideration makes cost assignment easier and more precise, overcoming one of the shortcomings of traditional MAS previously described.

Table 3.1 reports an example of VSC. Following a pull philosophy, since inventories are considered as waste in a lean environment, any material purchased is considered part of the value stream cost, even when it is stocked and unsold.

Moreover, due to the particular treatment of changes in inventories, the VSC allocates fixed and variable production costs (labour, depreciation etc.) only on sold products, instead of on the units produced. This mechanism is more coherent with the idea that inventories are waste, since their change is charged to the Value Stream Cost and reduces the Value Stream Profit.

Another aspect characterising VSC is that it includes only the cost of the space actually used (Row 7, Table 3.1); as a consequence, when a value stream requires less space – thanks to inventory reduction, process realignment etc. – its cost also decreases, highlighting lean benefits and encouraging the transformation.

3.3.2 Focus on a few key performance indicators

LA approaches pursue the strong reduction of financial measures and data-gathering activities, which should be completely removed on the single work cell level and simplified on the value stream level.

With the exception of the value stream, LA encourages the use of non-financial measures in both strategic and operational contexts. In particular, on a single work cell level it suggests very few technical measures that are quickly available and familiar to the personnel. Indeed, on the value stream level, financial information should be enriched by quality, efficiency, etc. measures in a Value Stream Box Scorecard (VSBS) (Kennedy and Huntzinger, 2005).

Table 3.2 shows an example of VSBS; thanks to the lean transformation of the accounting processes described, this report could be drawn up very quickly and thus with high frequency (i.e., every week).

Table 3.1 An example of value stream costing

	Items	Value Stream 1	Value Stream 2	Total
1	Revenues	4,380,000	3,999,000	8,379,000
2	Purchased raw materials	2,151,780	1,710,223	3,862,003
3	Industrial services	450,900	501,000	951,900
4=2+3	Total variable cost	2,602,680	2,211,223	4,813,903
5=1−4	Contribution Margin	1,777,320	1,787,777	3,565,097
6	Labour cost	876,400	540,700	1,417,100
7	Space capacity cost	120,900	110,100	231,000
8	Value Stream commercial cost	101,343	109,222	210,565
9	Value Stream administrative cost	87,777	56,555	144,332
10=6+7+8+9	Total VS overhead cost	1,186,420	816,577	2,002,997
11=5−10	Value Stream profit	590,900	971,200	1,562,100
12=11/1	VSP%	0.134908676	0.242860715	18.6%
13	Change in inventories	56,789	71,222	128,011
14	Unused space capacity cost			128,300
15	General overhead cost			591,000
16=11+13−14−15	EBIT			970,811
17=16/1	Return on Sales			11.6%

Finally, objectives and key success factors also have to be identified at the strategic level, together with their relationship with the value stream level and the work cell level. A sort of strategic map (adapted to lean management targets and actions) could help in controlling lean at a strategic level (Kennedy and Huntzinger, 2005).

3.4   Weaknesses of the lean accounting models developed

3.4.1   Is lean accounting new?

Some authors (Van Der Merwe and Thomson, 2007) assert that in principle LA does not introduce a very innovative approach and that it is rather better applied to a specific environment. First of all, LA only proposes a different

Table 3.2   An example of a value stream box scorecard (adapted from Kennedy and Huntzinger, 2005)

	Week t-2	Week t-1	Week t	Annual Target
Operational performance indicators				
On time delivery (%)	94.3%	94.5%	93.0%	97.0%
Lead time (days)	14	13.7	13.4	10.0
Quality problems (PPM)	12.5	14.8	11.2	9.0
Stock level (no. of items)	300	290	280	190
Capacity indicators				
Used capacity for production	37.4%	38.0%	38.0%	55.0%
Used capacity for commercial and administrative activities	40.0%	37.3%	37.0%	30.0%
Unused capacity	22.6%	24.7%	25.0%	15.0%
Financial performance indicators				
Revenues	650,000	670,000	590,000	8,160,000
Raw materials	390,000	400,000	340,000	4,320,000
Value Stream Profit %	15.30%	15.10%	14.90%	16.50%

use for well-established tools and techniques. In particular, VSC can be seen as direct costing that has the value stream as the single cost object. Other similarities link VSC with Throughput Accounting (Goldratt, 1984). Moreover, VSBS in a lean environment would only be an implementation of the Balanced Scorecard model or other performance measurement system theories (Kaplan and Norton, 2004; Lorino, 1991; Hines *et al.*, 1997).

The second main criticism highlights that recent advanced theories have already developed more powerful tools and techniques, such as Target Costing, Activity-based Costing and Resource Consumption Accounting that are not considered by LA developers and supporters.

3.4.2   What about value?

A main constraint of LA is its strong focus on the efficiency dimension to the detriment of the value dimension, which is one of the main pillars of LM. In sum, LA does not deal with important questions such as: (1) what is value in the eyes of the customer? (2) which activities and processes are value adding? In other words, a distinction should be made between the activities on the basis of their value content.

3.4.3   What about lean profit potential?

Finally, another important criticism focuses on the lack of support for companies that are only evaluating a potential LM transformation.

Indeed, LA does not provide any financial tools for the analysis of the expected results of lean projects, which are instead a crucial aspect in obtaining top management's attention and approval.

For instance, the VSC is suitable only for lean environments due to the very simplified allocation process of indirect costs, which could even be dangerous if the company is not yet lean and still facing significant overhead costs and inventories.

3.5 A new lean accounting model

Taking into consideration the abovementioned concerns of the current LA approaches, a more effective model should pursue the two following main objectives: (1) Exploring Lean Potential; (2) Controlling Lean Management.

The following two sections explore possible LA tools for these two purposes.

3.5.1 Exploring lean potential: approaches and tools

A fully comprehensive LA framework should also support companies that are only just approaching the idea of implementing LM. In order for the project to be successful, middle management (usually based in the manufacturing or logistic departments) wanting to implement one or more lean tools needs the commitment of the top management.

In sum, in this context, the most relevant accounting needs of LM teams are: (1) to explore the lean profit potential, i.e., the financial impact of the suggested programmes; (2) to identify priorities and to set targets, thanks to an understanding of where waste is embedded; and (3) to produce relevant and effective information for managers (who are often used to only receiving financial data).

In order to obtain appreciation of the project benefits, firstly, the lean team needs specific tools focused on the potential impact on the company's financial performance (in terms of costs savings, cash flow, profitability, financial strength etc.). This additional financial information can also help persuade accounting personnel and conservative owners of small and medium-sized companies, who tend to resist change.

Second, Process Costing and Mapping Tools (Morrow and Hazell, 1992; Hines *et al.*, 2002) help map micro-activities with details on their time and cost implications, cost drivers and value content. A comparison between the cost and time profile of activities before ('as is', Table 3.3) and after ('to be', Table 3.4) the lean programme measures their profit potential.

Table 3.3 Process cost map before the lean programme ('as is')

Micro-activity (1)	Driver (2)	Annual driver value (3)	Time (seconds)/d river (4)	Total time (hours) (5)=(3)×(2)/3600	Cost/hours (6)	Total cost (7)=(6)×(5)
Arrival of materials	No. of movements	35,000	50	486	17.00	8,264
Documents to accountant	No. of movements	35,000	30	292	17.00	4,958
Login to the system	No. of movements	35,000	20	194	20.00	3,889
Delivery paperwork in the system	No. of document rows	172,715	10	480	20.00	9,595
Materials unloading	No. of items	95,555	90	2,389	17.00	40,611
Materials to inspector	No. of items to be tested	10,550	50	147	17.00	2,491
Stock of items not to be tested	No. of items not to be tested	85,005	90	2,125	17.00	36,127
Quality inspection	No. of tests	31,700	600	5,283	21.00	110,950
Positive test outcome into the system	No. of positive tests	27,040	90	676	21.00	14,196
Negative test outcome into the system	No. of negative tests	4,660	360	466	21.00	9,786
Stock of checked items	No. of positive tested items	9,000	90	225	17.00	3,825
Materials to non conformity area	No. of negative tested items	4,660	60	78	17.00	1,320
Return administrative procedure	No. of negative tests	4,660	600	777	20.00	15,533
Total				13,617		261,546

As an example, Table 3.3 reports the Process Cost Map of the 'goods inwards process'. The activity driver and its annual value, the time per driver (in minutes), the total time, the cost per hour and the total cost are described for each micro-activity. The comparison between the 'as is' map and the 'to be' map can explore the improvement in terms of savings of a just-in-time program (for example, 3.700 hours, i.e., €81.000, as shown in the last row of Table 3.4). In particular, the 'to be' Process Cost Map shows the savings linked to the testing and non-conformity management activities. The resources saved could be directed towards more value adding activities.

This costing model has other advantages: (1) it allows the operations personnel to fully comprehend the reporting, consistent with organisational learning logic, and (2) it helps in forecasting and simulating process and cost configurations.

As in established Lean Enterprises, MAS have to support the start-up stage of LM programs. In this context, the VSC is not fully applicable since most resources are still related to several value streams and allocation problems can arise. An activity-based Accounting System is therefore more suitable, as it measures activity costs and allocates them to the value streams through appropriate activity drivers. This treatment would:

- simplify the Activity-based Costing implementation, since the allocation process would be applied to a reduced number of activities in considering the value streams as cost objects;
- measure both the used and unused capacity of the value streams and, thereafter, quantifying efficiency improvements due to the lean programmes in terms of both time savings and less space used (see Table 3.5).

However, value stream performance does not depend only on its cost; it is also a function of its revenue. Nevertheless, a key constraint of the LA models developed is simply the lack of focus on the value dimension, which is driven by customer value perception.

An LA approach could thus include value analysis tools (McNair, 1994), imported from SCM (Shank and Govindarajan, 1989, 1993a, b). According to the SCM approach, activities can be classified as follows (McNair *et al.*, 2001a, b):

- Value Adding Activities (VA), which the customer is willing to pay for;
- Future Value Adding Activities (FVA), i.e., activities representing an investment in future customer value adding activities;

Table 3.4 Process cost map after the lean programme ('to be') Controlling lean management: approaches and tools

Micro-activity (1)	Driver (2)	Annual driver value (3)	Time (seconds)/driver (4)	Total time (hours) (5)=(3)×(2)/3600	Cost/hours (6)	Total cost (7)=(6)×(5)
Arrival of materials	No. of movements	70,000	50	972	17.00	16,528
Documents to accountant	No. of movements	70,000	30	583	17.00	9,917
Login to the system	No. of movements	70,000	20	389	20.00	7,778
Delivery paperwork in the system	No. of document rows	345,430	10	960	20.00	19,191
Materials unloading	No. of items	95,555	90	2,389	17.00	40,611
Materials to inspector	No. of items to be tested	3,165	50	44	17.00	747
Stock of items not to be tested	No. of items not to be tested	92,390	90	2,310	17.00	39,266
Quality inspection	No. of tests	9,510	600	1,585	21.00	33,285
Positive test outcome into the system	No. of positive tests	8,112	90	203	21.00	4,259
Negative test outcome into the system	No. of negative tests	1,398	360	140	21.00	2,936
Stock of checked items	No. of positive tested items	2,700	90	67	17.00	1,147
Materials to non conformity area	No. of negative tested items	1,398	60	23	17.00	396
Return administrative procedure	No. of negative tests	1,398	600	233	20.00	4,660
Total				9,898	–	180,720
Delta "to be" – "as is"				3,719	–	80,826

Table 3.5   The financial impact of efficiency improvement

	Item	Before	After
1	Time per invoice (minutes)	40	32
2	Total time (hours)	5,000	5,000
3	Total activity cost (€)	130,000	130,000
4=2/(1/60)	No. of potential invoices	7,500	9,375
5=3/4	Potential cost per invoice	17.33	13.87
6	Actual no. of invoices	7,500	7,500
7=3/6	Actual cost per invoice	17.33	17.33
8	No. of invoices for value stream A	4,500	4,500
9	No. of invoices for value stream B	3,000	3,000
10=5×8	Cost of value stream A	78,000	62,400
11=5×9	Cosl of value stream B	52,000	41,600
12=3−10−11	**Cost of unused capacity**	–	**26,000**

- Supporting Activities (SA), which do not directly add value but under the current process are necessary to support the value-adding proposition (they are thus a target for medium term containment or even elimination);
- Waste (W), which does not add value to the customer since it is due to misalignments and failures in processes (they are a target for short-term elimination or drastic reduction).

Value stream reporting should thus include both cost and value information (Table 3.6).

Value stream reporting emphasises some important results:

1. The *Contribution Margin* (Row 5), a function of the company's contractual power over suppliers, R&D process quality and efficient consumption of materials. This margin can be supported by the *Contribution Index* (Row 23) – the Contribution Margin divided by the revenues;
2. The *Value Stream Profit Potential* (Row 7). As the difference between value stream revenues, value stream direct costs and value adding activity costs, this margin describes in financial terms the idea of perfection, i.e., a pillar of the LM paradigm. This profit potential measures ideal performance, after the total elimination of waste

Table 3.6 Value stream reporting

	Items	Value Stream 1	Value Stream 2	Total
1	**Revenues**	4,380,000	3,999,000	8,379,000
2	Purchased raw materials	2,151,780	1,710,223	3,862,003
3	Industrial services	450,900	501,000	951,900
4 = 2 + 3	**Total variable cost**	2,602,680	2,211,223	4,813,903
5 = 1 − 4	**Contribution margin**	1,777,320	1,787,777	3,565,097
6	**Value activities**	346,777	355,555	702,332
7 = 5 − 6	**Profit potential**	1,430,543	1,432,222	2,862,765
8	Supporting activities	490,888	254,444	745,332
9 = 7 − 8	**Efficient value stream profit**	939,655	1,177,778	2,117,433
10 = 9/1	**EVSP%**	21.5%	29.5%	25.3%
11	Waste	207,555	156,005	363,560
12	**Value stream profit**	732,100	1,021,773	1,753,873
13	Unused space capacity cost			128,300
14	Unused capacity for value adding activities			345,698
15	Unused capacity for not value adding activities			369,223
16 = 13 + 14 + 15	**Unused capacity cost**			843,221
17	Overhead cost			67,852
18 = 12 − 16 − 17	**Revised EBIT**			842,800
19 = 18/1	**Revised return on sales**			10.1%
20	Change in inventories	56,789	71,222	128,011
21 = 18 + 20	**EBIT**			970,811
22 = 21/1	**Return on sales**			11.6%

Indicators

	Index	Value Stream 1	Value Stream 2	Total
23=5/1	Contribution Index	40.6%	44.7%	42.5%
24=7/5	Value Index	80.5%	80.1%	80.3%
25=9/7	Efficiency Index	65.7%	82.2%	74.0%
26=23×24×25	EVSP%	21.5%	29.5%	25.3%
27=12/9	Value Stream Profit Index			82.8%
28=18/12	Capacity Index			48.1%
29=21/18	Inventory Index			11.5%
30=26×27×28×29	ROS			11.6%

and non-value adding activities. This margin can be associated to the *Value Index* (Row 24), which is measured by dividing the Profit Potential by the Contribution Margin;

3. The *Efficient Value Stream Profit* (Row 9), which can be enhanced by reducing only used capacity, and supporting activities, together with the *Efficiency Index* (Row 25), i.e., the Efficient Value Stream Profit divided by the Value Stream Profit Potential;

4. The *Value Stream Profit* (Row 12), which is affected also by waste activities and can be divided by the Efficient Value Stream Profit to obtain the *Value Stream Profit Index* (Row 27);

5. The *Value Stream Revised EBIT* (Row 18), which does not include the increase or decrease in inventories, and the *Capacity Index* (Row 28) – the Value Stream Revised EBIT divided by the Value Stream Profit;

6. The *Value Stream EBIT* (Row 21), which also includes changes in the inventories and that can be divided by the Value Stream Revised EBIT to obtain the *Inventory Index* (Row 29).

By putting together the preceding value stream performance indexes, we obtain the following equation (Row 26):

$$\begin{aligned} & \textit{Efficient Value Stream Profit \%} \\ & = \textit{Contribution Index} \\ & \times \textit{Value Index} \times \textit{Efficiency Index} \end{aligned}$$

In Table 3.6, value stream no. 1 and value stream no. 2 show very close Contribution and Value Indexes, but the first reports an Efficiency Index of just 65.7 per cent, compared to the second with 82.2 per cent. This difference is due to a larger portion of non-value adding activities in value stream no. 1 and highlights the potential benefits of programs focused on efficiency improvement.

Table 3.6 (Row 30) also shows the following relationship:

$$\begin{aligned} & \textit{Value Stream EBIT \% (ROS)} \\ & = \textit{Efficient Value Stream Profit \%} \\ & \times \textit{Value Stream Profit Index} \times \textit{Capacity Index} \\ & \times \textit{Inventory Index} \end{aligned}$$

Since the Capacity Index in Table 3.6 is 48.1 per cent, unused capacity absorbs more than 50 per cent of the Value Stream EBIT.

Finally, SCM offers other useful and well-known techniques for a lean environment such as Cost Driver Analysis (Shank and Govindarajan,

1993), Capacity Cost Management (McNair, 1994; McNair and Vangermeersch, 1998), Total Cost of Ownership and Life Cycle Costing (Ansari and Bell, 1997; Berliner and Brimson, 1988), and Target Costing (Ansari and Bell, 1997).

3.6 Conclusions

This chapter is focused on the following questions:

1. Are traditional MAS a constraint for the development of LM programs?
2. In that case, how should they be revised in order to better support managers in lean or future lean environments?

Section 3.2 highlighted the weaknesses of traditional MAS, while Section 3.4 described the reasons why LA models developed by theory do not introduce a very innovative approach.

Section 3.5 introduced an innovative and more flexible LA approach, importing tools and techniques from SCM that should be able to overcome a number of criticisms thanks to:

1. a focus on the evaluation of the potential impacts of a future lean transformation on a company's financial performance (in terms of costs and benefits, cash flow, profitability, financial strength etc.). In fact, a fully comprehensive LA framework should also support companies that are only just approaching the idea of implementing LM. Middle management wanting to implement lean tools needs the commitment of the top management. In order to make the project benefits appreciable, the lean team also has to use a financial language;
2. the role of the value analysis, which considers the value dimension as an LM principle and not solely efficiency, lead times, inventories, waste, costs etc.;
3. the process orientation of the mapping and costing tools, consistent with the LM principle of creating lean flows of activities along the value streams;
4. progressive LA, taking into consideration that a lean transformation can be a long process including numerous different stages with their own information needs;
5. the opportunity to provide management control targets.

Finally, LA systems themselves should be lean. As a consequence, simplified and customised versions of the suggested SCM tools and techniques are recommended, most of all in small and medium-sized companies or in the very early stages of a lean transformation. In particular, LA implementation can give rise to issues relating to the specific company context, such as the measurement attitude, the amount of standardised activities, the degree of extension and flexibility of the information system.

References

Ansari, S. L. and Bell, J. E. (1997). *Target Costing: The Next Frontier in Strategic Cost Management*, McGraw-Hill, New York.

Anthony, R. (1965). *Planning and Control Systems*, Harvard University, Boston.

Berliner, C. and Brimson, J. A. (eds.) (1988). *Cost Management for Today's Manufacturing: The CAM-I Conceptual Design*, Harvard Business School Press, Boston.

De Luzio, M. C. (2006). 'Accounting for Lean', *Manufacturing Engineering*, 137 (6), 83–9.

Goldratt, E. M. and Cox, J. (1984). *The Goal – Excellence in Manufacturing*, North River Press, New York.

Goldratt, E. M. (1990) *Theory of Constraints*, North River Press, New York.

Grasso, L. P. (2006) 'Barriers to Lean Accounting', *Cost Management*, March–April, 6–19.

Hines P., Dimancescu, D. and Rich N. (1997). *The Lean Enterprise; Designing and Managing Strategic Processes for Customer Winning Performance*, Amacom, New York.

Hines, P., Silvi, R. and Bartolini, M. (2002). *Lean Profit Potential*, Lean Enterprise Research Centre, Cardiff Business School, Cardiff, UK.

Johnson, H. T. (2006). 'To Become Lean, Shed Accounting', *Cost Management*, 20 (1), 6–17.

Johnson, H. T. and Kaplan, R. S. (1987). *Relevance Lost. The Rise and Fall of Management Accounting*, Harvard Business School Press, Boston.

Jusko, J. (2007). 'Accounting for Lean Tastes', *Industry Week*, 256 (9), 35–7.

Kaplan, R. and Norton, D. (2004). *Strategy Maps, Converting Intangible Assets into Tangible Outcomes*, Harvard Business School Press, Boston.

Kennedy, F. A. and Huntzinger, J. (2005). 'Lean Accounting: Measuring and Managing the Value Stream', *Cost Management*, September–October, 31–8.

Kennedy, F. A. and Brewer, P. C. (2005). 'Lean: What's It All About?' *Accounting, Strategic Finance*, November, 27–34.

Kroll, K. M. (2004). 'The Lowdown on Lean Accounting', *Journal of Accountancy*, July, 69–76.

Lorino, P. (1991). *Le contrôle de gestion stratégique*, La gestion par les acticités, Dunod, Paris.

MacInnes, R. (2002). *The Lean Enterprise Memory Jogger*, Salem, GOAL/QPC, NH.

Maskell, B. H. (2000). 'Lean Accounting for Lean Manufacturers', *Manufacturing Engineering*, December, 46–53.

Maskell, B. H. and Baggaley, B. (2003). *Practical Lean Accounting: A Proven System for Measuring and Managing the Lean Enterprise*, Productivity Press, New York.

Maskell, B. H. (2006). 'Solving the Standard Cost Problem', *Cost Management*, 20 (1), 27–35.

McNair, C. J. (1994). *The Profit Potential: Taking High Performance to the Bottom Line*, Oliver Wight Publications Inc, Essex Junction, VT.

McNair, C. J. and Vangermeersch, R. (1998). *Total Capacity Management: Optimising at the Operational, Tactical and Strategic Level*, St. Lucie Press, Florida.

McNair, C. J., Polutnik, L. and Silvi, R. (2001a). 'Outside-In: Cost and the Creation of Customer Value', *Advances in Management Accounting*, 9, 1–41.

McNair, C. J., Polutnik, L. and Silvi, R. (2001b). 'Cost Management and Value Creation, The Missing Link', *European Accounting Review*, 1, 33–50.

Merchant, K. A. (1985). *Control in Business Organisations*, Ballinger Publishing Company, Cambridge, MA.

Morrow, M. and Hazell, M. (1992). 'Activity Mapping for Business Process Redesign', *Management Accounting*, February, 36–8.

Ohno, T. (1988). *Toyota Production System: Beyond Large-Scale Production*, Portland, OR, Productivity Press.

Ostrenga, M. R. and Probst, F. R. (1992). 'Process Value Analysis: The Missing Link in Cost Management', *Cost Management*, 6 (3), 1–4.

Shank, J. and Govindarajan, V. (1989). *Strategic Cost Analysis: The Evolution from Managerial to Strategic Accounting*, Richard Irwin Inc., Homewood, IL.

Shank, J. and Govindarajan, V. (1993a). *Strategic Cost Management*, The Free Press, New York.

Shank, J. and Govindarajan, V. (1993b). 'What "Drivers" Cost? A Strategic Cost Management Perspective', *Advances in Management Accounting*, 2, 27–45.

Simons, R. (1995). *Levers of Control: How Managers Use Innovative Control System to Drive Strategic Renewal*, Harvard Business School Press, Boston, MA.

Van der Merwe, A. and Thomson, J. (2007). 'The Lowdown on Lean Accounting', *Strategic Finance*, 88 (8), 26–33.

Womack, J., Jones, D. and Roos, D. (1990). *The Machine that Changed the World*, Rawson Associates, New York.

Womack, J. and Jones, D. (1996). *Lean Thinking: Banish Waste and Create Wealth in Your Corporation*, Simon & Schuster, New York.

4
What *Really* Happens with Performance Management Systems

Noah P. Barsky and Garry Marchant

4.1 Introduction

CEOs are increasingly focusing on strategy implementation rather than strategy formulation as the key to ultimate success. The systems, processes and tools that managers adopt to manage organisational performance and align performance with strategic objectives form the core of strategy implementation. Otley (1999) argues that performance management frameworks provide a useful mechanism for examining holistically management control techniques used by organisations. Performance management systems span beyond simply *measuring* performance to include the related strategic planning and feedback processes. A key benefit of taking the performance management framework view of management control systems is that it allows for a complete rather than piecemeal evaluation of the system.

We examined hundreds of written descriptions prepared by senior and frontline managers about the perceived nature and use of performance management systems, processes, tools and techniques in place in their employers and (1) consider the management control components of performance management framework in terms of connections among three fundamental business processes: strategic planning, performance measurement and performance appraisal; (2) research considers data from the perspective of individual managers rather than the company; and (3) provide indications about the actual use of performance management processes and where and how the breakdowns from expectations occur.

4.2   Otley's performance management framework

Otley (1999, p. 5) defines the performance management framework around five main sets of issues that he represents as five key compelling questions:

1. What are the key objectives central to the organisation's overall future success, and how does it go about evaluating its achievement of these objectives?
2. What strategies and plans has the organisation adopted and which processes and activities has it decided will be required to successfully implement these? How does it assess and measure the performance of these activities?
3. What level of performance does the organisation need to achieve in each of the areas defined in the above two questions, and how does it go about setting appropriate performance targets for them?
4. What rewards will managers (and other employees) gain by achieving these performance targets (or, conversely, what penalties will they suffer by failing to achieve them)?
5. What are the information flows (feedback and feed-forward loops) necessary to enable the organisation to learn from its experience, and to adapt its current behaviour in the light of that experience?

The first question focuses on the organisation's transformation of its core mission to goals and objectives. Also contained within this question are issues related to how it determines success and the attainment of its goals. The second question is targeted at the formulation of strategy and the determination of strategic initiatives and key success factors. These two elements are connected through the strategic planning process. Strategic planning is the process through which organisations develop the mechanisms necessary to achieve their objectives. The third question is at the centre of much of the research in management accounting and management control. Strategic actions and key success factors are used to develop targets and performance measures through the performance management systems. The balanced scorecard is an example of a performance measurement system (Kaplan and Norton, 2009). The fourth question relates to rewards and their connection to performance measures and targets. The performance appraisal process connects targets, performance measures and rewards through the process of individual performance planning, appraisal and feedback. Feedback is the topic of the last question. Feedback is necessary for

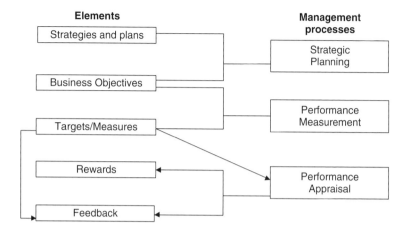

Figure 4.1   The performance management framework (adapted from Otley, 1999)

managers to learn from their experience and for the organisation to learn and adapt.

Extending Otley's model, three key organisational processes connect the performance management elements contained in these five questions:

1. Strategic Planning
2. Performance Measurement
3. Performance Appraisal

These elements and processes combined describe the performance management framework as shown in Figure 4.1. Each of the core elements is connected by one of these processes that provide a basis for ensuring alignment of the elements from corporate objective to individual objectives.

4.3   Three fundamental processes

Performance management provides an integrative framework that allows researchers to focus both on the whole performance management package, on its elements and on the three fundamental processes supporting these elements. The three processes are:

Strategic Planning This transforms corporate objectives into strategic initiatives, actions, plans and key success factors. Strategic planning typically starts with the organisation's objectives, and analyses the environment and organisational factors for success. From this is developed the strategic plans and actions. These plans and actions along with the associated key success factors form the inputs for the performance measurement system.

Performance Measurement System These systems play a key role in developing the strategic direction of the organisation and evaluating the achievement of the organisations objectives. Most performance measurement systems have historically been financially driven (Ittner and Larcker, 1998). Kaplan and Norton (2009) contend that the balanced scorecard performance measurement system is designed to facilitate the linking of strategic objectives and plans with manager behaviour and organisational performance.

Performance Appraisal Process This process involves evaluating the performance of each manager against some benchmark for performance. Performance appraisal systems are typically designed to communicate the organisation's objectives, to provide feedback for learning, to allocate rewards and for career development. Performance appraisals may be based on subjective or impression-based criteria (essentially impressions of a qualitative nature), or they may be objective requiring clear targets and measures drawn from the performance measurement system. Performance appraisal is often used to determine performance rewards. Alternatively, the performance appraisal process can be designed to provide feedback with the aim that both the individual and the organisation will learn and adapt for the future. Performance appraisal is important because it is the most prominent means by which individual managers receive feedback and rewards. Many organisations have implemented a number of tools and techniques that together represent a performance management package that covers the entire framework, but frequently the performance management elements and processes as practised do not reflect the designed system.

4.4 Aligning the performance management system

The prime directive of performance management is to align individual goals with corporate goals. This alignment should lead to organisations that are effective, committed and results driven (American Quality and Productivity Center, 2010). There is frequent discussion in the management control literature of the importance of alignment (Flamholtz *et al.*, 1985), but there is almost no examination of whether or not performance management systems are in alignment or not. Yet, this is the primary determinant of effectiveness of the systems. While the link between organisational achievement, targets and performance measures is well accepted, the connecting of targets and measures to achievement of organisational goals is complex and problematic. In part this is because of the inherent trade-offs implicit in multi-dimensional measurement frameworks where one cannot assess definitively whether the organisation is better than its competitors. Further, Slagmulder (1997) examined the use of performance management systems to align strategic investment decisions with strategy. Her research suggests that the primary driving force in the design of performance management systems is the alignment of strategy with strategic investment decisions.

4.5   Research issues

Summarising the preceding discussion, this study is focused on three exploratory research questions. The first question relates to the gap between normative models of performance management and the description of performance management in practice. This issue focuses on closing this gap by documenting and understanding control processes from managers' perceptions.

Research Question No. 1: From the perspectives of managers, to what extent (if at all) have today's organisations implemented components of the performance management system? There is a great deal of research and professional literature describing the various elements and processes of the performance management system which many organisations have adopted and yet there is some suggestion that practice may not reflect the normative textbook performance management systems adopted by many organisations. There may also be a gap between the rhetoric of performance management espoused by organisations and the practice of performance management as perceived by managers.

Research Question No. 2: From the perspectives of managers, is performance management practice consistent with the intended or designed utilisation of the performance management system, as espoused by the organisation? The primary purpose of performance management is to align corporate objectives with individual objectives and behaviour. Previous research has focused on individual tools and techniques for performance management and has as a result not been able to assess the overall effectiveness of performance management systems with regard to this primary objective. The performance management framework, with its holistic focus, provides an opportunity to evaluate whether alignment is occurring. In other words, are corporations implementing performance management programmes as designed and do managers perceive that these processes achieve the desired effects? Also, if the system is misaligned, the performance management framework makes it easier to determine where in the framework and why misalignment is happening.

Research Question No. 3: What connections among the performance management elements and processes are important to effectively align corporate objectives with individual objectives? These three questions, when considered together, provide the context for understanding the current state of practice at large and the reasons for (in)effectiveness of performance management programmes in specific organisations.

4.6 Data collection and analysis

Data were collected from participants in an Executive MBA (EMBA) Programme and an evening MBA programme at two US universities. As part of the course coverage on performance measurement topics, students were asked to complete a self-reflection exercise where they were asked to think about their employer's performance management programme. Specifically, participants were asked to consider how well their employer clearly articulated objectives and designed systems that effectively aligned employee incentives and actions with strategic goals. Memos were collected from 60 senior managers (EMBA students, averaging nine years of work experience) and 80 managers (MBA students, averaging five years of work experience).

Each participant prepared a two-page, single-spaced, typed memo that described the following information (if known): (1) their employer's line of business and their personal job responsibilities; (2) detail about the nature of their firm/business unit's strategic goals, plans and business objectives; (3) the performance measurement and target setting process; (4) the basis for periodic performance evaluation (by your boss); and (5) the nature and type of rewards and feedback. Participants were also asked to reflect on how their job contributes to the firm's strategic success and how well (if at all) the firm had aligned their personal performance objectives with the firm's strategic success factors. A benefit of collecting data from practising managers enrolled in an education programme is that managers are committed to spend time to offer complete and descriptive responses.

4.7   Data analysis

The participants represented a wide cross-section of industries, including telecommunications, pharmaceuticals, financial services, aerospace and industrial manufacturing: 53.4 per cent of participants were employed at service firms, while 46.6 per cent were employed at manufacturing firms. Of the managers, 59.3 per cent were employed at service firms, while 58.6 per cent of the senior managers worked at manufacturing firms.

4.7.1   Performance management elements and attributes

Otley (1999) defined performance management programmes in terms of five primary elements: (1) Business Objectives; (2) Strategies and Plans; (3) Targets and Measures; (4) Rewards and (5) Feedback. As depicted in Figure 4.1, these elements manifest themselves in organisations through three primary management processes: (1) Strategic Planning; (2) Performance Measurement; and (3) Performance Appraisal. The elements and attributes of each management process, as depicted in Table 4.1, provide the basis for supporting and structuring the data analysis.

In this study, 94.3 per cent of all participants, 91.5 per cent of managers and 100 per cent of the senior managers indicated that their firms had clearly defined strategic initiatives. Further, 90.8 per cent of all participants, 87.9 per cent of managers and 96.6 per cent of senior managers indicated that their firms had defined business objectives to support the strategic initiatives. Interestingly, only 5.7 per cent of all respondents, 1.7 per cent of managers and 13.8 per cent of senior managers participated in strategic planning. These results suggest that while almost all managers and senior managers can readily identify strategic initiatives and business objectives at their firms, participation in strategic planning can be characterised as an executive-level, top-down process at these firms.

While the data suggest that the strategic planning process seems to be the domain of corporate executives, some managers and senior managers do participate in developing performance measures and setting targets. In fact, 31.4 per cent of all participants, 28.8 per cent of all managers and 37.0 per cent of senior managers participated in setting targets. The data indicate that 9.6 per cent of all participants (3.5 per cent of managers

Table 4.1 Attributes of the performance management processes

Performance management processes	Attributes
Strategic planning	Does the firm have defined strategic initiatives? Do managers participate in strategy formulation and planning? Are strategies tied to specific business objectives?
Performance measurement	Do managers participate in developing performance measures? Does the firm use financial and/or non-financial measures of performance? Are targets set for each measure? Do managers participate in setting targets?
Performance appraisal	*Evaluation* Is there a formalised appraisal process? Are managers appraised according to the policies of the process? Are appraisals based on targets? Are managers appraised on personal competencies? How frequently are appraisals conducted?
	Rewards Are appraisals the basis for rewards? What form of compensation rewards does the firm offer?
	Feedback Do managers receive performance feedback? How often do managers receive performance feedback? Is the nature of feedback subjective, objective or both?

and 23.1 per cent of senior managers) helped to develop the performance measures used to evaluate strategic initiatives.

These results suggest that participation in designing the performance management system is extended from executive management to some managers and senior managers for the purposes of setting targets. However, the data in this sample indicate that senior managers, but not operating managers, participate in developing measures of performance. This offers important insights into the level of management participation across these firms.

Another important dimension to the performance measurement process relates to the types of measures used to evaluate business performance. Interestingly, 53.5 per cent of all firms are using both financial and non-financial measures and nearly one-fifth (19.8 per cent) of managers indicated that no performance measures are in place. Financial measures only were the basis of evaluation for 12.8 per cent of managers, and 14.0 per cent of managers were evaluated based on non-financial measures alone.

These results indicate that, consistent with broader survey-based research, many firms have broadened their performance measures beyond financial performance. However, an almost equal number rely on financial measures alone, non-financial measures alone or no measures at all. Of the participants using measures of some type, 76.1 per cent had established targets, while 19.3 per cent operated without set targets and 4.5 per cent of the managers indicated that targets in their firms emerge over time.

In terms of performance appraisal, virtually every firm (98.9 per cent) has a formal appraisal process and 96.5 per cent of the managers were appraised. Almost all participants have formal process and are evaluated routinely. However, great variability exists in terms of the nature, timing and use of this management process. For example, in terms of timing, 92.3 per cent of senior managers are evaluated annually. Alternatively, managers are evaluated more frequently, with only 76.3 per cent evaluated only once per year. The basis of the evaluations also differed across participants. For example, 61.9 per cent of all participants (57.9 per cent of managers and 70.4 per cent of executives) are appraised based on targets. While managers without targets could not possibly be evaluated based on targets, of the managers with established or emerging targets, 77.6 per cent were evaluated based on those targets. In other words, 22.4 per cent of managers with established or emerging targets are not appraised based on performance in comparison to those targets.

The nature of appraisals differed also. In our sample, 75.4 per cent of managers and 66.7 per cent of senior managers were evaluated based on personal competencies. This difference may be a reflection of the commitment that firms may make to measure and develop employee skills at lower levels of the organisation. Interestingly, of the participants appraised on competencies, 41 per cent were appraised on competencies alone, with no use of target-based appraisal. The performance appraisal process is an important element of the overall performance management system because it presents the opportunity to tie rewards and feedback at the individual level to corporate strategies, objectives and organisational performance. In terms of this research, the performance appraisal process points to the connections among the attributes of these processes. If employees lack proper and timely incentives and feedback, the best strategies may be difficult to implement and objectives impossible to achieve.

4.7.2 Connections among performance management elements and attributes

In preceding analysis, we measured the extent of implementation of various programme elements across businesses. The qualitative nature of the data offers detailed insights into how and why the participants may perceive a particular control process as a great aid in managing the business, or alternatively how and where breakdowns can occur across management processes. For example, a firm may have clear and appropriate measures with targets, yet performance appraisal is not based on these objectives. By reviewing some of the quotes in the context of each process and element of the performance management framework, we structure our analysis of connections among the quantitative data. Kaplan and Norton (2009) suggest that effective implementation should: (1) clearly communicate strategies, plans and business objectives; (2) effectively measure activities and link actions to value creation; (3) explicitly align employee incentives and rewards with company goals; and (4) create a sense of accountability at the individual manager level. Alternatively, performance management programmes may be ineffective if any of these links is not implemented or accepted in a meaningful sense by managers.

We find four key differences. First, of the firms with established performance targets, 22.3 per cent do not use them to assess managers. Of managers who set the targets, 16.0 per cent are not appraised using those targets. Further, 40.7 per cent of the firms that use competency-based appraisals do not use targets during appraisals. However, those firms that base rewards on appraisals are quite reliant (84.1 per cent) on targets during appraisals. The results show no significant difference between management levels for each of these links. The absence of these links may mute or diminish the credibility of these elements of performance management programmes.

An analysis of the qualitative data supports this notion and provides detailed insight into why and how performance management programmes may not be embraced by operating managers. In this section, we use managers' comments and supporting quantitative data to examine how the connections between performance management elements and processes may work to align corporate objectives with individual objectives.

4.7.3   Clear communication of strategies, plans and business objectives

The data analysed in the previous section indicates that almost all firms in the data set have strategies, plans and business objectives of some sort. The data also indicates that few managers participate in developing these strategies. Given the resulting top-down directive nature of these goals, it is essential that effective communication occur. Simons (2000) stresses the criticality of the link between strategy and control, indicating that performance measurement systems provide the primary mechanism for formalising and communicating business strategy and monitoring implementation.

Simply, the performance management programme presents the opportunity to communicate ideas and connect individuals to overall corporate goals. At some firms, these links and the importance of the links is made very clear to employees:

> An important element to this system is that by tying a person's performance appraisal and raise to evaluations that include outside assessments, there is more of a connection with the company's strategic objectives.
>
> Senior Manager 1010, Model Manager,
> Aircraft Engines Manufacturer

Conversely, failure to communicate strategies and objectives can alienate employees:

> Any overall strategic goals [of my firm] have never been communicated to me.... The perception is that accounting does not contribute to the strategic success of the firm, but, is a drag upon that success.
>
> Manager 38, Accounting Manager,
> Medical Supplies Manufacturer

Given the finding about the widespread lack of participation of managers and senior managers in developing strategies and objectives, effective communication gains heightened importance. Mechanisms to achieve effective communication include (1) developing measures that demonstrate the link between actions and valued outcomes; (2) aligning employee incentives with goals; and (3) creating a sense of accountability through meaningful and directed feedback.

Simply put, the performance management process is important to managers because it is personal and highly visible. One manager summed up its importance:

> Improving the performance process would not only boost employee morale, it would also help employees understand how they are being evaluated and what behaviour or criteria is important to the company.
>
> Manager 55, Product Manager, Technology Firm

In terms of developing measures, aligning interests and providing appropriate and timely feedback, our data provide significant insights about these connections.

4.7.4   Developing measures that matter

There is significant variability in the types of measures (if any) in use and the nature of target setting. In some cases, while targets are not negotiated, they can provide specific direction and appropriate challenge and motivation for employees. For example, the supply chain manager at a major chemicals manufacturer described target setting as follows:

> My manager develops a [individual and team] Performance Agreement that lists objectives, measures and targets that are specific to our group, but are in alignment with the objectives, measures and targets set by the [divisional senior managers].
>
> Manager 36, Supply Chain Specialist, Chemical Manufacturer

Likewise, a manager at a pharmaceutical manufacturer reported a high level of satisfaction with the nature of measurement and target setting by his management team. As described in his memo, his company subscribes to a policy of creating 'SMART' goals – Specific, Measurable, Agreed upon, Realistic and Tied to the business. This explicit mechanism results in commitment and satisfaction.

> These metrics are handed down from the director and VP levels as attainable objectives and all managers in the department/division need to be evaluated against them at year's end. Overall my position is very strongly tied to all the basic principles that serve to accomplish

[my company's] ultimate goal of improving business performance and stimulating employee satisfaction.

Manager 39, Production Supervisor,
Pharmaceutical Manufacturer

Alternatively, some firms have focused on clearly developing measures that are aligned with performance objectives, but employees lack measures and/or targets to assess progress.

Even though my performance objectives are closely aligned with the company's strategic success factors, my company needs to do a better job of tying the 'triggers' to a measure more associates have the ability to influence.

Manager 77, Industrial Engineering Manager,
Materials Manufacturer

4.7.5   Aligning individual goals with corporate objectives

Performance appraisals provide a highly visible and personal way for firms to tie individual accountability to company objectives. Our data show that breakdowns can occur when the appraisal is not timely, explicitly tied to objectives, and/or linked to rewards. For example, a closer examination of the data indicates that, of the firms with established targets, 22.2 per cent do not use those targets in the appraisal process. For example, in a technology resource manufacturer the division had goals, but individual accountability was not defined.

from a financial perspective [my firm] has adopted two standpoints; cost reduction and productivity improvement, yet none of these objectives have funneled down into our individual objectives.

Manager 55, Product Manager, Technology
Resources Firm

Likewise a development engineer at telecommunications firm added,

The success of products which are launched is typically measured by whether or not they work or create headaches for our customers and operations group. There is little or no effort to match achieved revenue and subscriber targets for a product to the projections made in the business case. This leads to a lack of accountability in the product development process. There are also no direct incentives to achieve the numbers in the business case. The overall bonus plan is tied to corporate goals, and does not account for individual goals. There is a general feeling, therefore, that an individual has little ability to control or impact their getting the bonus.

> Manager 7, Development Engineering Manager,
> Telecommunications Firm

Some firms may use a subset of the targets and measures for evaluation. In these cases, we see performance evaluated in terms of financial targets, despite the use of a broader set of measures. A bank manager at a bank with an overt customer service strategy, commented that personal evaluations seemed to be based on deposit growth:

> The 'official' categories on which my performance is judged include Leadership, Profit and Cost Sensitivity, Training & Development, Business Development, Business Judgement, Teamwork... the 'unofficial' category on which my performance is based is solely focused on deposit growth within my branch... there is no measurement system for the majority of categories on which our performance is rated. This is what leads Branch Managers 'unofficially' being rated on deposit growth alone. Without measurements, there is no motivation and no real fair evaluation.
>
> Manager 49, Branch Manager, Retail Bank

Likewise a manager at a financial services firm that uses the Balanced Scorecard remarked:

> The problem that I see with my company's approach, however, is that individuals in different job functions are evaluated annually according to the broad-based measures of the Balanced Scorecard, but they are actually compensated based on a much more narrow set of objectives for their particular job. In other words, the company seems to pay lip-service to the Balanced Scorecard without really tying compensation to these measures.
>
> Manager 10, Sales Representative, Financial Services Firm

Another problem can be a lack of alignment between personal goals/rewards and corporate objectives. For example, this breakdown can occur in the sales function.

> For the sales people at [my firm] the performance is based on eight behavioral characteristics that are important to being a successful

salesperson. In addition to these qualitative categories is the quantitative evaluation of sales achieved versus goals…. . Right now [my firm] is focusing on growth, which means achieving higher market share, but the sales people are receiving commission based on how much profit they secure.

Manager 31, Account Manager, Construction
Products Manufacturer

In one case, the misalignment was so severe that it resulted in outright manipulation of the system, as this sales manager reported:

The firm's strategic goals differed greatly from the sales division. Virtually no emphasis was placed on anything related to the profitability of the firm. The firm paid commission based on the quantity of orders. Managers and reps stood to lose thousands of dollars if their order numbers fell below a certain amount, even if the orders generated a lot of revenue. This caused reps to make up phony orders, and manipulate orders from customers with bad credit histories in order to meet their minimum quotas.

Manager 76, Sales Manager, Telecommunications Firm

Lastly, in many cases, many managers indicated that while their firm had clear business objectives, these objectives were never related to job expectations or evaluation.

Bluntly stated, there are essentially no links between performance measurement and company strategy at [my firm]. If there are links, they are only subjective and most employees there would probably be unable to directly articulate the strategy, or what part they play in its achievement.

Senior Manager 1000, Engineering,
Industrial Manufacturer.

The success of products which are launched is typically measured by whether or not they work or create headaches for our customers and operations group. There is little or no effort to match achieved revenue and subscriber targets for a product to the projections made in the business case. This leads to a lack of accountability in the product development process. There are also no direct incentives to achieve the numbers in the business case. The overall bonus plan is tied to corporate goals, and does not account for individual goals. There is a general feeling, therefore, that an individual has little ability to control or impact their getting the bonus.

> Manager 7, Development Engineering Manager,
> Telecommunications Firm

As the quotations indicate, the presence of elements and attributes of the performance management framework are not effective unless tied to appraisal and rewards.

4.7.6   Meaningful and useful feedback

Appraisals must be conducted in a timely and meaningful manner to have a positive motivational effect. As the primary form of personal feedback, it is important to recognise several aspects of the appraisal process that promote the effectiveness of the performance management framework. In some cases, the appraisal may be impersonal and not timely. For example, one senior manager describes the uncomfortable nature of the task at his firm:

> Admittedly, I feel so uncomfortable having to review people subjectively on these basis, that I procrastinate until many are three months late. Obviously I am not alone. My boss dropped my review off on my desk as he was leaving for a two-week vacation (it was five and a half months late). The more amazing thing is that this was not a ploy to avoid bad news, my 'scores' were high, and my increase was more than double the 'infamous' guideline.
>
> Senior Manager 1000, Engineering Manager,
> Industrial Products Manufacturer

In many cases, the appraisal can be impersonal or not consistent with policy:

> My performance evaluation is conducted on an annual basis. Although my boss is supposed to review my evaluation with me, it is often sent through interoffice mail. I am then instructed to read it, make comments and sign it. Within a couple of weeks of the review, I am notified of my bonus as well as my salary increase.
>
> Manager 49, Branch Manager, Retail Bank

What is supposed to take place is that you are to sit with your supervisor and set your objectives for the year. At a six-month interval, you should formally sit with your supervisor and perform an interim review. At the end of the year, you would sit with your supervisor and review your year's performance. This doesn't sound that bad, except that this is not how it typically happens. You don't sit with your supervisor at the beginning of the year or at the mid-point. At the end of the year your supervisor sets and reviews some generic objectives for the *past* year and you get a met or exceeds expectations. In my case for the past three years, I wrote my objectives *and reviews* for my supervisor to sign. Although I have never asked my associates to write their own review, I have been guilty of conducting informal reviews through the year and using generic objectives.

> Senior Manager 1041, Manufacturing Engineering,
> Industrial Equipment Manufacturer.

Performance appraisals are frequently not used to determine rewards. The words of a few managers support this concept:

Outside of yearly increases, few 'rewards' are distributed. As a member of management, I have received a yearly grant of stock options from the board of directors for the last four years. A congratulatory letter accompanies these options from our CEO, but the magic by which they are granted has never been revealed. There is certainly no openly stated policy about how stock options are meted out.

> Manager 1000, Engineering Manager,
> Industrial Products Manufacturer

Another manager commented that performance appraisal is not linked to rewards by design.

[Our] performance evaluations are supposed to have no bearing on raises or bonuses, they are meant to be informative only.

> Manager 52, Fund Project Head, Financial Services Firm

These excerpts from the managers' memos illustrate a frequent breakdown of the performance appraisal process, particularly when the system attempts to evaluate for rewards and provide feedback at the same time.

4.8 Conclusions

As the analysis indicated, all five elements and three primary processes of the performance management framework seem to be consistently in place at the firms in the sample. Interestingly, despite the extensive literature on participation, there remains very little participation by either senior managers or managers in the strategic planning process and in the setting of performance targets and the development of performance metrics. The processes seem to be top-down in nature.

Despite the widespread implementation of the balanced scorecard, the number of firms using both financial and non-financial measures is only just above 50 per cent. Almost one-fifth of managers indicated there were no measures at all and almost a quarter of the managers in the sample were evaluated on something other than specific performance targets, even when those targets existed.

There is however a great deal of diversity in practice in both the nature of those elements and the processes used to develop them. There is a great deal of variety in the types of measures and targets used, with some managers indicating that there are no specific targets of perform-ance measures. The performance appraisal process also reflects a great deal of variety in terms of nature, timing and use. Only 61.9 per cent of managers are based on performance targets. Indeed, there is an increasing trend for appraisal to be based on evaluation of competencies rather than performance with 41 per cent of participants evaluated solely on competencies. Our analysis also reveals a performance management system that is often practised differently from what is prescribed by the firm. A good example of this is the following:

> What is supposed to take place is that you are to sit with your super-visor and set your objectives for the year. At a six-month interval, you should formally sit with your supervisor and perform an interim review. At the end of the year, you would sit with your supervisor and review your year's performance. This doesn't sound that bad, except that this is not how it typically happens.... In my case for the past three years, I wrote my objectives <u>and reviews</u> for my supervisor to sign.
>
> Senior Manager 1041, Manufacturing Engineering,
> Industrial Equipment Manufacturer

Thus there is a risk of designing and communicating initiatives but not actually employing those programmes. This example demonstrates the gap between rhetoric and reality that can occur throughout the performance management framework. Firms encourage participation in setting targets, but then use some other basis for evaluation; firms say that rewards are based on performance, but then pay bonuses before the performance appraisal process is complete.

Performance Management is critical for communicating business strategy and aligning individual goals with corporate goals. Our analysis reveals that firms are often very poor communicators of strategy, with managers frequently feeling that they have no idea where their organisation is heading. There are also frequent breakdowns in the alignment of the performance management process so that individuals are often not behaving consistently with corporate objectives. Sometimes the wrong measures are used, ones unrelated to the objectives, sometimes there are no measures at all. Frequently rewards are not based on performance evaluations and feedback is not given or is inconsistent with other signals within the system. Sometimes these problems can lead to goal incongruence or, as in the following case, to outright manipulation of the system:

> The firm's strategic goals differed greatly from the sales division. Virtually no emphasis was placed on anything related to the profitability of the firm. The firm paid commission based on the quantity of orders. Managers and reps stood to lose thousands of dollars if their order numbers fell below a certain amount, even if the orders generated a lot of revenue. This caused reps to make up phony orders, and manipulate orders from customers with bad credit histories in order to meet their minimum quotas.
>
> Manager 76, Sales Manager, Telecommunications Firm

Sometimes rewards are given and the recipient is unaware of the reasons for the reward or who else received an award. One participant spoke of a system where once a year his boss would hand him secretly a plain brown sealed envelope inside which would be stock options. There was no discussion of why the reward was given or the amount of the reward, no feedback, no connection to performance and complete secrecy surrounding the whole process. From the individual manager's perspective, the performance appraisal links incentives to performance measurement and represents a personalised means of providing evaluation, rewards and feedback.

A performance management system can break down when there are missing components or elements or there is a lack of connection between the elements. In terms of the three major processes, the data indicate that almost all firms have defined and communicated strategies and objectives to managers. However, the data indicates that supporting these goals with effective measurement and feedback can be problematic if: (1) firms do not develop targets or measures to evaluate performance,

(2) measures are developed, but targets are not set, (3) the objective targets are not incorporated into performance appraisals or rewards are allocated based on metrics that are not aligned with strategic goals, and (4) performance appraisals are either not conducted; are not timely; or do not provided the basis for rewards.

Any particular component of a performance management system or element should be considered in light of the overall system. For example, designing and implementing an appropriate performance measurement programme is dependent on connecting measures to meaningful rewards and feedback at the individual level. It is valuable to consider managers' perspectives. The results as a whole indicate that it is important to appreciate the inter-relationships between components and elements of performance management systems. These connections are vital to the effectiveness of the overall programme and provide a broader context for interpreting individual elements. Otherwise firms run the risk of investment with little, no or (worse) negative returns.

References

American Quality and Productivity Center (2010). Houston, Texas at http://www.apqc.org/.

Flamholtz, E. G., Das, T. K. and Tsui, A. S. (1985). 'Toward an Integrative Framework of Organizational Control', *Accounting, Organizations and Society*, 10, 35–50.

Ittner, C. D. and D. F. Larcker (1998). 'Are Non-Financial Measures Leading Indicators of Financial Performance? An Analysis of Customer Satisfaction', *Journal of Accounting Research*, 36 (Supplement), 1–46.

Kaplan, R. and Norton, D. (2009). *The Execution Premium*, Harvard Business School Press, Cambridge, MA.

Miles, M. B. and Huberman, A. M. (1994). *Qualitative Data Analysis*, Sage, New York.

Otley, D. T. (1999). 'Performance Management: A Framework for Management Control Systems Research', *Management Accounting Research*, 10 (4), 363–82.

Simons, R. (2000). *Performance Measurement & Control Systems for Integrating Strategy*, Prentice Hall, Upper Saddle River, NJ.

Slagmulder, R. (1997). 'Using Management Control Systems to Achieve Alignment Between Strategic Investment Decisions and Strategy', *Management Accounting Research*, 8, 103–39.

5
Recent Progress in Management Control Depiction

Jim Rooney

5.1 Overview

Following exhortations in the mid-1990s to investigate the use of management controls within inter-organisational relationships (Hopwood, 1996; Tomkins, 2001), there has been a range of theoretical and empirical research treatments employed in response (Anderson and Dekker, 2005. As a result, this area of research has attracted theories sourced from a number of academic disciplines ranging from accounting to sociology, social psychology and related social sciences (Langfield-Smith, 2008). Given recent literature reviews illustrating considerable progress in understanding drivers of management control design (for example, Vosselman and v. d. Meer-Kooistra, 2008), a detailed bibliography is not included here.

In broad terms, primary concerns to date have focused on the nature of the controls operating in networks (e.g., v. d. Meer-Kooistra and Vosselman, 2000) and explaining these in terms of contingent factors comprising characteristics of the transaction, the environment and the contracting parties, and the question of whether formal controls and informal controls are substitutes or complements (e.g., Das and Teng, 1998; Poppo and Zenger, 2002; Langfield-Smith and Smith, 2003; Dekker, 2004, 2008; Cuganesan, 2006).

However, the nature of accounting research to date may have limited the opportunities to develop a more detailed understanding of the complex behavioural interactions and effects associated with the use of this accounting technology (Caglio and Ditillo, 2008). While theoretical diversity has advanced our understanding, it has also increased the risk of concept misspecification (Bisbe *et al.*, 2007) and difficulties with interpretation of the research outcomes (Caglio and Ditillo, 2008).

This has been partly due to material inconsistency in the definition and application of theoretical constructs employed in this research (Caglio and Ditillo, 2008), including those associated with the identification of management control archetypes (Malmi and Brown, 2008). Consequently, management control research in this inter-organisational context is yet to provide deep understanding of the multi-dimensional and evolving nature of control design; the interaction between transaction characteristics and control; and the decision-making processes that shape it. Furthermore, detailed understanding of the impact of other drivers of management control design, including organisational life cycle, has not been explored in detail (Caglio and Ditillo, 2008).

In response, researchers tend to advocate the study of alternative theoretical and empirical perspectives as a means of gaining a deeper understanding of the changes in management control design (Malmi and Brown, 2008). In contrast, the alternative view is that research on this subject requires greater clarity in terms of unit of analysis and theoretical control constructs (Caglio and Ditillo, 2008) as well as the underlying purpose or informational characteristics of the management controls being studied (Chenhall, 2005) in order to yield consistent management control research outcomes.

Accordingly, this chapter addresses the academic and practitioner literature on management control in more detail in order to understand current perspectives on the management control of inter-organisational alliances. Starting with a definition of management control, an overview of the roles and interactions between management and accounting control is provided, followed by a discussion on the emergence and specification of control problems. The chapter concludes with an outline of alternative control schema before continuing with discussion of the implications for the thesis.

5.2   Definition of management control

Dekker (2004) defines accounting controls as a subset of formal control mechanisms comprising either action controls or results controls, whereby the behaviours or the results of these behaviours are respectively measured. Action controls in inter-organisational relationships both specify how the partners should act and monitor whether actual behaviour is in accordance with that pre-specified. In contrast, results control mechanisms specify the outputs or outcomes to be realised by the alliance and its partners and monitors the achievement of performance targets. Results controls in particular enable a level of management flexibility and innovation to be preserved in the relationship, as they do not require adherence to pre-specified procedures or behaviours but specify only the end results required from the outsourcing arrangement.

Separately from accounting controls, contract controls focus on clauses included in the design and modification to the terms of the inter-organisational contract developed and formally agreed by both parties. Such controls 'include formal rules, procedures and policies to safe-guard, monitor and reward desirable performance that ... are codified in a contractual arrangement' (Vosselman and v. d. Meer-Kooistra, 2008, p. 3).

Accounting controls, through measurement of how the inter-organisational relationship management process is enacted (known as action controls) or what it achieves (results controls), can enable communication and alignment of interests between firms in an inter-organisational alliance. It includes monitoring of outsourcing service providers compliance with pre-specified conditions (contract controls). They may change as the nature of, or the parties to, the exchange alter (Caglio and Ditillo, 2008).

Socio-cultural controls have been defined as 'Management control practices targeting minds, through norms, emotions, beliefs and values, are intended to affect behaviour indirectly' (Alvesson and Karreman, 2004, p. 425). These notions are expanded by Dekker (2004) in describing social controls.

Among others in the recent accounting literature, Cuganesan and Lee (2006) have also highlighted the role of market controls within inter-organisational relationships. This largely involves the use of market alternatives to guide behaviour including credible threats of substitution with alternative suppliers for part/all of in-scope services.

5.3   Overview of current theory and practice on formal controls

Before exploring these various types of management control and their uses, the following paragraphs will discuss recent rescarch findings on accounting and contract controls. A contract 'refers to a formal written contract between two or more competent parties, which creates obliga-tions, whereby one party becomes bound to another to do or omit to do certain acts that are the subject of that contract' (Blomqvist *et al.*, 2005, p. 498). The contract thus provides a *'frame'* for the outsourcing relationship, outlining the nature and term of the relationship, what is to be provided and the rights and obligations of parties to the contract.

Prior empirical research (e.g., Whang, 1992; Anderson and Dekker, 2005) into contract design is consistent with this definition, finding that contracts define the exchange (detailing the product/service to be provided, the price and the associated payment terms) as well as the rights and obligations of the parties to the exchange (comprising the assignment of rights and defining mechanisms of legal recourse).

In terms of ongoing management of an inter-organisational relationship, contracts are often used to mitigate potential opportunistic behaviour through formal pre-specified mechanisms that bind the parties together, such as requiring parties to undertake transaction-specific investments or credible commitments to the relationship (Williamson, 1983). Ex-post mechanisms may also be incorporated into the contract, providing parties with rights and sanctions over others in the event of non-performance or other pre-specified situations. Specification of these mechanisms in the context of limited information and uncertainty leads to the notion of 'incomplete contracting' where, given possibilities for opportunism as well as the bounded rationality of parties, costs of both describing possible future states of the economic exchange in the contract and verifying realised ex-post states leads to incomplete contracting (Williamson, 1995; Klein, 2002).

It is this notion of 'contract completeness' or 'contract extensiveness' that has received interest among researchers investigating formal management controls. Within the accounting discipline, Anderson and Dekker (2005) found that more extensive written contracts are associated with transactions of greater size, asset specificity and complexity. In marked contrast, environmental complexity, technological uncertainty and remote dates for contract performance have also been found to result in less complete contracts (Crocker and Reynolds, 1993) while difficulties in measuring performance drives a more collaborative and relationship-based contracting approach (Krishnan *et al.*, 2007).

While there is mixed evidence on the use of contracts in managing control problems and the transaction hazards of outsourcing, these studies also overlook that exchange parties may utilise other forms of formal control such as accounting mechanisms either in conjunction with or separate from the contract. Given the difficulties of incomplete contracting, alternative control mechanisms may become more attractive (Cuganesan, 2007). In spite of this, the issue of interactions between contracts and accounting controls has only limited empirical examination despite issues of choice in control design. This choice occurs not only in terms of the mix of formal–informal controls, but also the interaction between formal controls in terms of contracts and accounting. The next section discusses the extent to which management control problems drive changes in management control design in order to explore this trade-off between management control mechanisms in more detail.

5.4 Management control problems

Recent development of a number of competing works of theory-building in the accounting literature are worthy of note, such as Kamminga and v. d. Meer-Kooistra (2007), Langfield-Smith (2008), v. d. Meer-Kooistra and Scapens (2008) and Vosselman and v. d. Meer-Kooistra (2008). The Caglio and Ditillo (2008) model is unique within this group as being founded on theories (and the resulting construct operationalisation) that have a significant measure of empirical support within the accounting community of scholars. While there is merit to the view that the aforementioned works deserve further research attention, the explicit focus on control problems and the resulting typology described in Caglio and Ditillo (2008), based on existing theory with a material, albeit incomplete, level of empirical support to date, is arguably more likely to facilitate focused academic debate on the ongoing drivers of control design in this complex business environment. The specific intent is to increase the likelihood that empirical findings are capable of focused review and future empirical replication by focusing on control problems as drivers for evolution in management control (Dekker, 2004).

A defining characteristic of this typology is the use of existing theory to specify the three relationship problem constructs (labelled cooperation, coordination and appropriation concerns) as a foundation for exploring the dynamics of ongoing inter-organisational relationships. Specifically, cooperation problems are defined using constructs taken from a combination of Transactional Cost Economics and Agency Theory. Contingency Theory forms the basis of constructs used to identify coordination problems. Finally, Resource Based Theory is used to identify appropriation concerns, moderated by the coordination constructs described by Dekker (2004). The combination of multiple theories to explore complex phenomena is consistent with the approach outlined by Chenhall (2003) as a means of addressing concerns about model misspecification, a common criticism of contingency-based models of management control (Chenhall, 2003), as well as concerns about construct definition and measurement (Auzair and Langfield-Smith, 2005). These constructs are outlined below.

Firstly, based on a combination of TCE and Agency Theory, **cooperation problems** are broadly defined in terms of the existence of threats of opportunism and moral hazard whereby 'partners may have incentives to cheat and free-ride in order to attain their own specific goals at the expense of the objectives of the collective undertaking, so they need to introduce mechanisms to align their objectives' (Caglio and Ditillo, 2008, p. 891). Comprehensive coverage of the extant literature on opportunism has been addressed elsewhere (Deeds and Hill, 1998) identifying three key aspects, namely:

- *The Threat of Opportunism* considers the existence of self-interest seeking behaviour either for short-term gain or strategic gain by deviating from contractual expectations where it is advantageous, as described in Deeds and Hill (1998);
- *Transaction Characteristics* – known transaction-level drivers of opportunistic behaviour identified by Transaction Cost Economics (TCE) and related literature such as asset specificity, uncertainty (Williamson, 1985) and governance inseparability (Argyres and Liebeskind, 1999); and
- *Relationship Cooperation* – the degree to which both parties to a transaction agree that reciprocity of benefits has been achieved as a result of the transaction, including complementary activities jointly undertaken to achieve mutual benefits (Goles and Chin, 2005).

In addition to the above, Dekker (2008) also found that prior partnership experience moderates the impact of transaction-based management control exposures, reducing the requirement for extensive governance structure. This is reinforced by the concept of governance inseparability that occurs when a firm's past governance choices significantly influence the range and types of governance mechanisms it can adopt in future periods.

Other examples of research exploring this aspect of control include Cuganesan and Lee (2006), who found similar inter-organisational precedents using an Actor Network Theory approach, and Poppo and Zenger (2002), who investigated the precedents for the adoption of relational governance structures. In discussing opportunism and its antecedents, transaction is taken to mean the entire outsourcing transaction rather than an individual outsourced operational process. Further, in eschewing discussion of specific TCE-based transaction antecedents, it should be noted that one of these antecedents, uncertainty, has been identified by Caglio and Ditillo, 2008, p. 12) as an under-researched area. The investigation of environmental and task uncertainties has been treated as a secondary consideration to conventional TCE constructs, with the sole exception being Dekker (2004).

Consistent with Agency Theory, the focus is on the contract to bind the relationship (Eisenhardt, 1989) rather than the inter-organisational relationship itself. This aspect of opportunism is concerned with the degree to which both parties to the transaction agree that the parties' attempt to achieve reciprocity of benefits as a result of the inter-organisational relationship, including complementary activities jointly undertaken to achieve mutual benefits (Goles and Chin, 2005). This concern is in contrast to the achievement of actual factor endowments addressed in the appropriation construct discussed later. In particular, the focus is on two specific Agency problems explored in both the accounting and organisational science literature, namely the hold-up (Goldberg, 1976) and moral hazard problems (Saam, 2007). Accordingly, the mechanisms for addressing these agency problems are also sourced from the same literature and are consistent with the management control mechanisms described elsewhere in this section, namely monitoring systems (generally a buyer or principal-initiated response) and signalling (a supplier or agent-initiated response).

Other dimensions of cooperation mentioned in the management control literature, such as incentive/rewards systems (Jensen and Meckling, 1976, 1992; Eisenhardt, 1989), vertical integration (Klein *et al.*, 1978), game theoretics (Rasmusen,1990), self-selection (Arrow, 1986), bonding (Jensen and Meckling, 1976) and screening (Spence, 1974), are excluded from discussion because of their limited applicability to the inter-organisational unit of analysis (e.g., vertical integration being an alternative to outsourcing, screening being a human resources tool).

Coordination problems between firms are the second type of relationship issue identified. Based on Contingency Theory, these problems are related to lack of clear inter-organisational relationship boundaries. The result is failure to achieve the relationship outcomes agreed by the parties to a 'level of mutual satisfaction' (Caglio and Ditillo, 2008, p. 891). Measurement of coordination problems is focused on two constructs, namely asymmetry and interdependence. Where considered in the extant literature, these constructs have been analysed largely as unidimensional (Caglio and Ditillo, 2008). Accordingly, the use of a more complex mix of measures is called for, covering the following dimensions:

- *Asymmetry*: The degree to which both parties to the transaction agree that power and relevant information are perceived to have been shared as a result of the transaction (Vincent-Jones, 1999);
- *Interdependence*: The degree to which the products and services provided are related to one another, increasing the complexity of the transaction (Milgrom and Roberts, 1992; Dekker, 2008).

Consistent with Hakansson and Lind (2004, p. 53), the key parties in the inter-organisational relationship 'must be matched, both qualitatively and quantitatively'. The market is not always suitable for this matching (Richardson, 1972) as the functional and organisational context of an inter-organisational relationship, particularly joint ventures, is more complicated than the alternative forms of coordination identified in the organisational science literature (namely market and hierarchy forms). In matching plans and processes within this relationship focus coordination is not centrally orchestrated, as in the hierarchical situation, or carried out by the total structure, as in the market situation. In contrast, buyer and supplier firms work interactively, seeking a suitable solution. The firms involved in the inter-organisational relationship 'match their activities and resources to each other'.

The third and final relationship problem, **appropriation concerns**, can be understood in terms of Resource Based Theory (RBT). It highlights differences in resource endowments as a key motivator for the establishment of inter-organisational relationships. In the presence of such differences, partners in an inter-organisational relationship 'need to ensure that the value of the joint output is perceived by the parties to be clearly and fairly distributed and that the resources exchanged are not misappropriated by their counterparts'(Caglio and Ditillo, 2008, p. 891). Dekker (2004) had earlier broadened the scope of analysis for appropriation concerns, developing a typology of management controls that cover formal and informal designs. However, this construct may need revision as it focuses mainly on partner selection rather than the ongoing management of the relationship.

Given the three key control problems outlined above, the next section discusses the management control mechanisms available to address these problems as they emerge.

5.5 Management control types

As described by Caglio and Ditillo (2008), accounting literature on inter-organisational control has identified three key management control archetypes or models:

- *Market Models* rely on market institutions and mechanisms to provide alternative partners in the case where one party acts opportunistically;
- *Hierarchy Models* utilise detailed contracts and related 'hostage' arrangements to ensure legal compliance;

- *Alternative/Social Models* focus on the use of social controls such as coordination, information sharing and trust.

Further, the accounting literature recognises the practice of hybrid control system design utilising a combination of these distinct archetypes (Spekle, 2001). Each of these archetypes has been broadly identified with broad transaction characteristics (e.g., use of market model in relationships with low asset specificity and high task programmability). Given that these characteristics and their links to specific control archetypes are described in Caglio and Ditillo (2008), including the limitations and ambiguities with specification of the related constructs in the existent literature, they are not described here.

However, it is difficult to disagree with Caglio and Ditillo (2008) that a focus on control archetypes rather than mechanisms would 'offer limited insights into the multi-faceted reality of practice; only "simple" archetypes of control are investigated, whereas "more complex" and varied combinations of control traits empirically observed are not fully explained'.

Accordingly, recognition of multiple controls in the more recent accounting literature has been encapsulated in the notion of management control typology described in Dekker (2004), addressing the following control mechanisms:

- *Behaviour Controls*: these are directed at guiding behaviour, excluding changes to contract terms associated with these items (Dekker, 2004);
- *Outcome Controls*: quantitative measures, standards and feedback processes, excluding changes to contract terms associated with these items (Dekker, 2004);
- *Socio-Cultural Controls*: 'Management control practices targeting minds, through norms, emotions, beliefs and values, are intended to affect behaviour indirectly'. (Alvesson and Karreman, 2004, p. 425);
- *Contract Controls*: Clauses included in the design and modification to the terms of the outsourcing contract developed and formally agreed by both parties. Such controls 'include formal rules, procedures and policies to safeguard, monitor and reward desirable performance that... are codified in a contractual arrangement' (Vosselman and v. d. Meer-Kooistra, 2008, p. 3).

Given the relationship between institutional trust, credible exit threats and market institutions addressed in the paper by Vosselman and

Meer-Kooistra (2008), the use of market controls is another separate aspect of the control design process that is of interest. The use of market controls was explored in research by Cuganesan (2007) in discussing the prerequisites and uses of market controls and evoking earlier research by Ring and Van der Ven (1992).

5.6   Comparison of recent approaches to management control

Although far from exhaustive, the list of management control schemas considered here represents the development of comprehensive management control theory addressing predefined criteria. The key criteria are: coverage of a range of control types across a range of perspectives from the accounting literature (e.g., formal and informal; market and bureaucratic); alignment with relationship problems; and published no earlier than 2008 using the latest research and theory-based multidisciplinary constructs. A comparison of these three selected schemas is provided below.

Given the standing of *Accounting, Organizations and Society* (*AOS*) and *Management Accounting Research* (*MAR*) as leading accounting research journals and their demonstrable fit with the selection criteria described below, two papers from the 2008 *AOS* special edition on management control and one published in *MAR* the following year describe three separate management control schemas suitable for the purposes of this chapter with relevant background to the respective management control schemas outlined below:

- Management Control Types – based on a synthesis of the extant accounting literature by Caglio and Ditillo (2008);
- Management Control Package – based on a synthesis of the extant accounting literature by Malmi and Brown (2008);
- Trust-Building Management Control – based on a synthesis of the extant control literature by Vosselman and v. d. Meer-Kooistra (2008).

Other papers published in the same *AOS* special edition addressed management control theory but were focused on specific aspects, such as organisational design or the role of trust within inter-organisational relationships. The three schemas selected had the specific purpose of integrating or extending the extant accounting literature.

There are broad similarities between a number of the subcategories used across the three control schemas. For example, the subcategories of behaviour controls (Management Control Type schema) and administrative controls (Management Control Package schema) use similar construct definitions and are significant forms of change in response to post-contract control problems. This relationship is reinforced on review of the more detailed constructs, given that change to procedures associated with an inter-organisational relationship are major constructs evidenced in the many outsourcing case studies. There is a similar relationship between organisational norms/trust combined (Management Control Type schema) and cultural controls (Management Control Package schema).

However, while generally equivalent in concept, the Management Control Package schema of Malmi and Brown (2008) may under-represent the importance of informal controls, as evidenced case studies of outsourcing relationships in the practitioner literature. This may also evident with regards to behavioural and outcome controls – two significant formal control mechanisms used in outsourcing relationships.

Hence, a central issue is that, while there are a plethora of theoretical frameworks developed for the measurement, management and reporting of control, these frameworks are not clearly operationalised in order to be consciously adopted by firms, despite the potential benefits. This key insight into current management control theory is discussion below.

As mentioned previously, management control research on inter-organisational relationships to date has provided only a limited measure of understanding of the detailed, multi-dimensional and evolving nature of control design; the interaction between transaction characteristics and control; and the decision-making processes that shape it. Furthermore, detailed understanding of the impact of other drivers of control design, including performance improvement, has not been explored (Caglio and Ditillo, 2008). This limitation highlights a need to investigate the concurrent use of, as well as interaction between, control problem antecedents, alliance transaction characteristics, control mix (including its purpose or role) and the business environment in which the alliance operates.

While detailed theory-building is beyond the scope of this chapter, recent findings in the accounting literature may be assimilated into a schema that reflects the consistency in theoretical constructs in the three schemas mentioned above. In addition, the relationship between the control problem constructs, control indicators and other opportunities described below can potentially be used as the basis to form a more comprehensive management control framework. Specifically, other theoretical schema described in the accounting literature but targeted at specific aspects of control, such as inter-organisational partner selection (Dekker, 2008) and initial post-contract control selection (Langfield-Smith, 2008) can be analysed for potential for incorporation of applicable constructs or indicators.

This approach involves further empirical testing of management control constructs and exploration of potential to combine constructs from different schemas to reflect responses to control problems, which may provide greater academic and practitioner confidence in management control theory in the future. This would include critical analysis of competing schemas to summarise the impact on the development of a multi-theory, multidisciplinary typology of management control as well as practice. The emphasis of this chapter is on the multidimensional nature of control problem constructs, consistent with the views of Luft and Shields (2002, p. 33) whereby 'Failing to take the multiple properties of practice-defined variables into account can result in invalid conclusions from research'. To that end, the management control systems research mentioned above provides a basis for examination of the key management accounting constructs associated with post-contractual relationships based in relevant theory.

5.7   Implications for accounting theory

The key implication for theory is the requirement for tighter definitions of the key constructs based on combinations across the three control schema used for the purpose of this chapter, which would assist with clear identification of management control responses to control problems. Following Luft and Shields (2002, p. 32), 'theory-defined variables are more likely to have defined, stable, unitary meanings, making it possible to identify consistent cause-and-effect relations'. This is a area for follow-up research.

To date, there has been limited understanding of the links between emergent relationship problems and changes in control design (Caglio and Ditillo, 2008). Reversal of prior research focus on a subset of controls or control solutions rather than control problems found in the extant accounting literature is likely to reflect research literature in non-accounting disciplines as well as industry practice (Caglio and Ditillo, 2008). Expanding on the above gap, a limited analysis of the processes that lead to change in the configuration of management control packages (v. d. Meer-Kooistra and Scapens, 2008) or the development of long-term trust (Langfield-Smith, 2008; Vosselman and van der Meer-Kooistra, 2008) needs to be addressed in order to explore the connection between control problems and the redesign of control solutions.

5.8   Implications for practice

As highlighted by Caglio and Ditillo (2008), a focus on control problems rather than solutions has potential to incorporate alternative control theories and identify potential improvements in current practice. This approach may also provide an opportunity to explore the interactions between control design and inter-organisational transaction characteristics as well as the resulting relationship outcomes. Accordingly, there is a need to address the limitations and biases identified by Caglio and Ditillo (2008) for the constructs and indicators identified above in order to help clarify and confirm the impacts of these identified determinants of inter-organisational controls on practice as well as the interaction between these variables (see Caglio and Ditillo, 2008).

In the meantime, the implications for practitioners include the need to ensure an appropriate focus on the early identification of control problems based on intra- and inter-organisational and environmental influences. There appears to be benefit in focusing on emergent control problems rather than the achievement of ideal control solutions, and in recognising that an alternative mix of management controls can address control problems. In addition, intra-organisational factors play an important role at both the relationship and process operations level. Notwithstanding this approach, the use of performance measurement systems to help identify and participate actively in joint planning activities also helps develop enhanced behavioural controls.

The deployment of these competencies is an example of the influence of supplier-generated intra-firm factors in terms of both performance measures and the use of intra-organisational experts and processes consistent with those identified by Cuganesan and Lee (2006), albeit as supplier- rather than buyer-initiated activities. Thus, within the limitations of research to date, there is no 'one right way' to control.

5.9   Conclusions

The description of current research and practice in inter-organisational management control in this chapter is intended to encourage further research on this subject in order to address the limitations listed below. There is an opportunity to incorporate a more diverse range of inter-organisational relationships across the key dimensions described earlier in this chapter, allowing more detailed exploration of changing management control practice. This may help address a common weakness in the outsourcing literature, best expressed by Bigelow and Argyres (2007, p. 5) 'While a large number of make-or-buy and related studies have been carried out, to our knowledge no study has to date been conducted on data from an entire population of firms in an industry'. Such an expansion of scope would also support better understanding of the linkage between organisational design, MCS and financial performance in an attempt to address concerns of the type expressed by Fritsch *et al.* (2007, p. 23) that 'no clear conclusions on the impact of outsourcing or vertical integration on firm performance can be drawn'.

References

Alvesson, M. and Karreman, D. (2004). 'Interfaces of Control: Technocratic and Socio-ideological Control in A Global Management Consultancy Firm', *Accounting Organizations and Society*, 29 (3–4), 423–44.

Anderson, S. W. and Dekker, H. C. (2005). 'Management Control for Market Transactions: The Relation between Transaction Characteristics, Incomplete Contract Design and Subsequent Performance', *Management Science*, 5 (12), 1734–52.

Argyres, N. S. and Liebeskind, J. P. (2002). 'Governance Inseparability and the Evolution of US Biotechnology Industry', *Journal of Economic Behavior and Organization*, 47, 197–219.

Arrow, K. (1986). 'Agency and the Market' in Arrow, K. J. and Intriligator, M. D. (eds), *Handbook of Mathematical Economics*, Bd. III, North-Holland, Amsterdam, 1183–95.

Auzair, S. Md. and Langfield-Smith, K. (2005). 'The Effect of Service Process Type, Business Strategy and Life-cycle Stage on Bureaucratic MCS in Service Organisations', *Management Accounting Research*, 16, 399–421.

Bigelow, L. S. and Argyres, N. S. (2008). 'Transaction Costs, Industry Experience and Make-or-buy Decisions in the Population of Early U.S. Auto Firms', *Journal of Economic Behavior & Organization*, 66 (3/4), 791–807.

Bisbe, J., Batista-Foguet, J.-M. and Chenhall, R. (2007). 'Defining Management Accounting Constructs: A Methodological Note on the Risks of Conceptual Misspecification', *Accounting, Organizations and Society*, 32, 789–820.

Blomqvist, K., Hurmelinna, P. and Seppanen, R. (2005). 'Playing the Collaboration Game Right – Balancing, Trust and Contracting', *Technovation*, 25, 497–504.

Caglio, A. and Ditillo, A. (2008). 'A Review and Discussion of Management Control in Inter-Firm Relationships: Achievements and Future Directions', *Accounting, Organizations and Society*, 7–8, 865–98.

Chenhall, R. H. (2003). 'Management Control Systems Design Within Its Organisational Context: Findings from Contingency-Based Research and Directions for the Future', *Accounting, Organizations and Society*, 28 (2–3), 127–68.

Chenhall, R. H. (2005). 'Integrative Strategic Performance Measurement Systems, Strategic Alignment of Manufacturing, Learning and Strategic Outcomes: An Exploratory Study', *Accounting, Organizations and Society*, 30 (5), 395–422.

Crocker, K. and Reynolds, K. (1993). 'The Efficiency of Incomplete Contracts: An Empirical Analysis of Air Force Engine Procurement', *RAND Journal of Economics*, 24 (1), 126–46.

Cuganesan, S. (2006). 'The Role of Functional Specialists in Shaping Controls Within Supply Networks', *Accounting, Auditing and Accountability Journal*, 19 (4), 465–92.

Cuganesan, S. (2007). 'Accounting, Contracts and Trust in Supply Relationships', *Journal of Accounting and Organizational Change*, 3 (2), 104–25.

Cuganesan, S. and Lee, R. (2006). 'Intra-Organisational Influences in Procurement Network Controls: The Impacts of Information Technology', *Management Accounting Research*, 17, 141–70.

Das, T. K. and Teng, B. S. (1998). 'Between Trust and Control: Developing Confidence in Partner Cooperation Alliances', *Academy of Management Review*, 23, 491–512.

Deeds, D. L. and Hill, C. W. L. (1998). 'An Examination of Opportunistic Action within Research Alliances: Evidence from the Biotechnology Industry', *Journal of Business Venturing*, 14, 141–63.

Dekker, H. C. (2004). 'Control of Inter-organizational Relationships: Evidence on Appropriation Concerns and Coordination Requirements', *Accounting, Organizations and Society*, 29, 27–49.

Dekker, H. C. (2008). 'Partner Selection and Governance Design in Inter-Firm Relationships', *Accounting, Organizations and Society*, 33, 915–41.

Eisenhardt, K. (1989). 'Agency Theory: An Assessment and Review', *Academy of Management Review*, 14, 57–74.

Fritsch, M., Hackethal, A., Wahrenburg, M. and Wuellenweber, K. (2007). 'The Impact of Business Process Outsourcing on Firm Performance and the Influence on Governance: A Long Term Study in the German Banking Industry', http://ssrn.com/abstract=1076422.

Goldberg, V. P. (1976). 'Regulation and Administered Contracts', *Bell Journal of Economics and Management Science*, 7, 439–41.

Goles, T. and Chin, W. W. (2005). 'Information systems outsourcing relationship factors: Detailed conceptualization and initial evidence'. *The DATA BASE for Advances in Information Systems*, 36 (4), 47–67.

Hakansson, H. and Lind, K. (2007). 'Accounting in Inter-Organisational Settings', in Chapman, C. S., Hopwood, A. G. and Shields, M. D. (Eds). *Handbook of Management Accounting Research*, 2, 885–902.

Hopwood, A. G. (1996). 'Looking Across Rather than Up and Down: On the Need to Explore the Lateral Processing of Information', *Accounting, Organizations and Society*, 21, 589–90.

Jensen, M. and Meckling, W. (1976). 'Theory of the Firm: Managerial Behavior, Agency Costs and Ownership Structure', *Journal of Financial Economics*, 3, 305–60.

Jensen, M. and Meckling, W. (1992) in Werin, L. and Wijkander, H. (Eds), *Contract Economics*, Blackwell, Oxford.

Kamminga, P. E. and v. d. Meer-Kooistra, J. (2007). 'Management Control Patterns in Joint Venture Relationships: A Model and an Exploratory Study', *Accounting, Organisations and Society*, 32 (1–2), 131–54.

Klein, B. (2002). 'The Role of Incomplete Contracts in Self-reinforcing Relationships', in Brousseau, E. and Glachant, J. (eds), *The Economics of Contracts*, Cambridge University Press, Cambridge.

Klein, B., Crawford, R. G. and Alchian, A. A. (1978). 'Vertical Integration, Appropriable Rents and the Competitive Contracting Process', *Journal of Law and Economics*, 22, 297–326.

Krishnan, R., Miller, F. and Sedatole, K. L. (2007). 'An Empirical Examination of the Relationship Between Performance Measurement, Collaborative Contracting and Asset Ownership', AAA MAS meeting paper. Available at SSRN: http://ssrn.com/abstract=1004126.

Langfield-Smith, K. (2008). 'The Relations between Transactional Characteristics, Trust and Risk in the Start-up Phase of a Collaborative Alliance', *Management Accounting Research*, doi: 10.1016/j.mar.2008.09.001.

Langfield-Smith, K. and Smith, D. (2003). 'Management Control Systems and Trust in Outsourcing Relationships', *Management Accounting Research*, 14 (3), 281–307.

Luft, J. and Shields, M. (2002). 'Mapping Management Accounting: Graphics and Guidelines for Theory-Consistent Empirical Research', *University of Michigan Papers*.

Malmi, T. and Brown, D. A. (2008). 'Management Control Systems As A Package – Opportunities, Challenges and Research Directions', *Management Accounting Research*, 19, 287–300.

Meer-Kooistra, J. v. d. and Scapens, R.W. (2008). 'The Governance of Lateral Relations Between and Within Organisations', *Management Accounting Research*, doi: 10.1016/j.mar.2008.08.001

Meer-Kooistra, J. v. d. and Vosselman, E. G. J. (2000). Management Control of Inter-organisational Transactional Relationships: The Case of Industrial Renovation and Maintenance', *Accounting, Organizations and Society*, 25 (1), 51–77.

Milgrom, P. and Roberts, J. (1992). *Economics, Organization and Management*, Englewood Cliffs, NJ, Prentice-Hall.

Poppo, L. and Zenger, T. (2002). 'Do Formal Contracts and Relational Governance Function as Substitutes or Complements?' *Strategic Management Journal*, 23, 707–25.

Richardson, G. B. (1972). 'The Organization of Industry', *Economic Journal*, 82, 883–96.

Rooney, J. and Cuganesan, S. (2009). 'Contractual and Accounting Controls in Outsourcing Agreements: Evidence from the Australian Home Loan Industry', *Australian Accounting Review*, 19 (2), 80–92.

Rasmusen, E. (1990). *Games and Information. An Introduction to Game Theory*, Blackwell, Oxford.

Ring, P. and Van de Ven, A., (1994). 'Developmental processes of cooperative inter-organizational relationships'. *Academy of Management Review*, 19 (1), 90–118.

Saam, N. J. (2007). 'Asymmetry in Information versus Asymmetry in Power: Implicit Assumptions of Agency Theory?', *The Journal of Socio-Economics*, 36, 825–40.

Spekle, R. (2001). 'Explaining Management Control Structure Variety: A Transaction Cost Economics Perspective', *Accounting, Organisations and Society*, 26 (4–5), 419–42.

Spence, A. M. (1974). *Market Signaling: Informational Transfer in Hiring and Related Screening Processes*, Harvard University Press, Cambridge, MA.

Tomkins, C. (2001). 'Interdependencies, Trust and Information in Relationships, Alliances and Networks', *Accounting, Organisations and Society*, 26 (2),161–91.

Whang, S. (1992). 'Contracting for Software Development', *Management Science*, 38 (3), 307–24.

Vincent-Jones, P. (1999). 'Competition and Contracting in the Transition from CCT to Best Value: Towards a More Reflexive Regulation?', *Public Administration*, 77, 273–91.

Vosselman, E. G. J. and Meer-Kooistra, J. v. d. (2008). 'Accounting for Control and Trust Building in Inter-organisational Transactional Relationships', *Accounting, Organisations and Society*, 34, 267–83.

Vosselman, E. G. J. and van Sonsbeek, J. (2008). 'Formal Control and Action Nets in Inter-firm Transactional Relationships: Field Study Evidence', GMARS Conference, Sydney.

Whang, S. (1992). Contracting for software development, *Management Science*, 38 (3): 307–24.

Williamson, O. (1983). 'Credible Commitments: Using Hostages to Support Exchange', *American Economic Review* (September), 519–40.

Williamson, O. E. (1995). *The Economic Institutions of Capitalism: Firms, Markets, Relational Contracting,* Free Press, New York.

Part II
Environmental Management

6
Corporate Social Responsibility and Sustainability Reporting

Nigel Finch

6.1 Introduction

This chapter has four key sections. It commences with a brief overview of the historical development of the concept of sustainability and an analysis of the five major frameworks covered in the literature: (1) agency view; (2) corporate social performance view; (3) resource-based view; (4) supply and demand view; and (5) the stakeholder view, which is the dominant view.

Section 6.2 looks at understanding stakeholders and their importance in sustainability and provides some observations about sustainability frameworks and (importantly) the motivations of companies for increased disclosure with their stakeholders.

Section 6.3 briefly outlines the background to the development of new reporting frameworks which have been developed to facilitate sustainability disclosure.

Finally, Section 6.4 focuses triple bottom line reporting on the development of one particular framework designed to assist in sustainability disclosure: the Global Reporting Initiative (GRI).

6.2 Historical development of sustainability

The concept of social responsibility, or social responsiveness, is an evolving concept (Mays, 2003, p. 12) and means different things to different stakeholders (Arlow and Gannon, 1982). However, the concept of social responsibility has been with us since the beginning of mankind (Anderson, 1989).

A comprehensive approach to Western contemporary social responsibility came in 1953 with the publication of Howard R. Bowen's book,

Social Responsibilities of the Businessman. Here, Bowen described the social responsibility of the businessman as 'the obligation of businessmen to pursue policies, to make those decisions, or to follow those lines of action that are desirable in terms of objectives and values in our society' (Bowen, 1953, p. 6).

The Committee for Economic Development (CED) (1971) used the term 'social contract' to define the relationship between business and society, with business's major obligation being the provision of goods and services for the benefit of society.

A significant amount of research has been undertaken over the past decades in understanding the nature of and motives for corporate social responsibility (e.g., Anderson, 1989; Arlow and Gannon, 1982; Carroll, 1979; Clarkson, 1995; McWilliams and Siegel, 2001; Pava and Krausz, 1996; Waddock and Graves, 1997; Wood, 1991) Increasingly, the importance placed on corporate social responsibility by investors, analysts, commentators and academics has grown, indicating a shift in attitudes.

This shift started with the agency view, which is the first framework identified in the literature. The next framework in the literature is the corporate social performance (CSP) view, followed by the resource-based view (RBV) and the supply and demand view. Finally, the stakeholder view is identified.

6.1.1   The agency view

Initially, the idea that a corporation was using shareholders' funds to engage in social projects was criticised (Gelb and Strawser, 2001, p. 3).

Milton Friedman (1962, 1970) is generally credited with the 'agency view' of the corporation and its responsibility to society. Friedman, recipient of the 1976 Nobel Memorial Prize for economic science, proposed that engaging in CSR is symptomatic of an agency problem or a conflict between the interests of managers and shareholders. Friedman argues that managers use CSR as a means to further their own social, political or career agendas at the expense of shareholders (McWilliams and Siegel, 2001, p. 118).

According to Friedman's agency view, the business entity is accountable only to its shareholders and its sole social responsibility is to maximise the value of the firm (Gelb and Strawser, 2001, p. 3). To paraphrase from *Capitalism and Freedom* (Friedman, 1962, pp. 133–5): ·

> The view has been gaining widespread acceptance that corporate officials and labour leaders have a 'social responsibility' that goes beyond serving the interest of their stockholders and their members... few

trends could so thoroughly undermine the very foundation of our free society as the acceptance by corporate officials of a social responsibility other than to make as much money for their stockholders as possible. This is a fundamentally subversive doctrine... the claim that business should contribute to the support of charitable activities... is an inappropriate use of corporate funds in a free enterprise society.

The agency view started to lose favour in the literature as the corporate social performance view gained attention in the 1980s.

6.1.2   The Corporate Social Performance (CSP) view

Early research by Preston (1978) and Carroll (1979) outlined a 'corporate social performance' (CSP) framework, which includes the philosophy of social responsiveness, the social issues involved, and the social and economic responsibilities. Waddock and Graves (1997) empirically tested the CSP model and reported a positive association between CSP and financial performance (McWilliams and Siegel, 2001, p. 118). Researchers such as Pava and Krausz (1996) hypothesised that, according to the agency view, greater levels of CSR would lead to reduced levels of financial performance. Their findings persistently showed the opposite: that firms perceived as socially responsible performed as well as or better than their counterparts that do not engage in costly social activities. The authors concluded that 'sometimes a conscious pursuit of corporate social responsibility goals causes better financial performance' (Pava and Krausz, 1996, p. 333).

Building upon Preston and Carroll's framework, another view, the resource-based view (RBV) argues that CSP not only improves financial performance but also adds a competitive advantage to the firm.

6.1.3   Resource-based View (RBV)

Another framework has been developed by Russo and Fouts (1997). They examined CSR from a 'resource-based view' (RBV) of the firm perspective. Using this framework, they argue that CSP (especially environmental performance) can constitute a competitive advantage, especially in high-growth industries.

Using the RBV framework as a foundation, the next framework, the supply and demand view, introduced the notion of optimising sustainability investment.

6.1.4   Supply and demand view

McWilliams and Siegel (2001) developed a 'supply and demand' framework and proposed that there is a level of CSR investment that maximises profit, while also satisfying stakeholder demand for CSR. While focusing on the level of CSR investment is seen as important to maximise profits, the literature favours stakeholders as the primary focus.

6.1.5   Stakeholder view

A widely used framework for examining CSR is the 'stakeholder' perspective. Developed by Freeman (1984), the stakeholder theory asserts that firms have relationships with many constituent groups and that these stakeholders both affect and are affected by the actions of the firm. Freeman (1984) argued that systematic attention to stakeholder interest is critical to a firm's success and management must pursue actions that are optimal for a broad class of stakeholders, rather than those that serve only to maximise shareholder interests (Gelb and Strawser, 2001, p. 3).

6.2   Understanding stakeholders

Freeman (1984, p. 46) defines a stakeholder as '… any group or individual who can affect or is affected by the achievements of an organisation's objectives'. This definition is still widely acknowledged as the landmark position in stakeholder theory (Wood, 1991; Clarkson, 1995; Vos, 2003). The distinction between those who 'can affect' (i.e., the involved) and those who 'are affected' (i.e., the affected) is considered crucial in understanding and defining stakeholders. The involved have the possibility to directly influence the actions of the firm, while the affected do not have any influence over the actions of the firm.

From the firm's perspective, stakeholder identification is not easily solved, because it comprises, at least, a modelling issue and a normative issue (Vos, 2003, p. 141). The modelling issue refers to identification issues for management, such as 'who are our stakeholders?' and 'to what extent can we distinguish between stakeholders and non-stakeholders?'. The normative issue refers to managerial implications, such as 'what stakeholders will we take into account?' or 'to which stakeholders are we willing to listen?'. Vos (2003) argues that in order to identify stakeholders, both the modelling and the normative issues need to be resolved.

Mitchell *et al.* (1997) stresses the importance of risk in identifying stakeholders and points out that, without risk, there is no *stake* (a stake in this sense is something that can be lost). As such, a stakeholder is a risk-bearer, and from this perspective, the distinction can be made between voluntary and involuntary stakeholders. Voluntary stakeholders bear some form of risk as a result of having invested some form of capital (human or financial) or something of value in the firm. Involuntary stakeholders are placed at risk as a result of the firm's activities (Mitchell *et al.*, 1997).

The dominance of the shareholder among all stakeholders is consistent with Friedman's (1962, 1970) agency view, which is largely seen as untenable in the context of CSR. There is no denying that shareholders deserve their special position as voluntary stakeholders because of the property rights they enjoy with the organisation, and the fiduciary duty (which is based on trust) between management and the shareholders. However, the organisation should acknowledge that it also owes a moral obligation to all non-shareholder stakeholders (including involuntary stakeholders) where the freedom and well-being of stakeholders are affected by the organisation's activities (Goodpaster, 1998).

Donaldson and Preston (1995) refined the stakeholder paradigm by arguing that three aspects of this theory – normative, descriptive/empirical and instrumental – are 'mutually supportive'. Jones and Wicks (1999) propose converging the instrumental (social science) and normative (ethics) components of stakeholder theory to arrive at a normative theory that describes how managers can create morally sound approaches to business and make them work (Jones and Wicks, 1999, p. 206). For more recent developments in stakeholder theory, see Gelb and Strawser (2001).

To a certain extent, the management of CSR has become stakeholder management (Donaldson and Preston, 1995). In dealing with stakeholder identification and management, there are two generally accepted positions: the firm-centred or instrumental perspective; and the system-centred or social responsibility framework (Vos, 2003, p. 144).

The firm-centred or instrumental perspective (Vos, 2003) is where the organisation identifies all its stakeholders for firm-centred purposes, such as economic prosperity, risk management, economic dependency, and brand and image building. In general, these are the 'involved' stakeholders who can potentially affect the organisation's achievements.

Using stakeholder theory as a dominant paradigm, CSR may be defined as 'the obligation to a specific system of stakeholders to carry out actions that appear to further some social good, beyond the interest of the firm and that which is required by law to do' (Vos, 2003; McWillams and Siegel, 2001).

CSR means going beyond obeying the law; merely abiding by the law does not necessarily constitute a CSR activity. Some examples of CSR actions include going beyond legal requirements in adopting progressive human resource management programmes, developing non-animal testing procedures, recycling, abating pollution, supporting local businesses, and embodying products with social attributes or characteristics such as product or process innovation (McWillams and Siegel, 2001, p. 117).

Over the past few decades, the attitudes of some companies have changed, rejecting the agency view (Friedman, 1962, 1970), and instead embracing stakeholders (Freeman, 1984) and sustainability concepts in their business practice.

This has been motivated by a belief that adopting sustainability practices in the long run will lead to the improved financial performance of the firm (McWilliams and Siegel, 2001; Pava and Krausz, 1996), increased competitive advantage (Russo and Fouts, 1997), profit maximisation (McWilliams and Siegel, 2001) and the long-term success of the firm (Freeman, 1984).

To achieve these goals, companies need to demonstrate to their stakeholders that they are meeting or exceeding those stakeholders' expectations of performance in the area of sustainability. To facilitate this, companies have adopted new reporting and disclosure frameworks to help them communicate with their stakeholders. This will be the focus of the next sections.

6.3   The introduction of new reporting frameworks

Traditional accounting has long been criticised for providing an incomplete account of business. It fails to present the dynamics of business-value-creating activities and how socio-political factors may affect or be affected by those activities. This is evidenced by increased research into intellectual capital reporting (ICR) and corporate social responsibility reporting and the introduction of new disclosure frameworks.

From the perspective of the CSR research, the traditional accounting framework is too narrow (Guthrie and Parker, 1993). The business income concept needs to be expanded (Bedford, 1965) because economic performance is not an index of total welfare (Bedford, 1965; Pigou, 1938). Since business activities have both economic and social impacts (Estes, 1976), businesses must meet societal expectations of both profit generation and contributions to the quality of life in general. This is also consistent with the concept of social contract of the legitimacy theory (CED, 1971).

A plethora of alternative reporting methods have been proposed in the sustainability literature including the Balanced Scorecard, the Jenkins Report, the 21st Century Annual Report, Value Dynamics, Value Reporting, the Hermes Principles and the Global Reporting

Initiative (ICAEW, 2004, p. 9), however, there is no universally accepted framework.

The idea of combining extended reporting frameworks with the traditional accounting framework has recently attracted a great deal of attention. One example of this synergy is the triple bottom line (TBL) reporting approach.

TBL, a term coined by Elkington (1997), focuses corporations 'not just on the economic value they add, but also on the environmental and social value they add – and destroy'. The idea is rooted in the concept and goal of sustainable development, which is defined as 'development that meets the needs of the present world without compromising the ability of future generations to meet their own needs' (World Commission on Environment and Development, 1987).

As Deegan (1999) indicated, 'for an organisation or community to be sustainable (a long-run perspective), it must be financially secured (as evidenced through such measures as profitability), it must minimise (or ideally eliminate) its negative environmental impact, and it must act in conformity with society's expectations'. That is, it is inadequate to measure and present only economic performance, which is the focus of intellectual capital (IC) research. To be sustained in the long run, organisations must strive to achieve better performance across the three dimensions of TBL.

An alternative is the codification of guidelines such as those of the Global Reporting Initiative 2002, which is heading towards a common and acceptable reporting framework that combines the reporting of financial, environmental and social performance within the same format. In addition, as stated in GRI (2002), the initiative has enjoyed the active support and engagement of representatives of key constituencies, and in the GRI's view, its guidelines provide the most updated consensus on a reporting framework at this point.

6.4 Triple bottom line and development of the Global Reporting Initiative

The publication of *Cannibals with Forks* (Elkington, 1997) focused the business community on the links between environmental, economic and social concerns that had been highlighted previously in the Brundtland Report (WCED, 1987). Elkington coined the term triple bottom line and has convinced many leading companies to embrace sustainability using his triple bottom line theory. The Global Reporting Initiative (GRI) builds upon the foundations of triple bottom line to provide a framework for reporting and social accounting.

The Coalition for Environmentally Responsible Economies originally launched the GRI in 1997. The GRI is a voluntary set of guidelines for reporting on the economic, environmental and social aspects of an organisation's activities.

The GRI was established with the goal of enhancing the quality, rigour and utility of sustainability reporting. The initiative has enjoyed the active support and engagement of representatives from business, non-government organisations, accounting bodies, investor organisations and trade unions. Together, these different constituencies have worked to build a consensus around a set of reporting guidelines with the objective of obtaining worldwide acceptance (Fowler, 2002).

The sustainability reporting guidelines are a framework for reporting on economic, environmental and social performance. They (a) outline reporting principles and content to help prepare organisation-level sustainability reports; (b) help organisations gain a balanced picture of their economic, environmental and social performance; (c) promote comparability of sustainability reports; (d) support benchmarking and assessment of sustainability performance; and (e) serve as a key tool in the overall process of stakeholders' engagement.

Sometimes referred to as triple bottom line reporting, the term *sustainability reporting* is used throughout the GRI guidelines.

The guidelines can be used simply as an informal reference document to assist organisations in developing a framework and indicators for measurement and reporting in an environmental fashion. Alternatively, the organisation may choose to adopt them and prepare its report 'in accordance' with the guidelines.

The GRI recognises the complexity of implementing a sustainability reporting programme and the need for many organisations to build their reporting capacity in an incremental fashion. Such organisations may choose not to prepare a complete GRI-based report in their initial effort. Instead, they may choose a step-by-step approach to adopting the guidelines over a period of time. Increasingly, these voluntary guidelines are being adopted by companies worldwide, providing a common framework for sustainability reporting.

6.5   Conclusion

Over the past few decades, the attitudes of some companies have changed, rejecting the agency view (Friedman, 1962, 1970), and instead embracing stakeholders (Freeman, 1984) and sustainability concepts in their business practice.

With a new-found focus on disclosure to stakeholders, there has been growing concern in the academic literature that the traditional financial disclosure framework by organisations is insufficient because: (a) it has failed to adapt to the changing nature of business; (b) it no longer meets the changing needs of investors; and (c) it fails to recognise a wide enough circle of users (ICAEW, 2004, p. 6).

In attempting to satisfy this deficiency in traditional reporting, several new alternative sustainability reporting frameworks have been developed, but there is no universally accepted framework that allows universal comparison of sustainability performance.

In the absence of legislative prescription, organisations have been adopting these new disclosure frameworks on a voluntary basis only to help them communicate with their stakeholders. The Global Reporting Initiative is one such framework being adopted which has attracted significant comment and attention. With the help of these extended reporting frameworks, many leading companies are demonstrating to their stakeholders that they are meeting or exceeding those stakeholders' expectations of performance in the area of sustainability.

References

Anderson, J. W. (1989). *Corporate Social Responsibility*, Greenwood Press, Connecticut.

Arlow, P. and Gannon, M. J. (1982). 'Social Responsiveness, Corporate Structure and Economic Performance', *Academy of Management Review*, 7 (2), 235–41.

Bedford, N. M. (1965). *Income Determination Theory: An Accounting Framework*, Addison-Wesley, Massachusetts.

Bowen, H. R. (1953). *Social Responsibilities of the Businessman*, Harper & Bros, New York.

Carroll, A. (1979). 'A Three Dimensional Model of Corporate Performance, *Academy of Management Review*, 4, 99–120.

Caswell, T. (2004). 'Sustainability: A Vital Agenda or 21st Century Good Governance', *Journal of Chartered Secretaries Australia*, 56 (2), 85–90.

Clarkson, M. (1995). 'A Stakeholder Framework for Analysing and Evaluating Corporate Social Performance, *Academy of Management Review*, 20 (1), 92–117.

Committee for Economic Development (CED) (1971). *Social Responsibilities of Business Corporations*, US Government Printing Office, Washington DC.

Deegan, C. (1999). 'Implementing Triple Bottom Line Performance and Reporting Mechanisms', *Charter*, 70, May, 40–2.

Donaldson, T. and Preston, L. (1995). 'The Stakeholder Theory of the Corporation: Concepts, Evidence and Implications', *Academy of Management Review*, 4, 65–91.

Elkington, J. (1997). *Cannibals with Forks: The Triple Bottom Line of 21st Century Business*, Capstone Publishing.

Estes, R. (1976). *Corporate Social Accounting*, Wiley, New York.

Fowler, G. (2002). 'Sustainability Reporting – A Global Framework, *Company Director*, November, Sydney.

Friedman, M. (1962). *Capitalism and Freedom*, University of Chicago Press, Chicago, IL.

Friedman, M. (1970). 'The Social Responsibility of Business is to Increase its Profits', *New York Times*, September 13, 122–6.

Freeman, R. (1984). *Strategic Management: A Stakeholder Perspective*, Prentice-Hall, New Jersey.

Gelb, D. S. and Strawser, J. A. (2001). 'Corporate Social Responsibility and Financial Disclosures: An Alternative Explanation for Increased Disclosure', *Journal of Business Ethics*, 33 (1), 1–13.

Goodpaster, K. E. (1998). *The Corporation and Its Stakeholders*, University of Toronto Press, Toronto.

Guthrie, J. and Parker, L. D. (1993). 'The Australian Public Sector in the 1990s: New Accountability Regimes in Motion', *Journal of International Accounting, Auditing and Taxation*, 2 (1), 57–79.

ICAEW (2004). *New Reporting Models for Business*, Institute of Chartered Accountants in England & Wales, London.

Jones, T. and Wicks, A. (1999). 'Convergent Stakeholder Theory', *Academy of Management Review*, 24, 206–21.

Mays, S. (2003). *Corporate Sustainability – An Investor Perspective; The Mays Report*, Department of the Environment and Heritage, Canberra.

McWilliams, A. and Siegel, D. (2001). 'Corporate Social Responsibility: A Theory of the Firm Perspective', *Academy of Management Review*, 26 (1), 117–27.

Mitchell, R. K., Agle, B. R. and Wood, D. J. (1997). 'Toward A Theory of Stakeholder Identification and Salience: Defining the Principle of Who and What Really Counts, *Academy of Management Review*, 22 (4), 853–86.

Pava, M. L. and Krausz, J. (1996). 'The Association between Corporate Social Responsibility and Financial Performance: The Paradox of Social Cost', *Journal of Business Ethics*, 3 (15), 321–57.

Pigou, A. C. (1938). *The Economics of Welfare*, Macmillan and Co., London.

Preston, L. (1978). *Research in Corporate Social Performance and Policy*, JAI Press, Greenwich.

Russo, Michael V. and Fouts, Paul A. (1997). 'A Resource-Based Perspective on Corporate Environmental Performance and Profitability', *Academy of Management Journal*, 40, 534–59.

Vos, J. F. (2003). 'Corporate Social Responsibility and the Identification of Stakeholders', *Corporate Social Responsibility and Environmental Management*, 10, 141–52.

Waddock, S. and Graves, S. (1997). 'The Corporate Social Performance – Financial Performance Link', *Strategic Management Journal*, 18, 303–19.

Wood, D. J. (1991). 'Corporate Social Performance Revisited', *Academy of Management Review*, 16 (4), 691–719.

World Commission on Environment and Development (WCED) (1987). *Our Common Future*, Oxford University Press, Geneva.

7
Management Accounting Practices for Sustainability

Jayanthi Kumarasiri

7.1 Introduction

With growing sensitivity towards social and environmental issues, modern businesses are increasingly under pressure to perform their business activities in an environmentally friendly manner. A widely accepted view among many different professionals and the general public is that companies – the key players in the modern global economy – are the entities which cause greatest damage to our ecological sustainability (Ball *et al.*, 2009). Global warming, ozone depletion, deforestation, acid rain and toxic wastes are examples of ecological damage caused by corporations (Shrivastava, 1995). Governments and regulatory bodies across the world are tightening the relevant rules and regulations in an attempt to coerce companies towards becoming socially responsible and to pay greater attention to the environmental and social impact of their corporate actions. In this context, companies are compelled to look for the means that enable them to run their businesses in a socially and environmentally sustainable manner. However, they face the challenge of achieving this objective without sacrificing their economic well-being and performance.

Balancing a company's economic performance with its social and environmental performance may not be an easy task. The economic performance may not always coincide positively with environmental and social performance (Milne, 1996). Therefore it is important for companies to base managerial decisions on reliable information and to perform business activities with a greater strategic focus. In this respect, by providing relevant, accurate and timely information for managers, management accounting can play a vital role in achieving organisational sustainability.

The academic literature which evaluates corporate sustainability performance provides mixed evidence in support of the argument that companies are getting the message about the importance of being environmentally concerned when conducting their business activities. Researchers who have observed the evolution of environmental reporting have witnessed a vast improvement in the disclosure of environmental policies, environmental performance and future environmental plans by companies during the last two decades (Kolk, 2003; Dammak, 2009). However, researchers who have analysed the quality of environmental reporting have had some concerns about the genuineness displayed by the companies in being environmentally sensitive (Belal, 2002; Gray and Milne, 2002; Adams, 2004). On the other hand, those researchers who have investigated the motives behind the environmental performance of companies and the benefits of those performances have found that companies were motivated to be environmentally friendly not just to obey the regulatory requirements (Al-Tuwaijri *et al.*, 2004; Cormier *et al.*, 2005). They have observed many benefits that companies can achieve through improved environmental performance. Such benefits include financial benefits from cost reductions through eco-efficiency and the achievement of competitive advantages by building their images as green companies (Al-Tuwaijri *et al.*, 2004; Burnett and Hansen, 2008).

The literature which discusses the relationship between economic and environmental performance and eco-efficiency highlights that, in order to improve environmental performance while enjoying economic benefits, companies need to be innovative, environmentally sensitive and be able to integrate environmental information into their business strategies. For this purpose, companies need to have a proper information system which integrates all relevant information and provides such information for managerial decision-making. The purpose of management accounting is to provide relevant information for managers in their planning, evaluating, controlling and decision-making processes (Bartolomeo *et al.*, 2000). In that context, management accounting can play a significant role in an organisation by integrating all the core functions and providing relevant information for managerial decision-making. The objective of this chapter is to review research that has investigated the performance-related benefits that companies can realise by using management accounting techniques to integrate environmental considerations into the business decision-making process. The chapter also discusses leading examples of companies which use advanced management accounting techniques, such as capital budgeting, performance measurements and incentives to manage and execute their environmental strategies. Further, it presents emerging evidence on how companies attempt to overcome the challenge of managing carbon emissions and how they respond to the critical issue of climate change.

7.2 Environmental sustainability to economic sustainability

A considerable number of researchers have observed a positive association between the environmental and economic performance of companies (Konar and Cohen, 2001; Nakao *et al.*, 2007; Mahoney and Roberts, 2007). Researchers who have documented a positive relationship argue that by being socially and environmentally responsible, companies acquire a competitive advantage as their efforts are valued in the marketplace (Konar and Cohen, 2001). Konar and Cohen (2001) argue that the main motivation for large, publicly traded companies to invest in environmental reputation capital (i.e., voluntary disclosure of environmental performance and environmental research and development) is because they reap the rewards of such actions in the marketplace.

More recent studies conducted by Nakao *et al.* (2007) provide evidence from Japan for the positive association between environmental performance and competitive advantages achieved by companies. They analysed the financial reports of 300 listed Japanese firms over the five-year period from 1999 to 2003, together with Nikkei Environmental Management Survey Reports. They found a significant positive relationship between environmental performance and financial performance; this two-way interaction was found to have become more prevalent in recent years. The perception of companies on environmental performance has changed over time; modern Japanese companies perceive environmental issues not as a 'cost factor' but as an 'important strategic factor'.

It has been found that by being eco-efficient, companies can create more economic value while continuously reducing the ecological impact and use of natural resources (Burritt and Saka, 2006). According to the World Business Council for Sustainable Development (WBCSD), eco-efficiency can be defined as 'the delivery of competitively priced goods and services that satisfy human needs and bring quality of life, while progressively reducing ecological impacts and resource intensity throughout the life cycle, to a level at least in line with the earth's estimated carrying capacity' (World Business Council for Sustainability Development, 1998, p. 3). A reasonable number of researchers have examined the relationships among eco-efficiency, economic benefits and the environmental benefits for the firm.

Pagan and Prasad (2007), who investigated the 'Queensland Food Processing Eco-Efficiency Project' in Australia, uncovered evidence of significant savings achieved by companies by being innovative and by integrating environmental information into their business strategies. After implementing the eco-efficiency project, Queensland food processing companies were able to reduce significantly the amount of water and energy used in their production processes. This eco-efficiency project highlighted the importance of a collaborative approach between industry associations, individual companies, government and external consultants to achieve eco-efficiency objectives.

A similar study by Burritt and Saka (2006), which employed a sample of Japanese companies, also found that by being eco-efficient companies can improve their production efficiency and reduce costs while reducing the environmental pollution of their business activities. The researchers emphasised the importance of promoting eco-efficiency benefits in the process of environmental sustainability. According to Sinkin *et al.* (2008), companies that implement eco-efficiency strategies have consistently higher market values than those that do not pursue such a strategy.

In sum, when looking at the literature which discusses the relationship between environmental efficiency and economic benefits, it is clear that by being environmentally friendly and eco-efficient companies can enjoy economic benefits.

7.3 The role that management accounting can play in achieving economic and environmental sustainability

The literature discussed in the previous sections highlights that, in order to improve environmental performance while enjoying economic benefits, companies need to be innovative, environmentally sensitive and able to integrate environmental information into their business strategies. To do this, companies need to have a proper information system which integrates all the relevant information and provides such information for managerial decision-making. According to the Chartered Institute of Management Accountants (CIMA), Management Accounting is 'the process of identification, measurement, accumulation, analysis, preparation, interpretation and communication of information used by management to plan, evaluate and control within an entity and to assure appropriate use of and accountability for its resources'.

In that context, it is clear that there is significant potential for the management accounting function to play a role in driving the environmental strategies and actions within organisations. The objective of this particular section is to discuss the role that management accounting can play in achieving economic and environmental sustainability for an organisation. As there is very little research that has directly addressed the role of management accounting in doing this, this review will synthesise some related academic literature which discusses the different management accounting techniques used by companies in integrating environmental issues into management decision making process.

As highlighted by Langfield-Smith and Thorne (2009) and Epstein (2008), management accounting techniques such as capital budgeting, balanced scorecard, performance measurement and reward systems can facilitate the integration of environmental matters into management's decision-making process. Here we will discuss the different management accounting techniques used by companies to do this. Some examples of how leading companies use such techniques are also provided.

7.4   Capital budgeting

Capital budgeting is a management accounting tool used by companies to plan their capital expenditure projects. In the past two decades, growing concern about environmental effects on business activities has forced companies to consider these effects when evaluating their business projects. Companies are therefore compelled to incorporate environmental costs into the traditional capital budgeting process. The importance of incorporating environmental costs arises from the moral obligation towards environmental sustainability, but also because companies are held financially liable for negative environmental impacts. Therefore, it is important for managers to incorporate environmental costs and liabilities into the management decision-making processes. As highlighted by Epstein (2008), even though the evaluation of social and environmental impacts on capital investments is difficult (because of the changing climate of social and environmental awareness, changing technologies, future government regulations, long-term horizons etc.), it is crucially important for businesses to have better awareness of such costs.

Bartolomeo *et al.* (2000) found an increase in managerial concern over environmental matters in capital budgeting. The study analysed the present and potential future links between the environmental management and management accounting functions of European companies. The study sample consisted of 84 companies and detailed case studies were conducted on 15 companies selected from Germany, Italy, the Netherlands and the UK. The researchers found that the linkage between management accounting and environmental management helped companies to enhance their decision-making process. Most of the companies recognised the superiority of pollution prevention at source over the 'end-of-pipe' solution. They believed that proper integration of environmental information into their normal decision-making process allows them to identify the potential environmental costs and take corrective action in early stages. Further, these companies identified management accounting techniques, such as capital budgeting and operating budgeting, as important tools for environmental management. For example, 48 per cent of the respondents considered capital budgeting to be of either considerable or crucial importance to their current environmental management processes, and 61 per cent of them believed that it would be considerably or crucially important in the future. Perez *et al.* (2007), Epstein (2008) and Henri and Journeault (2010) also identified capital budgeting as an important tool that management could use to evaluate the environmental costs and benefits of capital investment projects. The following example (Coca-Cola Amatil Ltd Australia) provides some guidance on how environmental factors may be incorporated in capital budgeting.

7.4.1   Example: Coca-Cola Amatil Ltd Australia

> For each major capital project an environmental impact assessment is performed. Under the energy use and greenhouse gas emissions category the expected amount of energy use/GHG emitted is factored in. These estimated costs are considered as part of a holistic capital expenditure review and approval process from the project manager up to the director of operations in most cases. For projects above a certain cash threshold this approval goes to the Managing Director.
>
> Carbon Disclosure Project (2009): Coca-Cola Amatil Ltd

However, the incorporation of environmental costs and liabilities into traditional capital budgeting is not without its problems. Changing government regulations, changing technologies, lack of measurements to evaluate the environmental effect and the long-term horizon involved make that task more complicated. Nevertheless, because of the stakeholder pressure and financial risk attached, companies are no longer able to ignore the environmental effect of their capital projects. Milne (1996) argues that businesses may have to reject their profitable and efficient projects if such projects bring negative effects to the environment. Therefore it is essential to incorporate environmental aspects into project evaluation and to evaluate projects continually in order to make sure that such projects absorb the effects of changing environmental regulations, technology and economics.

7.5   Performance measurements

The Balanced Scorecard (BSC) is a performance measurement tool used by companies to evaluate their financial and non-financial performances. As explained by Langfield-Smith and Thorne (2009), many companies use BSC and include sustainability success factors and key performance indicators to evaluate the sustainability performance of their companies. Figge *et al.* (2002) highlight the sustainability balanced scorecard (SBSC) as a valuable management tool that helps significantly to overcome the shortcomings of the parallel approaches of environmental, social and economic management systems within the organisation; the sustainability balanced scorecard (SBSC) can be used to integrate sustainability matters into the business.

Perez *et al.* (2007), who studied the role of Environmental Management Systems (EMS) in improving environmental performance, found that companies which used advanced management accounting techniques to incorporate environmental issues into organisational strategies showed a solid improvement in their environmental performance. Accordingly, Perez *et al.* (2007) identified the more advanced use of management accounting practices, such as capital budgeting and the balanced scorecard, as a key intangible asset that companies possess when they deal with environmental issues. Management accounting was also identified as a key intangible asset which facilitated and assured further environmental embeddedness and a solid improvement in the environmental performance of companies.

7.5.1   Example: Nike develops a 'balanced scorecard' for ethics integration

Global sportswear brand Nike has been hit by accusations over the labour conditions in its contracted factories in Vietnam and other Asian countries in recent years. In order to incorporate social responsibility as an integral part of its manufacturing contracts, it has added ethical factors into its BSC.

'The sports goods manufacturer has said it intends to introduce corporate responsibility as an integral part of its contract manufacturing business. It is creating a balanced scorecard to meet this end. The company will now make sourcing decisions based not just on price, quality and delivery but also a contractor's pledge towards labour management and environmental, health and safety programmes. Nike says that in order to extract a commitment to corporate responsibility from its contractors and hold them accountable to the company's corporate responsibility goals, it has incorporated these targets within its own business systems'.

Ethical Corporation (2010).

The identification and measurement of the costs and benefits of social, environmental and economic impacts of business activities are critically important for business sustainability. According to Neely *et al.* (2002) (cited by Cocca and Alberti (2010)), 'A Performance Measurement System is the set of metrics used to quantify the efficiency and effectiveness of past actions' and 'it enables informed decisions to be made and actions to be taken because it quantifies the efficiency and effectiveness of past actions through the acquisition, collation, sorting, analysis and interpretation of appropriate data'.

Perego and Hartmann (2009) view performance measurements as a crucial factor ensuring the effective implementation of an environmental strategy and its execution according to the expectations of the business. They found that companies with more proactive environmental strategies rely more on performance measurement systems. Additionally, the researchers observed that increased quantification of environmental performance (and their increased sensitivity to managers) helps achieve the alignment between strategies and performance measurers which allows the companies to achieve their objectives.

7.5.2 Sustainability performance rulers

Watercare Ltd is the largest water and wastewater company in New Zealand. It is the most consistent and leading sustainability reporter in New Zealand. Watercare has been following a systematic way of measuring its social, environmental and economic performance enabling management to compare the current year's performance with that in previous years.

Watercare has been looking for a clearer, more rigorous way of evaluating the company's performance. Bearing in mind the axiom 'what you measure, you can manage', the company has devised a new reporting method based on six sustainability polices and 18 objectives.

The sustainability performance rulers are a visual representation of performance against the company's stated objectives. They are not absolute or universal measures- they are broad indicators. They are not intended as benchmarks to compare Watercare with other organisations. Rather, they provide an internal standard that will allow management to compare future performance against this year's. The crux is to demonstrate improvement over time.

Watercare Ltd (2009), Annual report.

As highlighted by the above literature, performance measurements are important for businesses to evaluate their past performance and to take the necessary corrective actions. If companies use their performance measures just for the purposes of reporting, it can be seen as a waste of business resourses; each and every measure has some cost (collection of data, analysis and reports etc.) associated with it. Thus it is vital for companies to make sure that measured performances are communicated to the right individuals who are responsible for taking corrective actions. Well-designed and properly directed performance measures can make a significant difference to the performance of a business.

7.6 Reward system

As highlighted by Epstein (2008), performance evaluation and reward systems are crucially important in creating a culture in which employees understand and work towards corporate social and environmental goals. A proper reward system motivates employees to align their behaviour with the environmental goals of the organisation and to exert additional effort; it will contribute to improve environmental performance.

The study conducted by Henri and Journeault (2010) on the influence of management control systems on environmental and economic performance also stressed the importance of the integration of environmental goals and indicators to the reward systems of the companies. The researchers highlighted the important role and contribution that management accounting techniques can play by developing specific performance indicators, frequently using them to monitor compliance, using budgeting techniques to capture the environmental effect and linking environmental goals to reward systems. Adams and Frost (2008) also observed an increase in the use of environmental performance indicators to reward employees. They found that managers were evaluated not only based on their financial performance but also on the environmental performance indicated by, for example, the reduction of CO^2 and efficient usage of energy.

Daily *et al.* (2007), who analysed the role of rewards in an EMS, found that environmental reward systems are positively associated with employees' perception of environmental performance. Massoud *et al.* (2008) identify three reasons for the lack of environmental rewards in organisations: (1) environmental management is relatively new and organisations have neglected to define rewards for environmental management efforts, (2) the scope for defining new environmental performance standards may be very broad and may cost the organisation an inordinate amount of time to do so, and (3) the cross-boundary nature of environmental problems makes it difficult to reward on an individual basis (Massoud *et al.*, 2008, p. 17). Based on these factors, Massoud *et al.* (2008) highlight the importance of the introduction of a group-based collective reward system to reward employees for environmental performance in order to overcome difficulties associated with individual reward systems. The following are two examples of companies which use their environmental reward system to improve their employees' environmental performance.

Example: Shell

> Shell scorecard uses a number of key indicators to evaluate the company's overall performance across financial, operational and sustainable development (SD) areas. This evaluation is then used to determine bonus levels for employees, including members of the Executive Committee.
>
> Shell (2009)

Example: Westpac

Westpac Bank Ltd. Australia is one of the leading banks in Australia, which has fully integrated corporate sustainability principles into the way that it does business. The following is a quotation from their responses to Carbon Disclosure Project, 2009.

> 'Emissions reduction targets are included in personal scorecards of a number of individuals across the organisation and directly impact on their bonus potential. Our Executive Team (ie our CEO and their direct reports) have a shared emissions reductions target and where appropriate to job role these have been cascaded to General Manager level and below. All employees have a sustainability component

within their personal scorecard relating to elements of Westpac's overall sustainability strategy as relevant to their individual role and agreed with their manager. As appropriate these will include a climate change element.'

Carbon Disclosure Project (2009)

The above literature highlights the necessity for companies to have an environmental reward system that motivates employees to contribute to improve the environmental performance of the company. However, the characteristics of environmental issues (such as the lack of standardised measures, complexity and their multi-dimensional nature) make it more difficult to develop a reward system for environmental performance. Thus the development of an organisational culture that facilitates and encourages better environmental performance could provide a good foundation to develop a better environmental reward system.

7.7 Conclusion

Modern businesses are increasingly under pressure to take their corporate social and environmental responsibilities seriously. In this context, companies are compelled to look for the means that enable them to run their businesses in a socially and environmentally sustainable manner. When evaluating the literature relating to the relationship between the economic and environmental performance of companies and the role that management accounting can play in improving ecological sustainability while achieving outstanding financial performance, it is clear that there is a significant potential for the management accounting function to play a role in driving the environmental strategies and actions within organisations.

The literature that discusses the importance of using management accounting techniques to integrate environmental issues into strategic decision-making identifies a number of management accounting techniques that are used by companies for this purpose. Capital budgeting, performance evaluation techniques and reward systems were some of the tools used by companies to do this. However, the incorporation of environmental issues into traditional management accounting techniques is not without its problems.

Significantly, the lack of standardised measures, uncertainty, complexity and the multi-dimensional nature of environmental issues pose challenges for companies when they attempt to incorporate environmental cost and liabilities into traditional management accounting processes.

However, such environmental issues open up new opportunities for companies to develop environmentally friendly products and to innovate new technology in order to improve efficiency and minimise environmental cost, and thus gain the financial benefits associated with them. Therefore the benefits reaped by companies in employing different management accounting techniques are enormous.

However, an evaluation of the related literature reveals a clear lack of direct research that examines in detail how different management accounting techniques are used by companies to integrate environmental issues into their strategic decision-making processes.

As highlighted by Henri and Journeault (2010), there is a scarcity of literature which examines the link between management control systems and the economic and environmental performance of an organisation. Thus there is a clear need for empirical research into the role of management accounting practice and practitioners in driving environmental strategy and action. Without such research, possible gaps or areas of improvement in either the practice or the skills, expertise and human capital of those seeking to deploy such practices may remain unidentified.

References

Adams, C. A. (2004). 'The Ethical, Social and Environmental Reporting – Performance Portrayal Gap', *Accounting, Auditing and Accountability Journal* 17 (5), 731–57.

Adams, C. A. and Frost, G. (2008). 'Integrating Sustainability Reporting into Management Practices', *Accounting Forum*, 32 (4), 288–302.

Al-Tuwaijri, S. A., Christensen, T. E. and Hughes, I. I. (2004). 'The Relations Among Environmental Disclosure, Environmental Performance and Economic Performance: A Simultaneous Equation Approach', *Accounting, Organizations and Society*, 29 (5–6), 447–71.

Ball, A., Masom, I., Miler, B. and Milne, M. (2009). 'Carbon Neutrality: A Management Control Strategy for Climate Change or Modern-day Hocus-Pocus?', AFAANZ Conference, Adelaide, Australia.

Bartolomeo, M., Bennett, M., Bouma, J. J., Heydkamp, P., James, P. and Wolters, T. (2000). 'Environmental Management Accounting in Europe: Current Practice and Future Potential', *European Accounting Review*, 9 (1), 31–52.

Belal, A. R. (2002). 'Stakeholder Accountability or Stakeholder Management? A Review of UK Firms' Social and Ethical Accounting, Auditing and Reporting (SEAAR) Practices', *Corporate Social Responsibility and Environmental Management*, 9 (1), 8–25.

Burritt, R. L. and Saka, C. (2006). 'Environmental Management Accounting Applications and Eco-Efficiency: Case studies from Japan', *Journal of Cleaner Production*, 14 (14), 1262–75.

Burnett, R. D. and Hansen, D. R. (2008). 'Eco-efficiency: Defining A Role for Environmental Cost Management', *Accounting, Organizations and Society*, 33 (6), 551–81.

Carbon Disclosure Project (2009). *Carbon Disclosure Project Report 2009*, Australia and New Zealand. Available at: https://www.cdproject.net/CDPResults/CDP_2009_Australia_New_Zealand_Report.pdf (retrieved November 2009).

Cocca, P. and Alberti, M. (2004). 'A Framework to Assess Performance Measurement Systems in SMEs', *International Journal of Productivity and Performance Management*, 59 (2), 186–200.

Cormier, D., Magnan, M. and Velthoven, B. V. (2005). 'Environmental Disclosure Quality in Large German Companies: Economic Incentives, Public Pressures or Institutional Conditions?', *European Accounting Review*, 14 (1), 3–39.

Daily, B. F., Bishop, J. W. and Steiner, R. (2007). 'The Mediating Role of EMS Teamwork as it Pertains to HR Factors and Perceived Environmental Performance', *Journal of Applied Business Research*, 23 (1), 110–16.

Dammak, S. (2009). 'Contribution on the Analysis of the Environmental Disclosure: A Comparative Study of American and European Multinationals', *Social Responsibility Journal*, 5, 83–93.

Epstein, M. J. (2008). *Making Sustainability Work: Best Practices in Managing and Measuring Corporate, Social, Environmental and Economic Impacts*, Greenleaf Publishing Ltd.

Ethical Corporation (2010). 'Nike Develops A 'Balanced Scorecard' for Ethics Integration', at http://www.ethicalcorp.com/content.asp?ContentID=3117 (retrieved July 2010).

Figge, F., Hahn, T., Schaltegger, S. and Wagner, M. (2002). 'The Sustainability Balanced Scorecard – Linking Sustainability Management to Business Strategy', *Business Strategy and the Environment*, 11 (5), 269–84.

Gray, R. H. and Milne, M. (2002). 'Sustainability Reporting: Who's Kidding Whom?', *Chartered Accountants Journal of New Zealand*, 81, 66–70.

Henri, J. F. and Journeault, M. (2010). 'Eco-control: The Influence of Management Control Systems on Environmental and Economic Performance', *Accounting, Organizations and Society*, 35 (1), 63–80.

Kolk, A. (2003). 'Trends in Sustainability Reporting by The Fortune Global 250, *Business Strategy and the Environment*, 12 (5), 279–91.

Konar, S. and Cohen, A. (2001). 'Does the Market Value Environmental Performance?', *The Review of Economics and Statistics*, 83 (2), 281–9.

Langfield-Smith, K. and Thorne, H. (2009). *Management Accounting, Information for Creating and Managing Value*, McGraw-Hill Australia Pty Limited.

Mahoney, L. and Roberts, R. W. (2007). 'Corporate Social Performance, Financial Performance and Institutional Ownership in Canadian Firms, *Accounting Forum*, 31 (3), 233–53.

Massoud, J. A., Daily, B. F. and Bishop, J. W. (2008). 'Reward for Environmental Performance: Using the Scanlon Plan as Catalyst to Green Organisations', *Int. J. Environment, Workplace and Employment*, 4 (1), 15–31.

Milne, M. J. (1996). 'On Sustainability, the Environment and Management Accounting, *Management Accounting Research*, 7 (1), 135–61.

Nakao, Y., Amano, A., Matsumura, K., Genba, K. and Nakano, M. (2007). 'Relationship between Environmental Performance and Financial Performance: An Empirical Analysis of Japanese Corporations, *Business Strategy and the Environment*, 16 (2), 106–18.

Pagan, B. and Prasad, P. (2007). 'The Queensland Food Eco-efficiency Project; Reducing Risk and Improving Competitiveness', *Journal of Cleaner Production*, 15 (8–9), 764–71.

Perego, P. and Hartmann, F. (2009). 'Aligning Performance Measurement Systems with Strategy: The Case of Environmental Strategy', ABACUS, 45 (4), 397–428.

Perez, E. A., Ruiz, C. C. and Fenech, F. C. (2007). 'Environmental Management Systems As An Embedding Mechanism: A Research Note', *Accounting, Auditing & Accountability Journal*, 20 (3), 403–22.

Shrivastava, P. (1995). 'The Role of Corporations in Achieving Ecological Sustainability', *Academy of Management Review*, 20, 930–60.

Sinkin, C., Wright, C. J. and Burnett, R. D. (2008). 'Eco-efficiency and Firm Value', *Journal of Accounting and Public Policy*, 27, 167–76.

Shell (2009). *Sustainability Report.* Available at http://sustainabilityreport.shell.com/2009/servicepages/downloads/files/all_shell_sr09.pdf (retrieved July 2010).

Watercare Service Ltd, New Zealand (2009). *Annual Report*, available at http://www.watercare.co.nz/watercare/publications/annual-report-2009_home.cfm (retrieved July 2010).

Westpac Australia (2009). *Annual Report*, available at http://www.westpac.com.au/about-westpac/investor-centre/annual_reports/ (retrieved July 2010).

Wood, D. and Ross, D. G. (2006). 'Environmental Social Controls and Capital Investments: Australian Evidence', *Accounting and Finance*, 46 (4), 677–95.

World Business Council for Sustainability Development (1998). *Cleaner Production and Eco-efficiency, Complementary Approaches to Sustainability Development*, United Nations Environment Programme.

8
An Integrated Package of Environmental Management Control Systems

Max L. Baker, David A. Brown and Teemu Malmi

8.1 Introduction

This chapter examines the issue of how management control systems (MCS) can be designed and used to address environmental concerns within organisations. This issue is motivated by the developing awareness of the environmental and social issues caused by industrial activity, as spawned by a scientific consensus that human activities are affecting the Earth's climate (Oreskes, 2004), levels of biodiversity and ecosystems (Hooper *et al.*, 2005). In response, accounting academics, policy makers and practitioners have developed a range of external sustainability reports which aim to account for environmental activity. However, concerns remain in relation to the completeness and credibility of these reports (Adams, 2004). Moreover, while some researchers argue that reported levels of social and environmental performance are correlated with economic performance (Margolis and Walsh, 2003; Orlitzky *et al.*, 2003), this 'work leaves unexplored questions about what it is that firms are actually doing' (Margolis and Walsh, 2003, p. 278).

To date only a small amount of research has sought to explore what firms are actually doing in relation to managing environmental issues. This research has studied a range of management control systems such as strategic planning, costing systems, capital budgeting, organisational structures, performance measurement systems, and organisational values and culture. Researchers have found that these systems have produced benefits such as improved decision-making, communication and coordination of resources; greater management accountability; and better relations with stakeholders and behavioural control (Epstein, 1996; Parker, 2000; Epstein and Wisner, 2005; Albelda-Pérez *et al.*, 2007; Adams and Frost, 2008; Perego and Hartmann, 2009; Sundin *et al.*, 2010). Researchers have also explicated the strategic value of incorporating environmental issues into MCS design and use, as it may improve an organisation's competitive context (Porter and Kramer, 2002, 2006), improve product design and differentiation, and reduce the costs and improve the efficiency of production (Hart, 1995).

However, while this research has been insightful for managers, to date the study of the operation of these elements has been in isolation (Epstein and Wisner, 2005; Perego and Hartmann, 2009; Sundin *et al.*, 2010). Little is known of how individual MCS elements complement and reinforce each other's functionality and effectiveness in order to successfully manage environmental issues. These interactions are of particular interest given that more recent research in management accounting has suggested that only 'by examining all the elements in the package, and the relationships between them, are [we] more likely to get a better understanding of the effectiveness of the individual elements' (Malmi and Brown, 2008, p. 289). This is particularly relevant to the environmental context, considering that prior research has shown that such environmental management control systems can remain inactive and decoupled from other systems (Durden, 2008) or captured by powerful interest groups within the firm that do not see environmental issues as being a priority for organisations (Larrinaga-Gonzalez and Bebbington, 2001; Gray *et al.*, 1995). Therefore it is of interest in the context of environmental issues to consider how the various control system elements operate as a whole (package) to produce positive benefits for the organisation, key stakeholders and the environment.

This chapter outlines the design and use of environmental MCS in a large Australian energy utility company. The case company was the knowledge leader and premier environmental educator within the industry and consequently considered to be an example of 'best practice'. We used the MCS package framework developed by Malmi and Brown (2008) to examine how this industry leader was able to manage environmental issues. An analysis of the case brings two key practical insights to light. The first is that while individual MCS elements (such as budgets or KPIs or policies and procedures) play a role in managing environmental concerns, the real embedding of environmental practices in an organisation at the operating level came from an integrated package of MCS whose multiple elements operated in a complementary manner. The second was that the organisation worked in partnership with regulators in a 'responsive regulation' (Ayres and Braithwaite, 1992) approach, which along with a well-developed MCS package enabled the case company to overcome regulation limitations by influencing micro- or operating-level issues and enabling the organisation to be 'self-regulating'. This proactive approach sheds light on the advantages of a package of MCS in achieving more effective and efficient regulatory compliance.

Section 8.2 outlines the research method used, which is followed by a description of the case organisation in Section 8.3. After this is an explication of the MCS used in the organisation (Section 8.4), which then informs the development of the practical lessons learned from the organisation.

8.2   Method

The method used in this research was an explorative case study of a large Australian energy utility. The main part of the field work was conducted over a period of four months, with ongoing observational data collection and extra interviews in the two years following the main data collection period. Three principal data collection methods were used in a triangulated approach: interviews with selected personnel; examination of archival documents; and observation of training sessions and work practices. Eleven semi-structured interviews (totalling 20 hours of interview time) were conducted with a range of operational, environmental and accounting staff across all levels of the organisation. Where possible, substantiation was made through collecting or citing alternative sources of data, such as internal management documents and external documents. Observations were also used to examine management-level environmental training, as well as to study the physical controls and processes in place during routine maintenance of a substation.

8.3   The case

The case organisation is InfraServe, which is a wholly owned subsidiary of EnergyUtility (both names are pseudonyms). EnergyUtility is a state-owned Australian electricity retailer that operates and maintains its own network infrastructure in order to distribute electricity within the state in which it is based. EnergyUtility explicitly stated its environmental strategy through both its environmental policy and annual reports, and InfraServe had a responsibility to operationalise these. Under Part 5 of the *Environmental Planning and Assessment Act 1979*, public sector companies like EnergyUtility have sole responsibility for 'all matters affecting or likely to affect the environment'.

During the period of data collection, InfraServe was widely accepted as the environmental management leader in the Australian energy industry, as demonstrated by the fact that it held environmental training for other energy utilities and contractors and that these courses were widely considered industry 'best practice'. EnergyUtility received a gold star rating in the annual Corporate Responsibility Index survey conducted by the St James Ethics centre after the completion of the case study – the report awarded EnergyUtility with an 'outstanding performance' in environmental management.

For InfraServe, perhaps the biggest factor influencing its adoption of an environmental focus was the significant increase in new environmental regulation in Australia around the time of the study (Bates, 2006). Due to the diverse nature of InfraServe's activities, environmental non-compliance emerged as a major risk for the organisation to manage. The key environmental risk areas in terms of InfraServe's activities included air, water and land contamination, flora and fauna impacts and social and heritage site impacts.

> We're an organisation on the most part has come from a culture of compliance. [An environmental focus] in certain areas has crept in and probably where it's been more compliance driven.
>
> (InfraServe Manager)

Management control systems emerged as an effective way of complying with these regulatory pressures as efficiently as possible. As a result the organisation developed and adapted a comprehensive set of management control systems for environmental purposes in an emerging process. In 1994, InfraServe was the first organisation in the industry to receive an ISO 14001 accreditation for its Environmental Management Systems (EMS). In 1995, InfraServe won an Australian Quality Award for the same system. Many interviewees were confident that InfraServe had the best EMS in the energy industry:

> In terms of a system in place this is pretty hard to beat.
>
> (InfraServe Engineer)

> [InfraServe] is somewhat ahead of most infrastructure service companies ... with... the practices of other similar organisations ... following along behind.
>
> (InfraServe Manager)

8.3.1 InfraServe's structure

It is useful at this stage to outline InfraServe's organisation structure in terms of managing environmental responsibility (see Table 8.1). This structure consisted of seven levels.

Extending this, Figure 8.1 outlines the MCS used within InfraServe for environmental management. The *y*-axis represents the organisational

Table 8.1   Organisational structure and responsibility

Organisation level	Responsibilities
Stakeholders	State government, various environmental regulators (e.g., the Environmental Protection Authority) and community groups.
Environmental Steering Committee (ESC)	A subcommittee of the executive team and was the highest-level monitor of InfraServe's environmental actions and impacts. Its main function was to endorse and facilitate the development of InfraServe's environmental plan and policies. They met monthly and had representation from all InfraServe branches, with InfraServe's General Manager at the head. The committee communicated the broader environmental objectives to the environmental group.
Environmental group (EG)	A subdivision consisting of 10 staff members, who each specialised in different environmental issues. As a centralised unit, the EG provided guidance to other functional areas of InfraServe in terms of their individual responsibilities, policies and activities. The EG also performed a consulting service for individual projects, where they prepared specialised environmental impact assessments and community consultations.
InfraServe departments	Segregated on functional capabilities (for example, design, substations and power lines). **Senior managers** represent the highest managers for each of these functional areas and were each responsible for a number of projects.
Project managers	Responsible for each project taking place in one functional area. These projects consisted of many individual jobs.
Superintendents	Operational-level managers responsible for the running of each individual job.
Field staff	At the operational level, the **field staff** were directly and physically impacting the environment under the command of superintendents.

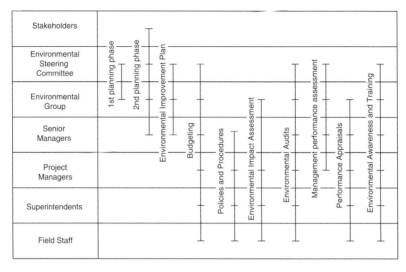

Figure 8.1 InfraServe's control elements

levels, while the lines/nodes between the organisational levels in the diagram represent the individual MCS elements and which level uses these elements. While all MCS elements were used continuously, they are ordered along the *x*-axis in the logical process of how each control affected one another, e.g., planning processes → updating policies, procedures and budgets → measuring and assessing performance against the plan → supporting this process with training. The design and operation of each of these MCS elements will now be described.

8.3.2 Environmental planning

Regulatory pressure required that InfraServe develop a coordinated and efficient approach to reducing environmental impacts. At the highest level, this coordination of activities started at the annual planning phase (See 1st and 2nd Planning Phases in Figure 8.1). In the **first planning phase** (one day), InfraServe's EG and the members of the ESC reviewed the full range of InfraServe's environmental impacts from a technical perspective. Environmental incident trends were analysed along with legislative requirements in order to understand and document the environmental risks facing InfraServe for the coming year.

After developing a technical understanding of the environmental concerns, the EG and the ESC then engaged a wider set of stakeholders in a **second planning phase** (two days). This process created a transparency for stakeholders in relation to InfraServe's environmental resources and the procedures it followed in order to act diligently in relation to its most environmentally sensitive operations. While the regulatory bodies benefited from increased control and transparency, InfraServe benefited from a clear communication of regulatory expectations. This also enabled InfraServe to manage their operations so that they stayed ahead of regulatory compliance.

The second planning phase also required that InfraServe measure and compare the risk level of its various activities and then coordinate the resources of each of its functional groups. Senior managers attended the second planning phase in order to discuss all the environmental aspects, impacts and legal changes affecting their functional area. These environmental aspects were then quantified using a universal scale. Comprehensive risk management tools were used to identify the probability (frequency of occurrence per year) and consequence (including business, social and environmental) for each environmentally hazardous action within each functional area. These risk management tools were used to develop an overall risk score (probability × consequence) for each functional group. Functional groups were then prioritised against each other on the basis of their overall risk.

An environmental improvement plan (EIP) (see Figure 8.1) was then developed where the EG and ESC defined a set of planned activities through matching stakeholder preferences, functional area risks and legal requirements with the resources available. An environmental budget was then developed to forecast the likely expenses incurred in relation to the activities detailed in the EIP as well as track actual expenses incurred in relation to these activities (see Figure 8.1). The EG was responsible for coordinating and allocating extra resources to functional areas, particularly if they were more environmentally risky.

8.3.3 Policies and procedures

The EIP set out the desired environmental actions for InfraServe as a whole and provided detailed procedures for conducting environmental activities in each functional area. In order to communicate these detailed environmental procedures, they were embedded as a specific environmental section within each functional area's policy document for conducting work. This policy document was called the 'network standard'. Therefore yearly changes to the EIP necessitated a change in each network standard.

While the environmental impact section of the network standard set the broader environmental guidelines for any maintenance or construction projects, each project needed a detailed Environmental Impact

Assessment (EIA) (see Figure 8.1). EIAs applied the broader environmental guidelines to each job or project by outlining the specific procedures that should be taken by the field workers to avoid or minimise environmental impacts. For maintenance work, the EIA was developed by project managers, and for construction projects, the EIA was developed in a consultation process between project design teams and the EG. The central advantage of the EIA was its ability to delegate responsibility and to communicate legal and regulatory issues to field workers.

8.3.4   Environmental audits

Environmental audits allowed the ESC to assess the success of the environmental improvement plan as well as monitor InfraServe's site operations on a random basis (see Figure 8.1). For site operations with higher environmental risk, audits were conducted by the EG frequently (once a year) and less frequently for areas with lower risk (once every three years). Adverse audit opinions required the EG to produce a quality action request for a change in the operation procedures. Quality action requests effectively put in place a list of required improvements and penalties applied if improvements were not fulfilled. For the EG, environmental audits were a vital source of information about specific environmental issues which occurred at the operational level. Audit information was used by the EG in the technical planning phase (first planning phase) of developing the EIP.

8.3.5   Management performance assessment

InfraServe measured its performance against Key Performance Indicators (KPIs) (see Figure 8.1). Management were assessed on meeting their individual KPIs and received an annual bonus based on their performance. These individual KPIs included non-financial KPIs with individual targets for environment, safety and customer performance. As most functional areas had environmental risks associated with their operations, they were addressed in the environmental planning process and EIP, and so became a component of each responsible manager's individual KPIs. Management bonuses were awarded on the basis of achieving their individual KPI targets.

> One of the elements of their bonus, one of the KPIs they have to meet is 100% compliance with our environmental improvement program each year. What ends up in their wallet depends upon how far they go with achieving that.
>
> (Long-serving InfraServe Employee)

Other levels of InfraServe staff were assessed through a Performance Development System (PDS). This performance appraisal system was conducted every six months and operated on a more individual and flexible basis than the KPI-based form of assessment. PDS focused on particular areas of the EIP which individuals had responsibility for, as well as the areas which they needed to improve. The PDS process also required that staff continually engage in training in order to take on new environmental responsibilities.

8.3.6 Environmental culture and training

Through the course of the interviews it became evident that an environmental awareness or culture had emerged in InfraServe. Environmental planning, budgeting, policies, procedures, auditing and performance measurement systems were used frequently in the course of each individual's everyday activities. In this way environmental responsibility was constantly reinforced. One manager commented on the increasing requirement for individuals to be environmentally conscious and proactive:

It comes back to the way social attitudes are changing towards the environment and the fact that the benchmark people are setting for environmental requirements nowadays is a lot tougher and a lot more stringent. There is that expectation that there is a level of environmental quality put into our operation and, like with any company, you have to keep that step ahead of what the baseline requirements are and ensure that we are keeping within stakeholder expectations as well.

(InfraServe Manager)

The secretary of the ESU was a champion of environmental issues and this also aided the development of environmental awareness in a number of ways. The secretary printed and distributed environmental awareness material to be posted up in staff offices and distributed as pocket manuals. These documents reinforced each functional area's environmental objectives as outlined in the EIP and attempted to 'get the message out and gradually change the culture' (InfraServe Environmental Manager). The secretary also encouraged any staff to contact him personally once a month via an 'environmental hotline' where confidential feedback about environmental issues could be communicated. The EG also facilitated the promotion of environmental awareness through constantly updating an environmental intranet site with information about changes to best practice and environmental regulatory requirements.

Environmental awareness was also reinforced by InfraServe's environmental training, which was designed to educate staff about their environmental responsibilities and roles within each project. The aim of the training was to teach staff the appropriate environmental actions and knowledge that would support an implementation of the EIP, network standard and EIA. While there was a focus in training on legal compliance (which stressed the fact that by law employees could be fined individually up to A$120,000 if they were associated with non-compliance), in general it was aimed at developing an understanding of the potential environmental risks and issues of each activity and to equip individuals with a knowledge of the appropriate procedures to mitigate these risks and comply with regulations. The increased frequency with which InfraServe conducted environment education was seen by many interviewees as a vital part of generating an environmental awareness in all staff members:

> Going back 6 years, there were ... virtually no training courses whatsoever. Since then we've got 6 or 7 training courses available. Every new employee goes through induction training, and every employee goes through annual refresher training. [This training is complemented when] every month we issue a team brief on a pressing environmental issue. Over the years, because I run the impact assessment training, I see the faces change, in the first course everybody was just dumbfounded saying 'we've got to do all this stuff?' Since then the types of questions have changed and you can just see an environmental change in people.
>
> InfraServe Environmental Manager

8.4   Practical implications

This case study provides two interesting insights for practitioners. The first insight is that MCS are more effective in managing environmental issues when they are designed as inter-related elements of a single MCS package. The second relates to the regulatory benefits of a well-designed MCS package. These practical implications will be elaborated on below.

8.4.1   MCS package

There are two interesting aspects of the environmental MCS as seen in InfraServe. The first is how different types of commonly used MCS elements operated together as an integrated package. The second is the effectiveness of this package in controlling a variety of activities in a number of contexts.

Consideration of the MCS used at InfraServe demonstrates a broad but integrated set of MCS which operated as follows. In a collaborative process with key stakeholders, environmental issues were prioritised and then addressed in a comprehensive environmental plan. This plan was developed by environmental experts and attempted to allocate resources in order to most effectively address the riskiest of InfraServe's activities. The cost of the planned activities was followed up against a budget and generated environmental requirements within each functional area's network standard (operational responsibilities, policies and procedures). In addition to these guidelines, each individual project/job had an environmental impact assessment, which clarified the particular and relevant issues. Two systems measured performance in relation to environmental actions: audits monitored the physical impacts on the environment; KPIs were used to measure management performance in relation to key environmental targets. Finally, both the ESC and the EG delivered constant communication and training, which created an environmental awareness culture which in turn facilitated the efficacy of the entire system.

InfraServe's case also reinforces the benefits of using social types of control within a package of controls. While the use of formal control mechanisms such as planning, policies and KPIs created an individual environmental awareness among staff (Albelda-Pérez *et al.*, 2007), there were also more explicit attempts to change the values of individuals through the high-level communication of environmental issues and training. These explicit attempts to change individual values or 'social controls' held two benefits for InfraServe. Firstly, they were an effective controls in their own right in terms of encouraging individuals to 'embrace common goals, which [were] essential to achieving alliance overall performance' (Langfield-Smith, 2008, p. 349). These social controls also 'reduce[d] the relationship to risk through encouraging the development of shared values, and hence reduce[d] the likelihood of opportunistic behaviour' (Langfield-Smith, 2008, p. 349). Secondly, InfraServe's social controls improved the function of formal controls; here social controls form the 'contextual frame for other controls' (Malmi and Brown, 2008, p. 295). This is specifically important in operational areas like the environment, as uncertainty is high and there is limited predictability in the outcomes of management decision-making as well as little ability to measure the impacts of decision-making (Langfield-Smith, 2008).

8.4.2   The reinforcing effects of MCS as a package

Perhaps the most striking feature of the design of environmental MCS was the way in which MCS elements operated in a complementary and reinforcing manner. InfraServe did not seem to set a hierarchy of importance for any MCS elements but designed and used an integrated set of MCS elements which improved the effectiveness of control in total. This has some interesting practical implications.

Alternative attempts to manage environmental issues have concentrated on implementing a single individual control system. Some scholars have suggested organisations adopt environmental performance measurement systems or environmental balanced scorecards (Johnson, 1998; Epstein and Wisner, 2001). This approach relies heavily on the 'what gets measured gets done' logic. However, a focus on environmental performance assessment alone may not assist managers in coordinating environmental activities or creating an environmental awareness. Additionally, not all activities or environmental impacts are directly measurable. Therefore reliance on a single MCS approach (such as a performance measurement system) may not enable environmental control, as the MCS becomes decoupled from other existing MCS elements or operations and does not form part of the everyday concerns or use for individuals. In this circumstance, standalone systems can become ceremonial in use (Meyer and Rowan, 1977). Instead, InfraServe extended the use and design of a range of pre-existing MCS elements in order to influence individual behaviour and activities in a wider variety of circumstances. These elements had a number of inter-related functions, including: measuring and assessing environmental impacts and risks; coordinating resources and activities; and creating a personal concern for the environment. In this way, it became very difficult for individuals to decouple their activities from the organisation's environmental agenda.

8.4.3   Environmental self-regulation

Regulation is a key mechanism motivating organisations to reduce their environmental impacts, particularly as environmental laws have increased dramatically in Australia over the course of the last 30 years (Bates, 2006). Aside from the somewhat coercive nature of complying with bureaucracy (Adler and Borys, 1996), regulation can have difficulty penetrating the micro- or operational levels of individual organisations. The cost of enforcing compliance can be very high and it is hard for regulators to create sufficient relevance to be meaningful in individual circumstances. As a consequence, at an operational level, ceremonial conformity to some broad-based regulation becomes more important than substantive changes in individuals' activity (Meyer and Rowan, 1977), rendering the regulation largely ineffective.

A variation in enforcement styles is needed to provoke polluters sufficiently to comply with regulation (Ayres and Braithwaite, 1992). 'Responsive regulation', for instance, requires a mix of voluntary and statutory regulatory instruments (Ayres and Braithwaite, 1992), and it is important to promote conciliatory styles of control where there is less distance and more frequency of contact between regulators and the regulated (Aalders, 1993).

In InfraServe's case they adopted a 'responsive regulation' approach by engaging the regulator into a process where concerns and regulating direction were raised early in the planning process and then translated into InfraServe operations through the use of MCS as outlined earlier. This enabled InfraServe to manage compliance with the ever-changing environmental regulatory requirements and allowed independent regulatory representatives to influence the micro- or operational levels in a conciliatory and cost-effective way, thus producing a type of 'partnership' for regulating environmental issues.

In general, the case study findings provide a novel insight into how organisations can use MCS to environmentally self-regulate, and bolster Aalders' (1993) claim that as an integrated part of regulatory engagement, these MCS serve to strengthen compliance with environmental regulations through allowing 'more manoeuvrability' while also assisting the state in withdrawing from the 'murky plain of overwhelming detail' involved in society's increasingly complex regulatory demands (Neave, 1988, p. 12). By establishing a responsive regulation approach, InfraServe was able to design and monitor its own regulatory compliant self-regulating system (Streeck and Schmitter, 1985).

8.5 Conclusion

This case study provides evidence that management control systems can operate effectively as an integrated system with a central part to play in the management of environmental issues. Practitioners can benefit from two important insights raised in this chapter. The first is that MCS elements operate most effectively as a package in which individual elements function in a complementary and reinforcing fashion as they are used to address the wide variety of environmental activities. The second is that a package of MCS also poses an effective part of regulatory control. MCS can be used to engage regulators and build their preferences into planning and risk management processes, which then determine the design of procedures and performance measurement. The use of MCS can also build an environmental awareness to support the regulatory function on a cultural/personal level.

References

Aalders, M. (1993). 'Regulation and In-Company Environmental Management in the Netherlands', *Law & Policy*, 15, 75–94.

Adams, C. A. (2004). 'The Ethical, Social and Environmental Reporting-Performance Portrayal Gap', *Accounting, Auditing & Accountability Journal*, 17, 731–57.

Adams, C. A. and Frost, G. R. (2008). 'Integrating Sustainability Reporting into Management Practices', *Accounting Forum*, 32, 288–302.

Adler, P. S. and Borys, B. (1996). 'Two Types of Bureaucracy: Enabling and Coercive', *Administrative Science Quarterly*, 41 (1), 61–89.

Albelda-Pérez, E., Correa Ruiz, C. and Fenech, F. C. (2007). 'Environmental Management Systems as an Embedding Mechanism: A Research Note', *Accounting, Auditing & Accountability Journal*, 20, 403–22.

Ayres, I. and Braithwaite, J. (1992). *Responsive Regulation*, Oxford University Press, Oxford.

Bates, G. M. (2006). *Environmental Law in Australia*, LexisNexis, Chatswood, NSW.

Durden, C. (2008). 'Towards A Socially Responsible Management Control System', *Accounting, Auditing & Accountability Journal*, 21, 671–94.

Epstein, M. J. (1996). *Measuring Corporate Environmental Performance: Best Practices for Costing and Managing an Effective Environmental Strategy*, Irwin Professional, Chicago.

Epstein, M. J. and Wisner, P. S. (2001). 'Using A Balanced Scorecard to Implement Sustainability', *Environmental Quality Management*, 11, 1–10.

Epstein, M. J. and Wisner, P. S. (2005). 'Managing and Controlling Environmental Performance: Evidence from Mexico', *Advances in Management Accounting*, 14, 115–37.

Gray, R., Walters, D., Bebbington, J. and Thompson, I. (1995). 'The Greening of Enterprise: An Exploration of the (Non) Role of Environmental Accounting and Environmental Accountants in Organizational Change', *Critical Perspectives on Accounting*, 6, 211–39.

Hart, S. L. (1995). 'A Natural-resource-based View of the Firm', *Academy of Management Review*, 20, 986–1014.

Hooper, D. U., Chapin, F. S., Ewel, J. J., Hector, A., Inchausti, P., Lavorel, S., Hawton, J. H., Lodge, D. M., Loreau, M. and Naeem, S. (2005), 'Effects of Biodiversity on Ecosystem Functioning: A Consensus of Current Knowledge', *Ecological Monographs*, 75, 3–35.

Johnson, S. D. (1998). 'Identification and Selection of Environmental Performance Indicators: Application of the Balanced Scorecard Approach', *Corporate Environmental Strategy*, 5, 34–41.

Langfield-Smith, K. (2008). 'The Relations Between Transactional Characteristics, Trust and Risk in the Start-up Phase of a Collaborative Alliance', *Management Accounting Research*, 19, 344–64.

Larrinaga-Gonzalez, C. and Bebbington, J. (2001). 'Accounting Change or Institutional Appropriation? A Case Study of the Implementation of Environmental Accounting', *Critical Perspectives on Accounting*, 12, 269–92.

Malmi, T. and Brown, D. A. (2008). 'Management Control Systems as a Package – Opportunities, Challenges and Research Directions', *Management Accounting Research*, 19, 287–300.

Margolis, J. D. and Walsh, J. P. (2003). 'Misery Loves Companies: Rethinking Social Initiatives by Business', *Administrative Science Quarterly*, 268–305.

Meyer, J. W. and Rowan, B. (1977). 'Institutionalized Organizations: Formal Structure as Myth and Ceremony', *American Journal of Sociology*, 83, 340–63.

Neave, G. (1988). 'On the Cultivation of Quality, Efficiency and Enterprise: An Overview of Recent Trends in Higher Education in Western Europe' (1986–1988), *European Journal of Education*, 23, 7–23.

Oreskes, N. (2004). 'Beyond the Ivory Tower: The Scientific Consensus on Climate Change', *Science*, 306, 1686.

Orlitzky, M., Schmidt, F. L. and Rynes, S. L. (2003). 'Corporate Social and Financial Performance: A Meta-Analysis', *Organization Studies*, 24, 403–41.

Parker, L. (2000). 'Environmental Costing: A Path to Implementation', *Australian Accounting Review*, 10, 43–51.

Perego, P. and Hartmann, F. (2009). 'Aligning Performance Measurement Systems With Strategy: The Case of Environmental Strategy', *Abacus*, 45, 397–428.

Porter, M. E. and Kramer, M. R. (2002). 'The Competitive Advantage of Corporate Philanthropy', *Harvard Business Review*, 80, 56–68.

Porter, M. E. and Kramer, M. R. (2006). 'Strategy and Society', *Harvard Business Review*, 84, 78–92.

Streeck, W. and Schmitter, P. C. (1985). *Private Interest Government: Beyond Market and State*, Sage Publications.

Sundin, H., Granlund, M. and Brown, D. (2010). 'Balancing Multiple and Competing Objectives with a Balanced Scorecard', *European Accounting Review*, 19(2), 203–46.

Part III
Intangibles and Non-financial Performance Measures

9
Efficiency Measurement for Supplier Selection and Control: A Data Envelopment Analysis Approach

Franco Visani, Riccardo Silvi and Klaus Möller

9.1 Introduction

Organisations should focus their supplier selection and control process on several different dimensions, including price, quality, service level, delivery and their ability to support the innovation process. (Dickson, 1966). Obviously, the roles that these dimensions play differ from one product/service to another. For example, the price dimension is more relevant for a low-tech and easy-to-replace commodity than for a high-tech component that might be crucial for the performance of the supplier's final product.

The issue is two-fold: first, companies need a model in order to select the suppliers for a specific product/service. Second, they need a tool for controlling the suppliers' performance. While many different conceptual frameworks have been proposed for these two purposes, many companies still consider price to be the main (if not the only) factor that influences their choice of a new supplier. The suppliers' performance control is often based on dashboards that represent different dimensions: price, quality, delivery and innovation. However, these dimensions do not include a single indicator that enables the organisation to draw a comparison between suppliers. Because of these shortcomings, Total Cost of Ownership (TCO) has been proposed as a better solution for the selection and the control process (Ellram, 1995). The possibility of evaluating the costs related to the selection of suppliers, transportation, receiving, inspection and rejection enables the firm to determine a single performance indicator (the TCO) for selecting and, subsequently, controlling the suppliers (see Section 9.2.1).

Although it is theoretically interesting and supported by many scholars and practitioners, TCO has not been implemented widely. The main reason is the model's complexity. Furthermore, it involves a huge information collection effort with regard to costs, activities and cost drivers.

This chapter aims to evaluate whether a statistical and less work-intensive technique such as Data Envelopment Analysis (DEA; see Section 9.2.2) could provide the same information as TCO, while being less costly and labour-intensive.

9.2   Background

A topic relevant to the current business environment is the identification of efficient criteria for selecting and controlling suppliers. Raw materials, components, external workings and other services represent more than 70 per cent of total costs for most manufacturing companies. Consequently, a reduction in direct and indirect purchasing costs is one of the most relevant methods for improving profitability.

Many different aspects must be considered in the suppliers' selection and control process (Dickson, 1966; Weber *et al.*, 1991), including price, quality, delivery, support to innovation, and flexibility. Degreave *et al.* (2000) classify selection and control models in the following four categories, on the basis of the specific selection criterion adopted:

- *Rating models* in which different aspects of the supplier's performance are given a different rating, weighted in order to reach a global performance index (Timmerman, 1986; Soukup, 1987; Thompson, 1990);
- *Total cost approaches* that recognise that price is only a part of the total cost, and this is determined by the relationship with the supplier; these models are aimed at identifying both internal and external costs driven by the supplier's behaviour (Monczka and Trecha, 1988; Smytka and Clemens, 1993);
- *Mathematical programming models* based on mathematical equations (Weber and Current, 1993; Sadrian and Yoon, 1994; Rosenthal *et al.*, 1995); and
- *Statistical models* that incorporate uncertainty in the decision (Ronen and Trietsch, 1988).

Although none of these methods is being used widely, TCO is undoubtedly the best known by practitioners. However, those that use it complain about TCO's labour-intensiveness: data related to the supplier's behaviour must be collected, analysed and reported (Ellram, 1995). This is therefore cited as the main cause of the low adoption rate. Mathematical frameworks, such as DEA, are far easier to use and less expensive to run, because they do not require analysis of costs, activities or cost drivers.

Based on these assumptions, this chapter investigates the following:

(a) Are the results of DEA coherent with the ones provided by TCO?
(b) Is DEA really much easier to use than TCO?

The following sub-sections describe the two methods in greater detail.

9.2.1 Supplier total cost of ownership

TCO provides a method for supplier selection and control based on a simple assumption – costs generated by suppliers are usually higher (sometimes much higher) than the price paid for them. Besides the price, organisations need to consider the internal costs related to supplier selection, order placement, quality checking and related rejections, downtime caused by failures etc.

Although this might seem like an obvious assumption, it is revolutionary for buyers and purchasing managers, who for years based their evaluations purely on PPV (purchasing price variance), or merely on their ability to obtain low prices from suppliers. For this reason, some scholars and practitioners say that TCO is a philosophy, rather than merely a tool for supplier selection (Ellram, 1995).

As a company can choose its target of analysis, there is not simply one single TCO approach. Rather, we can distinguish:

- TCO models that are aimed at supporting the supplier selection process for a single component/service (Ellram, 1995), from models targeted to the control of suppliers' performance (Carr and Ittner, 1992);
- *Unique* TCO models that are defined for a specific choice, from *standard* models used on a day-by-day basis for analysis and selections (Ellram, 1994); and
- TCO approaches that only consider costs derived from deviant behaviour of the supplier, year-by-year (Monczka and Trecha, 1988), based on models that analyse all the costs of managing the relationship within the life cycle approach (Jackson and Ostrom, 1980).

Ellram (1995) suggests that a standard TCO model should be used whenever possible, especially for suppliers' performance evaluation, while a unique method can be applied to specific and particularly relevant purchasing choices.

Many authors suggest the adoption of an activity-based costing approach for TCO evaluation (Ellram, 1995; Degreaeve and Roodhooft, 1999). Degreave and Roodhooft (1999), with an approach that clearly represents an ABC analysis, define four hierarchical levels of activities included in TCO:

- *supplier level costs*, assigned to each supplier in the same amount;
- *order level costs*, generated every time an order is placed;
- *batch level costs*, related to the management of each batch; and
- *unit level costs*, related to the costs for each product unit.

TCO is considered a complex and expensive tool (Ellram, 1994, 1995) and its adoption needs a radical cultural change inside the purchasing departments (Ellram and Siferd, 1993). These are the main reasons for its limited adoption.

9.2.2 Data Envelopment Analysis

Data Envelopment Analysis (DEA) is a linear programming-based technique that converts multiple input and output measures into a single comprehensive measure of efficiency (Epstein and Henderson, 1989). As a non-parametric approach, DEA provides an extensive model family. This contributes to the measurement of the relative efficiency of Decision Making Units (DMU). All models have in common their proposed efficiency measure, which is understood as the maximum of the ratio of weighted output factors to weighted input factors (Charnes *et al.*, 1978). Thus the quotient is solved in a separate optimisation process for each individual DMU, in which the weights of the various factors are not chosen arbitrarily, but represent a real object of optimisation. 'DEA calculates a maximal performance measure for each DMU, relative to all other DMUs in the observed population [...]' (Charnes *et al.*, 1994). The different approaches of DEA imply various conditions with regard to returns to scale and orientation of the projections on the efficiency frontier.

The BCC model used in this study evaluates the efficiency of suppliers in an input-oriented model. The applied BCC model assumes variable returns to scale. This model was chosen to eliminate the effect of scale when evaluating the efficiency of suppliers.

The applied DEA model can be defined as follows (Cooper, Seiford, Tone, 2006):

$$\max z = \sum_{r=1}^{s} u_r y_{r0} - u_0$$

subject to

$$\sum_{r=1}^{s} u_r y_{rj} - \sum_{i=1}^{m} v_i x_{ij} - u_0 \leq 0 \quad j = 1, ..., n$$

$$\sum_{i=1}^{m} v_i x_{i0} = 1$$

$$v_i \geq \varepsilon, \, u_r \geq \varepsilon, \, u_0 \text{ free in sign}$$

Within a comparative group, the best DMU (or the best DMUs) are called 'best in-class'. They are considered the most efficient, with the best combination of input and output measures. These above-mentioned DMUs dominate all other DMUs, which are in turn described as inefficient. In this case, the dominance tells us that there is no unit with the same output and lower input, and no unit with the same input and higher output, which relates to the definition of efficiency. Graphically, the best units represent a function that includes or envelops all inefficient units. The 'economies of scale' concept refers to the efficiency frontier on which a comparison unit and accordingly an inefficient unit is projected (Banker, 1984). Finally, the degree of inefficiency for each inefficient DMU is calculated. This is exactly the maximum distance to the efficient envelopment form.

9.3 Methodology

To test the research hypothesis, both TCO and DEA were applied to Alfa (a pseudonym for confidentiality reasons), an Italian mechanical company. Then the results obtained by the two methods were compared to determine whether or not DEA is able to supply the same information as TCO but at a lower cost.

Alfa is a medium-sized company (with almost €600 million in revenues and 3,000 employees in 2009) which has more than 600 active suppliers. We randomly chose 50 suppliers of external workings among the 'A class' suppliers that have sold more than €250,000 of products and services to Alfa. In the following sub-sections, the specific application of the two methods is described.

9.3.1   TCO

The TCO was calculated for each supplier, using four steps and an activity-based costing approach.

1. *Definition of the purchasing process boundaries.* The purchasing director helped us to define the boundaries of the purchasing process. The process starts when the specific component/external working is ordered and ends when the component is made available, in stock, for the manufacturing department.
2. *Definition of the activities included in the process.* The purchasing process involves four organisational units: the purchasing department, the quality management and control department, the inbound logistic department, and the accounting department. We interviewed all the directors and employees of the four departments (87 people in total), and identified 57 activities in total.
3. *Calculation of activity costs.* Activity costs were assessed twice, using an activity-based costing approach. Labour cost was calculated by determining the percentage of time dedicated to the different activities that were identified in the previous step. We maintained a high level of accuracy by asking both the concerned employees and the managers to tell us the percentage of time that they dedicated to each activity. We compared data only when discrepancies were higher than 10 per cent. We then multiplied the percentage of time that employees dedicated to each activity by their gross salary, with a view to assessing the labour cost of each activity. The other operational costs were subsequently allocated to activities with the use of different activity drivers, starting with values included in the cost centres that are related to the four organisational units included in the analysis. In total, the cost of the 57 activities of the purchasing process amounted to €13.9 million.
4. *Definition of the activity cost drivers.* In the final and probably most complex part of the analysis, we aimed to identify the cost drivers in order to allocate the cost of the activities to the suppliers. We tried to replicate the complexity of relationship management. This was a difficult task because we needed to solve a complex trade-off between complexity of the analysis and reliability of the final results. In other words, in order to reach the highest level of reliability, we needed to identify the cost drivers of all the suppliers. Considering that there were 1,129 suppliers, this was a hard, if not impossible, task. Regardless of the fact that the company uses SAP,

the ICT department was not always able to supply us with all the drivers we needed. Furthermore, in defining the TCO model, we simulated the process followed by companies in the real world, yet tried to keep the process as simple as possible. At the end, after many interviews and conversations with managers and employees, we defined six main cost drivers:

(a) *number of quality problems*: this driver was used to allocate the cost related to quality checking and management of quality issues (21 activities for a cost of €4.2 million);

(b) *late deliveries* to allocate the costs of all the delivery reminder activities (five activities for a cost of €693,000);

(c) *number of samplings* was used for the activities related to the analysis of the samplings and first supplies (two activities for a cost of €253,000);

(d) *number of pallets received* to allocate the costs of the activities related to inbound logistics (six activities for a cost of €2.7 million);

(e) *number of order lines* to allocate all the activities related to the accounting department, as well as the bureaucratic activities in the purchasing department (20 activities, €1.2 millions); and

(f) *number of pallets delivered to suppliers (when the company sends materials to suppliers)* to allocate the cost of delivering materials to suppliers (four activities; €4.8 millions, mainly due to transportation costs).

At the end of the sixth step, we calculated the cost of managing each supplier, summing up the allocated cost. This value was then divided by the amount purchased from the supplier for determining the 'Supplier Complexity Index'.

An example of the results that we obtained is presented in Table 9.1.

Table 9.1 shows that we do not propose that this method be used to measure the performance of the supplier, but the efficiency of the buyer–supplier relationship. What we mean is that a specific buyer–supplier relationship can be inefficient even while the supplier's performance is high. The supplier presented in Table 9.1 is performing very well, with a low level of quality and delivery problems. Regardless, its complexity index is very high because of outbound logistics costs. In other words, the company is spending a lot of money on the transport of materials to and from the supplier, when the supplier is in fact adding very little value.

Table 9.1 The TCO scoreboard

		Unit cost	Amount	Total Cost	% on total company costs
1	Amount purchased			409.541	0,1%
2	Quality management	277,21	17	4.805	0,1%
3	Orders management	6,07	49	297	0,0%
4	Late deliveries management	4,56	65	296	0,1%
5	Inbound logistics	7,97	5.690	45.336	2,1%
6	Outbound logistics	37,74	9.983	376.746	7,4%
7	Sampling and first supplies management	110,72	11	1.218	0,2%
8=2+3+4+5+6+7	Total supplier management costs			428.699	
9=8/1	Complexity index			104,7%	
10=1+9	Total Cost of Ownership			838.240	

In total, the TCO procedure took 14 days: 11 days for the interviews, two days for collecting the data about the activity drivers, and one day for running the analysis and obtaining the final results.

9.3.2 DEA

In the previous section, we showed that measuring the efficiency of the buyer–supplier relationship, using TCO, demands an extensive effort. Efficiency can be defined as the ratio of input and output. In order to measure the efficiency of the buyer–supplier relationship of the company with its suppliers, we defined several inputs and outputs that determine the relationship's efficiency. We applied the DEA in a procedure that we aligned with that of Golany and Roll (1989). In the first step, we interviewed directors and employees of the four departments to identify factors relevant to the efficiency of a buyer–supplier relationship. We identified these factors by judging each factor's contribution to the fulfilment of the objectives of the relationship, the conveyance of pertinent information, and the availability and reliability of data on the factor. For the remaining factors, data were collected for all suppliers using the company's ERP system.

In a second step, the identified factors had to be classified into inputs and outputs of the DEA model. The resources that units used to run their operations were considered typical inputs, while the measureable benefits that they generated constituted the outputs. Because of the underlying assumption of an isotonic relationship in DEA, undesirable outputs were moved from the output to the input side. In order to verify the straightforward classification of factors, a correlation analysis was conducted and data were checked for zero values because of DEA's weakness in handling them. The final DEA model, which was used to evaluate the efficiency in buyer–supplier relationships, is presented in Figure 9.1.

The input-oriented BCC-DEA was run for 50 buyer–supplier relationships, with an average efficiency score of 0.65, showing 22 efficient buyer–supplier relationships. The efficiency score is normalised to 1, where 1 means that the observation lies on the efficiency frontier.

The implementation of DEA took approximately three days: two for choosing the inputs or outputs and collecting the data, and one for running the analysis.

9.4 Findings

The application of TCO and DEA to the suppliers of mechanical external workings (50 suppliers) provided the results represented in Figure 9.2. In the figure, the DEA results are represented on the *x*-axis (ranging from

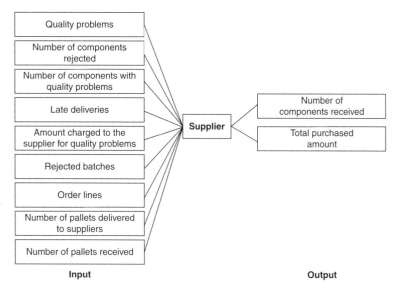

Figure 9.1 The DEA model

0 to 1), while the *y*-axis shows the TCO complexity index (ranging from 0 to 51.1 per cent).

We also calculated a Pearson correlation index. It provided a result of –0.522, significant at the 0.01 level (two-tailed). Both the graph and the correlation index show the presence of a correlation between the two variables, which was not high enough to conclude that DEA and TCO provide the same information on suppliers' efficiency level.

The results shift significantly when taking into account the position of the suppliers in the ranking derived by the two analyses, instead of the specific results of the analyses. The 50 suppliers were ranked from 1 to 50 on the basis of TCO analysis and DEA analysis, and the correlation between the two values was analysed. The results are presented in Figure 9.3.

In this second case, the Pearson correlation index between the two values was much higher: 0.718, still significant at the 0.01 level.

What emerges from this specific case is that DEA could provide a general understanding of a supplier's efficiency level inside a group of comparables, but it cannot be considered an adequate indication of suppliers' TCO, at least not without any procedure aimed at defining the weight of each input/output variable.

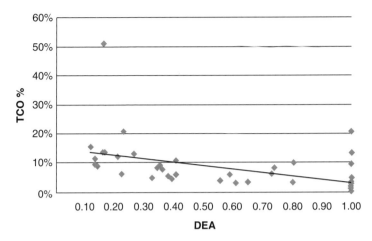

Figure 9.2   The relationship between TCO and DEA results

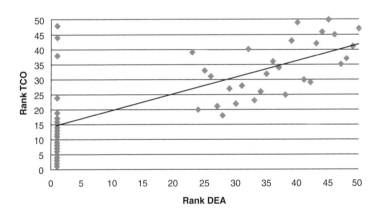

Figure 9.3   The relationship between TCO and DEA rankings

9.5   Conclusions and future research

To understand the ability of DEA to support decision-makers in the supplier selection process, we analysed the results of the TCO and the DEA of
the target organisation. Undoubtedly, TCO provides more useful results
than DEA, not only because the evaluation of the suppliers' performance

is more accurate, but also because it provides better support for decision-making. Indeed, the TCO report (Table 9.1) clearly represents the percentage of costs related to each driver (quality, reliability etc.), highlighting the root causes of a poor or good performance, thus providing a relevant basis for new initiatives of purchasing management (outsourcing, insourcing, aggregations, switches etc.).

As shown in the previous section, DEA proved to be only partially able to replicate TCO results. It supports the suppliers' control process, providing a useful indication of performance rankings between comparables, but does not provide information on the underlying causes of the different results. DEA is, however, simpler than TCO to run. While we needed only three days to run DEA, we needed 14 days to obtain the TCO results. The complexity and reliability of the two methods are influenced by the differences in approach used to weigh the cost drivers/inputs.

The TCO results relied on comprehensive ABC analyses to allocate costs. This can be considered a method of *ex ante* weighting of the different cost drivers. In the DEA analysis, the identified cost drivers needed no *ex ante* weighting. The cost drivers could be introduced into the model with different measurement dimensions. The weighting that used an ABC analysis in TCO was done inherently by the optimisation process of DEA. As DEA weighs the input or output in order to optimise each DMU's individual efficiency under the mentioned restrictions, the weightings are mathematical in nature. Therefore, they do not represent the cost caused by the factor, which the ABC analysis of TCO does.

From these results new research perspectives on this topic can arise. To improve the DEA analysis, the information produced by the ABC analysis can be introduced into the DEA model by weighting restrictions. Thereby, the degree of freedom when optimising factor weightings is reduced, so cost drivers with a high cost impact from the ABC analysis are not allocated low weightings in the DEA analysis. The effort of conducting a DEA analysis once the model is developed is reduced because no ABC analysis is needed. Therefore the DEA approach has potential as a managerial tool in the purchasing department, but it cannot be used without previous analysis of process costs and cost drivers.

References

Banker, R. D. (1984). 'Estimating Most Productive Scale Size Using Data Envelopment Analysis', *European Journal of Operational Research*, 17 (1), 35–44.

Carr, L. P. and Ittner, C. D. (1992). 'Measuring the Cost of Ownership', *Journal of Cost Management*, 6 (3), 19–27.

Charnes, A., Cooper, W. W., Lewin, A. Y. and Seiford, L. M. (1994). *Data Envelopment Analysis: Theory, Methodology, and Application*, Boston, Kluwer.

Charnes, A., Cooper, W. W. and Rhodes, E. (1978). 'Measuring the Efficiency of Decision-Making Units', *European Journal of Operational Research*, 2 (6), 429–44.

Cooper, W. W., Seiford, L. M., and Tone, T. (2006). *Introudction to Data Envelopment Analysis and Its Uses: With DEA-Solver Software and References*. Springer, New York, NY.

Degraeve, Z., Labro, E. and Roodhooft, F. (2000). 'An Evaluation of Vendor Selection Models from a Total Cost of Ownership Perspective', *European Journal of Operational Research*, 125 (1), 34–58.

Degraeve, Z. and Roodhooft, F. (1999). 'Improving the Efficiency of the Purchasing Process Using Total Cost of Ownership Information: The Case of Heating Electrodes at Cockerill Sambre S.A.', *European Journal of Operational Research*, 112 (1), 42–53.

Dickson, G. W. (1966). 'An Analysis of Vendor Selection Systems and Decisions', *Journal of Purchasing*, 2 (1), 5–17.

Ellram, L. M. (1994). 'A Taxonomy of Total Cost of Ownership Models', *Journal of Business Logistics*, 15 (1), 171–92.

Ellram, L. M. (1995). 'Total Cost of Ownership: An Analysis Approach for Purchasing', *Journal of Physical Distribution and Logistics*, 25 (8), 4–23.

Ellram, L. M. and Siferd, S. P. (1993). Purchasing: The Cornerstone of the Total Cost of Ownership Concept, *Journal of Business Logistics*, 14 (1), 163–84.

Epstein, M. K. and Henderson, J. C. (1989). 'Data Envelopment Analysis for Managerial Control and Diagnosis', *Decision Science*, 20 (1), 90–119.

Golany, B. and Roll, Y. (1989). 'An Application Procedure for DEA', *Omega*, 17 (3), 237–50.

Jackson, D. W. and Ostrom, L. L. (1980). 'Life Cycle Costing in Industrial Purchasing', *Journal of Purchasing and Materials Management*, 18 (4), 8–12.

Monczka, R. M. and Trecha, S. J. (1988). 'Cost-Based Supplier Performance Evaluation', *Journal of Purchasing and Materials Management*, Spring, 2–7.

Ronen, B. and Trietsch, D. (1988). 'A Decision Support System for Purchasing Management of Large Projects', *Operations Research*, 36 (6), 882–90.

Rosenthal, E. C., Zydiak, J. L. and Chaudhry, S. S. (1995). 'Vendor Selection with Bundling', *Decision Sciences*, 26 (1), 35–48.

Sadrian, A. A. and Yoon, Y. S. (1994). 'A Procurement Decision Support System in Business Volume Discount Environments', *Operations Research*, 42 (1), 14–23.

Smytka, D. L. and Clemens, M. W. (1993). 'Total Cost Supplier Selection Model: A Case Study', *International Journal of Purchasing and Materials Management*, Winter, 42–9.

Soukoup, W. R. (1987). 'Supplier Selection Strategies', *Journal of Purchasing and Materials Management*, 23 (2), 7–12.

Thompson, K. (1990). 'Vendor Profile Analysis', *Journal of Purchasing and Materials Management*, Winter, 11–18.

Timmerman, E. (1986). 'An Approach to Vendor Performance Evaluation', *Journal of Purchasing and Supply Management*, 1, 27–32.

Weber, C., Current, J. R. and Benton, W. C. (1991). 'Vendor Selection Criteria and Methods', *European Journal of Operational Research*, 50 (1), 2–18.

Weber, C. A. and Current, J. R. (1993). 'A Multi-objective Approach to Vendor Selection', *European Journal of Operational Research*, 68, 173–84.

10
Intangible Assets: Value Drivers for Competitive Advantage

Pankaj M. Madhani

10.1   Intangible assets: an introduction

Intangible assets are becoming increasingly vital to corporations, following the global shift from an industrially powered economy towards a knowledge-based one. With the stage set for competition to be largely based on intangibles, these assets become a critical resource for firms keen to build competitive advantage. As firms move towards becoming more knowledge- and information-based, intangible assets will comprise a significant percentage of the overall value of businesses. The concept of intangible assets is not always well defined (Marr and Chatzkel, 2004). According to Epstein and Mirza (2005), intangible assets are non-financial assets without physical substance, held for use in the production or supply of goods or services or for rental to others, or for administrative purposes, which are identifiable and are controlled by the enterprise as a result of past events, and from which future economic benefits are expected to occur.

According to the International Accounting Standards Committee (IASC), intangible assets are a resource, controlled by an enterprise as a result of past events, and from which future economic benefits are expected to flow to the enterprise (IAS 38). Others have defined intangibles as knowledge, skills and aptitudes at the individual level and as databases, technology and routines at the organisational level (Johanson *et al.*, 1998). The terms 'intangibles', 'knowledge assets' and 'intellectual capital' are used interchangeably and are non-physical sources of value (claims to future benefits) generated by innovation (discovery), unique organisational designs, or human resource practices. Different groups use different terms to indicate a non-physical claim to future benefits – intangibles in the accounting literature, knowledge assets by economists, and intellectual capital in management and legal literature – but they refer essentially to the same thing: a non-physical claim to future benefits (Lev, 2001). Intangible assets have become important resources in economic value creation of firms as compared to tangible assets of firms. Intangible assets are of increasing importance to the corporate value creation processes of all kinds of organisations.

10.2 Significance of intangible assets in a knowledge economy

There are two main ways of determining the value of a firm: internal valuation based on the firm's financial statements (such as balance sheet and income statement) or external valuation based on its market value in the stock market. These days, the two values differ widely (Andriessen, 2004). For most firms, market value is often much higher than accounting book value, as stock market value is derived mainly from assets that do not directly appear on the balance sheet of a firm. One explanation (among others) for the gap is the firm's intangible assets, which for the most part are not included in the financial statements. For example, the value of customer relationships, experience of employees or organisational culture cannot be determined on the basis of the balance sheet (Kujansivu and Lönnqvist, 2007). This highlights the growing significance of intangible assets and their accounting practices.

The value attached to intangible assets has increased many-fold in the current era of knowledge economy. For example, while firms like Microsoft or Coca-Cola only report traditional assets in their balance sheets, it accounts for less than 5 per cent of their total market value. In 1982, out of every $100 invested in stocks of US manufacturing and mining firms, an average of $62.30 (62 per cent) was spent on tangible assets. By 1999, the investment dipped to only 16 per cent (Lev, 2000). The market value of an asset is an appraisal based on an estimate of what a buyer would pay a seller for any such asset. The book value shown in a firm's financial statement reflects the value of firm-reported assets less liabilities. The market-to-book value ratio (M/B ratio) indicates how closely the traditional accounting assets included in the balance sheet of a firm relate to the firm's market value. M/B ratio for S&P 500 shows a shift in the relevance of the traditional accounting asset base (Ballow *et al.*, 2004).

Traditionally, the key resources of the firm were physical assets, such as land and machinery, or financial assets. However, in this knowledge era, intangible assets have been identified as key resources and sources of competitive advantage (McGaughey, 2002). In 1978, intangible assets constituted only 5 per cent of all assets, with traditional accounting assets comprising the majority of total assets. However, in 2008, intangible assets became 78 per cent of all assets, with traditional accounting assets comprising only a small portion of total assets (Chareonsuk and Chansa-ngavej, 2008) as firms become less dependent on physical assets for value creation.

In the new economy, value creation relies on the transformation from tangible assets to intangible assets, with firms likely to generate much of their value through intangible assets (such as proprietary processes, brands, strong relationships and knowledge) as differentiating factors (Nakamura, 2001). The drivers of value creation in modern competitive environments lie in a firm's intangible assets rather than its physical and financial capital as they underline future performance and growth. This resource is the main source of sustainable competitive advantage, and is rare, inimitable and non-substitutable.

10.3   Intangible assets: a resource-based view perspective

Until the 1980s, the mainstream of business economics focused on the external environment (industry structure) as the basis for understanding competitive advantage. According to this external environment theory, the role of management was to find a way to align the products of the firm with markets, given the bargaining power of suppliers and customers, entry barriers and potential substitute products and technologies. The core focus of this strategy is the external environment instead of the internal aspects of the firm. The global business environment has become more competitive, shifting from a seller's market to a buyer's market as customers become better informed and more demanding. This dynamic environment requires firms to take an internal perspective, examining their resources and capabilities, and identifying how to integrate them to gain core competencies and competitive advantages (Hamel and Prahalad, 1990). This internally focused view of strategy is based on the resource-based view (Wernerfelt, 1984) and the dynamic capability approach (Teece *et al.*, 1997) and emphasises the importance of matching any external opportunities with internal resources.

In the 1980s, a resource-based view of firms gained importance. A resource-based view focuses on resources and their deployment in organisations, leading to the development of value creation (Peppard and Rylander, 2001). According to this theory, competitive advantage was not reached only by different combinations of products and markets in a given industry structure but, on the contrary, it was mainly due to a variation in possession of different kinds of organisational resources (Wernerfelt, 1984).

Premised on the resource-based view of firms, Barney (1991) developed four criteria for determining what kinds of resources provided a sustainable competitive advantage:

1. Valuable in terms of value creation;
2. Rare in comparison to competence;
3. Inimitability of resources;
4. Non-substitutability.

The only resources that seem to pass this criteria test are intangible resources, whether they are named knowledge, invisible assets (Cohen and Levinthal, 1990), core competencies, core capabilities, strategic assets (Zander and Kogut, 1995), intangible resources (Hall, 1992) or any other denomination with a similar meaning. According to Itami and Roehl (1987), these assets are based on information and can include anything from customer loyalty to technological skills or internal goodwill. The concept of core competencies (Hamel and Prahalad, 1990) is another example of intangibles as a source of sustainable competitive advantage. One of the requirements for a competence to be considered 'core' is the difficulty of imitation by competitors, thereby fulfilling the criteria specified by Barney (1991). Intangibles are important in management processes, as they have become a crucial resource for the firm.

Organisations have realised that when formulating a corporate strategy it is not enough simply to focus on the competitive forces, opportunities and threats of the industry, as suggested by Porter (1979). In addition, organisations have to understand their competence and resources in order to evaluate those opportunities (Andrews, 1971). Intangible assets are primary drivers upon which a firm can establish its identity and frame its strategy (Kaplan and Norton, 2004). Intangible assets are of a strategic nature and need to be considered in the process of strategy development as well as strategy execution (Marr *et al.*, 2003).

10.4   Intellectual capital: major components

In a knowledge-based or information economy, intellectual capital creates value and drives demand. Intellectual capital consists of the non-physical sources of value related to employees' capabilities, organisational resources and operational methods, and relationships with stakeholders (Lönnqvist, 2004). Intellectual capital has been defined as the total stock of capital or knowledge-based equity possessed by the company (Dzinkowski, 2000). Petty and Cuganesan (2005) assert that the term 'intellectual capital' is often treated as being synonymous with 'intangible assets'. Intellectual capital is either the final product of a knowledge transformation process or the reserve of organisational knowledge itself. Some 50–90 per cent of the value created by a firm in today's economy is estimated to come from its intellectual capital rather than the use and production of traditional material goods (Guthrie and Yongvanich, 2004). Organisations have identified that they require intellectual capital assets in order to create sustainable competitive advantages and long-term value (Johanson *et al.*, 2001). Intellectual capital incorporates three main components that together form value and are distinguished as knowledge related to employees (human capital), knowledge related to customers (relational or customer capital) and knowledge related to the firm only (structural or organisational capital), as explained below.

10.4.1   Human capital

Human capital is defined as the knowledge that employees take with them when they leave the firm at the end of the day, including knowledge, skills, experiences, abilities, motivation and tasks (Hendry and Brown, 2005). Human capital embraces skills, expertise, problem-solving capability, creativity, education, attitude, entrepreneurial spirit, competence, commitment, innovation and loyalty of employees.

10.4.2   Relational capital

Relational capital is the knowledge embedded in relationships with any stakeholder that affects the organisation's life. Relational capital contains all the forms of relationship that an organisation has with its stakeholders. These relationships could be licensing and partnering agreements, contracts and distribution agreements or relationships such as customer loyalty and brand image as a fundamental link between the organisation and one of its key stakeholders. Finally, relational capital is also defined as all the intellectual capital linked with the firm's external relationships, for example the relationship with customers. Customers have become a new source of competence for the organisation by renewing its overall competence (Prahalad and Ramaswamy, 2000). Customer capital is a relationship between a firm and the people in contact with it, for example, the relationship of an enterprise and its upstream/downstream vendors (Stewart, 1997). The essence of customer capital is the knowledge embedded in relationships external to a firm (Bontis, 1998).

Edvinsson and Malone (1997) emphasised the association between all parties and the upstream/downstream link of a firm, and the integration of customers. Besides, a firm's value can be enhanced as a result of good relationships between a firm and its partners (such as customers, suppliers and other groups). For instance, British Petroleum was able to save 30 per cent of its transportation costs due to a good relationship with its suppliers (Roos *et al.*, 1998). The empirical research conducted by Bontis (1998), Tseng and Goo (2005) and Hermans and Kauranen (2005) proved that a positive correlation exists between customer/ relational capital and a firm's valuation. Therefore, good relationships can increase a firm's valuation.

10.4.3 Structural capital

Structural capital is defined as the pool of knowledge that stays with the firm at the end of the working day when employees leave the firm, for example infrastructures, information systems, routines, procedures and organisational culture (Cabriata and Vaz, 2006). It encompasses all non-human repositories of knowledge such as databases, organisational charts, process manuals, strategy routines and anything else with value to a company that outranks its material value (Bontis *et al.*, 2000). Structural capital means an organisation's capabilities to meet internal and external challenges. It also includes all intangibles that remain with the organisation, such as intellectual property comprising of patents, copyrights, trademarks and brands whose ownership is granted to the firm by law. Human capital interacts with structural capital to create, acquire and employ consumer capital to enable continued organisational success (Bontis, 1998). Some commonly identified elements of customer capital, such as loyalty and satisfaction, are dependent on the interaction between human and structural capital. Human capital does not directly affect a firm's performance, but influences it indirectly through customer or structural capital (Bontis *et al.*, 2000). The three components of intellectual capital are interdependent (Subramaniam and Youndt, 2005). Through the combination, utilisation, interaction, alignment and balancing of the three types of intellectual capital and managing the knowledge flow among the three components, intellectual capital renders the best possible value to organisations (Kong, 2007).

10.4.4 Accounting versus intellectual capital assets: recognition and characteristics

Firms need to identify and recognize different accounting and intellectual capital assets, depending on their strategic objectives. Table 10.1 shows

Table 10.1 Recognition of different asset types

Asset types/recognition	Accounting Assets		Intellectual capital assets		
	Physical	Financial	Human	Relational	Organizational
Tangible	• Plant • Property • Equipment • Inventory	• Cash • Investment • Receivables	• Contracts • Accessible skills	• Customer contracts • Formal alliance • Joint venture	• Systems • Formalized process • Codified knowledge
Intangible	• Plant flexibility • Access rights • Inventory (obsolete and redundant)	• Credit ratings • Borrowing capacity • Receivables certainty	• Employee loyalty • Employee engagement • Problem solving ability	• Customer loyalty • Quality of supply contracts • Networks	• Tacit knowledge • Know how • Informal processes • Firm reputation

Source: AssetEconomics Holdings.

Table 10.2 Characteristics of different asset types

Asset types/ characteristics	Accounting assets		Intellectual capital assets		
	Physical	Financial	Human	Relational	Organizational
Ownership	Yes	Yes	No	No	Yes
Additive	Yes	Yes	No	No	No
Type of economic return	Diminishing marginal returns	Diminishing marginal returns	Diminishing marginal returns	Increasing returns to scale	Increasing returns to scale
Applicability of network economics	Possibly	No	No	Possibly	Possibly

Source: AssetEconomics Holdings.

some examples of recognition of different asset types, distributed into accounting and intellectual capital assets and classified in the five categories: physical, financial, human capital, relational capital and organizational capital.

Similarly, Table 10.2 shows characteristics of these five categories of asset types: physical, financial, human capital, relational capital and organizational capital. Here, additive characteristics of assets refer to whether usage of assets decreases asset value, while, ownership refers to who owns the assets of the firm.

10.5 Identification, measurement and management of intangible assets

The main purpose of management of intangibles is to enhance the firm's value through the creation of competitive advantages. Intangible assets are critical for the future success of business organisations (Molnar, 2004); however, valuation approaches to measuring and managing them were either poor or non-existent. One key reason for measuring intangible assets is to assess drivers of performance and competitive advantage so as to make better strategic decisions. Another key interest for measuring intangibles comes from the broad gap between what firms disclose in their mandatory financial reports and what really matters for market valuation. Intangible assets have become, in recent years, the core focus of firms, investors, accountants, Wall Street analysts and regulators alike in their attempts to understand and reduce the huge gap between a firm's book and market values. Intangible asset valuation is critical from both accounting and business perspectives. The ability to clearly identify, measure, value and account for intangible assets is a serious problem for company managers, investors and governments (Blair and Wallman, 2001).

Intangibles are normally neither reported externally nor integrated in internal management accounting. Progressive and good practice firms are expected to identify, measure, report, communicate, evaluate and monitor important intangibles in the management control process. Financial profit alone cannot guarantee the long-term survival and growth of firms. To be sustainable, firms need to identify and be able to manage intangibles, including organisational learning and growth, internal processes and customer value propositions. The first phase in the analysis is thus the identification of the strategic objectives of the firm. Once this first phase has been accomplished, the measurement and monitoring of those related intangibles must be done (Sánchez *et al.*, 2000).

These phases can be distinguished in the management of intangibles as explained below:

1. Identification of intangibles;
2. Measurement of intangibles; and
3. Monitoring of intangibles.

10.6 Identification of intangibles

In the identification phase, firms usually focus only on those intangibles linked to the present or future value drivers of the firm, making it necessary to enquire about their strategic objectives. Every firm will identify a set of critical intangibles that might help to reach the strategic objectives of the firm or enhance the firm's competitive advantage. According to the Statement of Financial Accounting Standards (SFAS) 141 of the Financial Accounting Standards Board (FASB), most identifiable intangible assets fall into one of five categories – marketing-related, customer-related, artistic-related, contract-related or technology-related, as explained below:

1. Marketing-related intangible assets include trademarks, trade names, service marks, newspaper mastheads, Internet domain names, non-competition agreements.
2. Customer-related intangible assets include customer lists, order or production backlogs, customer contracts and customer relationships, including non-contractual relationships.
3. Artistic-related intangible assets include plays, operas, ballets, books, magazines, newspapers, pictures and photographs.
4. Contract-based intangible assets include licensing and royalty agreements, advertising, construction, service or supply agreements, lease agreements, franchise agreements and employment contracts.
5. Technology-based intangible assets include patented technology, computer software, unpatented technology (know-how), databases, and trade secrets such as secret formulas, processes and recipes.

The result of the identification phase is a network of intangibles related to the strategic objectives. Once an intangible asset has been identified, it needs to be measured and valued. Despite intangible assets' lack of physical substance and relationship to other assets, which makes them difficult to isolate and measure, there are several methodologies to measure and value an identified intangible asset.

10.7   Measurement of intangibles

As Peter Drucker has often said, 'If you can't measure it, you can't manage it'. Hence once critical intangibles have been identified, the firm needs to define specific indicators serving as a proxy measure for each intangible. There are three widely accepted valuation approaches towards intangible asset measurement: the income, market and cost approaches (Cohen, 2005). The appropriateness of each of these measurement approaches varies according to the type of asset, available data and the specific circumstance of different industries.

10.8   Different approaches for measurement of intangibles

10.8.1   Income approach

According to the income approach, income and expense data relating to the intangible asset are valued and estimated by using a discounted cash flow methodology (DCF), such as net present value (NPV), which is linked to the expected benefits from future returns on such assets. There are three basic steps to a feasible measurement of intangible assets:

1. Identify the asset from which the stream of expected future economic return occurs;
2. Estimate the expected future cash flows over time; and finally,
3. Assign an appropriate measure of risk to expected future cash flows by using the Capital Asset Pricing Model (CAPM), Arbitrage Pricing Theory (APT) or other financial approaches.

The income approach seeks to identify and quantify, in terms of present value, the future earnings attributable to the asset on the basis of future economic benefits derived from asset ownership. The main income methods are 'Relief from Royalty' and 'Excess Earnings'. 'Relief from Royalty' is based on estimating the price a business would pay for the use of an intangible asset if it did not own the asset, or the cost savings of not having to pay a royalty. The basis of the Excess Earnings methodology is that the value of an intangible asset is the present value of the earnings it generates, net of a reasonable return on other assets also contributing to that stream of earnings (Deloitte, 2007).

10.8.2   Market approach

The market approach estimates the fair value of intangible assets by comparing these assets with actual sales of similar assets in the marketplace.

The market approach is also called the 'sales comparison' approach. This approach generally assumes that intangible assets can be valued by observing transactions of comparable assets in the marketplace. The more heterogeneous assets are, the more difficult it is to apply this approach. Intangible assets such as brands cannot be sold separately from other business assets. It may therefore be difficult to observe benchmark prices paid in outright sales for comparable assets, as such transactions are infrequent and details are rarely fully disclosed. As there is no active market for some intangibles, this comparable approach has limitations. Many valuable intangibles are unique by nature and unless there are transactions of such specific assets under consideration, a price comparison approach may not be helpful for valuation. Therefore this approach can be difficult to apply in practice.

10.8.3 Cost approach

Under the cost approach, intangible assets are valued based on the 'cost to create' (development cost) or 'cost to recreate' (replacement cost) a similar kind of intangible asset, with comparable consumer appeal or equivalent commercial utility. The cost approach considers the book cost (reported in the traditional financial statements) or the replacement cost. For intangible assets such as brands these costs generally relate to naming, research and product design, packaging, design, advertising and promotional costs. In the case of IT services, costs may include development and implementation costs. For human capital assets, such as the workforce, it would include the costs of recruitment and training. The cost approach is one of the fundamental methods of valuing intangible assets; among several cost approach methods, the most common are the reproduction cost method and the replacement cost method (Reilly and Schweihs, 1998). Thus, for intangibles without an active market, this approach provides a useful benchmark for a valuation.

10.9 Different methods for measurement of intangibles

According to Williams (2000), there are four practical methods to measure intangible assets, as explained below.

10.9.1 ROA method

This method is based on the concept of return on assets (ROA). ROA is the average pre-tax earnings of a firm for a period of time divided by the average tangible assets of the firm. A firm can compare this ratio with the firm's industry average to calculate the difference between firm ROA and industry-average ROA. If this difference is positive, it is assumed that the firm has an excess value of intangibles in relation to the industry. If this excess is multiplied by the firm's average tangible assets, the result will be the average annual excess earning over the industry. An estimate of the current value of its intangibles is obtained by dividing this excess earning by the firm's weighted average cost of capital (WACC). WACC is equal to the after-tax weighted cost of debt plus the weighted cost of equity. This method is simple to use and the information needed is easily available from financial statements.

10.9.2   Market capitalisation method

This method is based on the concept of a valuation premium in the capital market and calculates the difference between a firm's market capitalisation and its stockholders' equity as the value of the intangible assets. The M/B ratio shows the excess of a firm's market capitalisation over its stockholders' equity and it can thus be deduced that this is due to the intangibles owned by the firm (Sveiby, 2001). To calculate the M/B ratio more accurately, the historical financial statements must be adjusted for inflation or replacement costs. This method provides a market measure of a firm's valuation of intangibles. The market information on the firm's stock price is readily available, but historical financial statements, as mentioned, should be adjusted for current replacement costs.

10.9.3   Direct identification method

The method is based on measuring the value of intangibles by first identifying its different components. Once these components are identified, they can be measured through indicators. This method is expensive and complex because of the large number of components that have to be identified and individually measured. However, this method is also the most accurate way to measure the value of intangibles, taking into account that the ROA and market capitalisation methods report the total value of intangibles but do not show any component.

10.9.4   Balanced Scorecard method

In the Balanced Scorecard method, various components of intangible assets are identified and indices are generated and reported in scorecards (Kaplan and Norton, 1992). The Balanced Scorecard concept is popular because it contains outcome measures and the performance driver of outcomes, linked together in cause–effect relationships (Wingren, 2004). There are linkages between customers, internal process and learning/growth, and financial performance. The Balanced Scorecard strategy map (Kaplan and Norton, 2004) may be used to provide a framework to illustrate how the strategy of firms links intangible assets to value-creating processes. The measures in the four perspectives are linked together by cause–effect relationships. The firm builds the core competence and training to support the internal process. The internal process creates and delivers the customer value proposition. When customers are satisfied, sales and profit are delivered in terms of financial performance. The financial performance is the outcome and visible to observers. Hence the Balanced Scorecard attempts to expand the focus of managers by encouraging them to look beyond short-term financial performance measures towards intangible items crucial in the value-generation process (Petty *et al.*, 2009). The Balanced Scorecard is the best known among all the methods, although its original intent was not for measuring intangible assets, as discussed by Marr and Adams (2004) and Mouritsen *et al.*, (2005).

10.10   Monitoring of intangibles

The final step in the whole process is monitoring. Once the measurement system is developed and implemented, firms must analyse their results internally. The management of intangibles involves identifying intangibles linked to the present and future value of the firm, their measurement, and finally, the implementation of those intangible activities that positively affect the level of critical intangibles, with the sole purpose of developing competitive advantages. Thus management's efforts are oriented towards the identification of those intangibles and their further measurement and management.

10.11   Value drivers of intangible assets: a source of competitive advantage

The economic value of intangible assets is the measure of utility it brings to the business enterprise (Sullivan, 2000). The value of intangible assets depends on the business enterprise's ability to transform intangible assets into financial returns. Intangible assets have been identified as the most critical resource of today's business firm, yet most firms cannot clearly define such business drivers. Businesses have not clearly defined the best approach to valuing intangible assets. The business enterprise in this knowledge era has a need to become receptive and intelligent about its environment so as to gain knowledge from it and subsequently value its intangible resources. Intangibles are significant factors in value creation within the business firm and need to be managed like the traditional input factors of labour, capital and raw materials (Von Krogh *et al.*, 1998). The intellectual capital can provide tangible bottom-line results if the sources of value are extracted.

Successful management of intangible assets within the organisation positively affects the performance and market valuation of a business enterprise. The main objective of intangible asset management is the establishment of tools and indicators to manage knowledge and increase earnings within the business enterprise (Sullivan, 1998). It has been stated numerous times, by Baruch Lev, Michael Porter, Robert Kaplan and David Norton to name a few, that the nature of value within the business enterprise has changed and that new assets such as intangible assets cannot be measured with old tools. It is important to analyse what factors can be considered to drive value of a firm. Green (2004) states that there are eight main value drivers of intangible assets, as described in Table 10.3.

The alignment of intangibles with strategic objectives and value drivers allows firms to focus their resources and activities on a set of objectives to achieve them more effectively and efficiently. A study by Green (2004) provides empirical evidence that the Balanced Scorecard model, developed by Robert Kaplan and David Norton, adequately represents all eight of the value drivers of intangible assets, explained in Table 10.3.

As intangible assets are often referred to as organisational performance drivers, they provide causal relationships between intangible resources and organisational value creation. Intangible assets such as customer relationships and employee skills often result in higher customer satisfaction and loyalty, which in turn delivers shareholder value. (Rucci *et al.*, 1998). Strategy maps (Kaplan and Norton, 2004) or success maps (Neely *et al.*, 2002) have been used as management tools to visualise the causal links between intangible value drivers and organisational performance outcome. Human capital, information capital and organisational capital are considered as value drivers for intangible assets in strategy maps.

10.12   Accounting practices for intangible assets

Conventionally, operating profit (or loss) information is used as the firm's main performance indicators and is reported in its financial reports. The accounting approach for tangible assets starts with categorising the various types of expense. Operating profit (or loss) is then derived

Table 10.3 Value drivers of intangible assets

No.	Value driver	Definition
1	Customer	Associations (e.g., loyalty, satisfaction, longevity) a firm has built with consumers of its goods and services
2	Competitor	Position (e.g., reputation, market share, name recognition, image) a firm has built in the business market place
3	Employee	Collective capabilities (e.g., knowledge, skill, competence, know-how) of a firm's employees
4	Information	Firm's ability to collect and disseminate its information and knowledge in the right form and content to the right people at the right time
5	Partner	Associations (financial, strategic, authority, power) a firm has established with external individuals and organisations (e.g., consultants, customers, suppliers, allies, competitors) in pursuit of advantageous outcomes
6	Process	Firm's ability (e.g., policies, procedures, methodologies, techniques) to leverage the ways in which the enterprise operates and creates value for its employees and customers
7	Product/service	Firm's ability to develop and deliver its offerings (i.e., products and services) that reflects an understanding of market and customer requirements, expectations and desires
8	Technology	Hardware and software a firm has invested in to support its operations, management and future renewal

from the difference between sales revenue and operating cost. The costs include the expenses in brand building, customer database, training, product design and development, etc. These are typically treated as part of the operating cost and marketing expenses. This simple accounting mechanism of maintaining records of revenue and expenses is no longer sufficient in the knowledge-based economy, since a growing share of a firm's market value in this era is not represented by inventory or physical assets, but by intangible assets. Investments in intangible assets are usually not documented and recorded in a systematic manner because of data non-availability or a difficulty in documenting. Therefore a firm's management may find it difficult to estimate performance in terms of its future financial potential.

Intangibles accounting is regulated by International Accounting Standard – IAS 38 issued by the International Accounting Standards

Board (IASB). IAS 38 sets down the criteria for intangibles to be recognised as assets in a firm's balance sheet. According to IAS 38, these criteria fulfil the requirement for an intangible resource to be recognised as an asset:

1. Expected to generate future economic benefits for the firm.
2. It should be controlled by the firm.
3. Outcome from past event or transaction.
4. Be identifiable with a cost or value that can be reliably measured.

IAS 38 prescribes the accounting treatment for intangibles that are not dealt with by another IAS. According to IAS 38, a firm can acquire an intangible asset by separate acquisition, internal generation or self-creation, acquisition as part of a business combination, or an exchange of assets. IAS 38 does not apply to financial assets and insurance contracts issued by insurance companies.

10.13 Conclusions

Firms are currently not required by accounting standards or by law to report on most of their intellectual capital; however they may voluntarily elect to disclose such information. Intangibles are among the organisational assets with market value which may be overlooked by current accounting practices. The management of intangible assets is a complex and perplexing task, not least because the prevailing accounting system is designed primarily for tangible assets, to the exclusion of most intangible and intellectual capital assets. Intangible assets are levers for competitive advantage and sustainable performance; firms should therefore find ways to identify, measure and manage their key intangible assets, as well as disclose them to their stakeholders. In today's knowledge-based economy, a firm's value is imperfectly measured by the value of its physical assets alone, as intangible assets create value and may decide a firm's future growth potential. New management methods are therefore instrumental in the valuation of intangible assets.

References

Andrews, K. (1971). *The Concept of Corporate Strategy*, Dow Jones-Irwin, Homewood, Ill.
Andriessen, D. (2004). *Making Sense of Intellectual Capital: Designing a Method for the Valuation of Intangibles*, Elsevier Butterworth-Heinemann, Oxford.

Ballow, J. J., Burgman, R. and Molnar, M. J. (2004). 'Managing for Shareholder Value: Intangibles, Future Value and Investment Decisions', *Journal of Business Strategy*, 25 (3), 26–34.

Barney, J. (1991). 'Types of Competition and The Theory of Strategy: Toward An Integrative Framework', *Academy of Management Review*, 11 (4), 791–800.

Blair, M. M. and Wallman, S. M. H. (2001). *Unseen Wealth*, Brookings Institution Press, Boston, MA.

Bontis, N. (1998). 'Intellectual Capital: An Exploratory Study that Develops Measures and Models', *Management Decision*, 36 (2), 63–75.

Bontis, N., Keow, W. C. C. and Richardson, S. (2000). 'Intellectual Capital and Business Performance in Malaysian Industries', *Journal of Intellectual Capital*, 1 (1), 85–100.

Cabriata, M. R. and Vaz, J. L. (2006). 'Intellectual Capital and Value Creation: Evidence from the Portuguese Banking Industry', *The Electronic Journal of Knowledge Management*, 4 (1), 11–20.

Chareonsuk, C. and Chansa-ngavej, C. (2008). 'Intangible Asset Management Framework for Long-term Financial Performance', *Emerald, Industrial Management & Data Systems*, 108 (6), 812–28.

Cohen, J. A. (2005). *Intangible Assets – Valuation and Economic Benefit*, John Wiley & Sons, New Jersey.

Cohen, W. and Levinthal, D. (1990). 'Absorptive Capacity: A New Perspective on Learning and Innovation', *Administrative Science Quarterly*, 35, 128–52.

Deloitte (2007). *Purchase Price Allocation (PPA) and Intangible Assets Valuation*. Deloitte SA, Luxembourg, available at http://www.deloitte.com/assets/Dcom-Luxembourg/Local%20Assets/Documents/Brochures/English/2007/lu_purchaseprice_13062007.pdf (accessed on 28 July 2010).

Dzinkowski, R. (2000). 'The Measurement and Management of Intellectual Capital: An Introduction', *Management Accounting*, 78 (2), 32–6.

Edvinsson, L. and Malone, M. S. (1997). *Intellectual Capital: Realizing Your Company's True Value by Finding Its Hidden Brainpower*, HarperCollins Publishers, New York, NY.

Epstein, B. J. and Mirza, A. A. (2005). *Interpretation and Application of International Accounting and Financial Reporting Standard*, Wiley, New York, NY.

Green, A. (2004). 'Prioritization of Sources of Intangible Assets for Use in Enterprise Balance Scorecard Valuation Models of Information Technology (IT) Firms' (Unpublished doctoral dissertation, George Washington University, Washington, DC).

Guthrie, J. and Yongvanich, K. (2004). 'Intellectual Capital Reporting: Comparison of Various Frameworks' (Working paper, Macquarie Graduate School of Management, Sydney).

Hall, R. (1992). 'The Strategic Analysis of Intangible Resources', *Strategic Management Journal*, 13, 135–44.

Hamel, G. and Prahalad, C. K. (1990). 'The Core Competence of the Corporation', *Harvard Business Review*, 68 (3), 79–91.

Hendry, C. and Brown, J. (2005). 'Probing the Intangible Drivers of Innovation Performance and Their Representation in Performance Measurement Systems' (EBK working paper).

Hermans, R. and Kauranen, I. (2005). 'Value Creation Potential of Intellectual Capital in Biotechnology-empirical Evidence from Finland', *R&D Management*, 35 (2), 171–85.

Itami, H. and Rochl, T. (1987). *Mobilizing Invisible Assets*, Harvard University Press, Cambridge, MA.

Johanson, U., Eklov, G., Holmgren, M. and Martensson, M. (1998). 'Human Resource Costing and Accounting Versus the Balanced Scorecard: A Literature Survey of Experience with the Concepts', Stockholm School of Business, Stockholm University, Stockholm.

Johanson, U., Martensson, M. and Skoog, M. (2001). 'Mobilizing Change Through The Management Control of Intangibles', *Accounting, Organisations and Society*, 26 (7/8), 715–33.

Kaplan, R. and Norton, D., (1992). 'The Balanced Scorecard: Measures that Drive Performance', *Harvard Business Review*, 70 (1), 71–9.

Kaplan, R. and Norton, D. (2004). *Strategy Maps: Converting Intangible Assets into Tangible Outcomes*, Harvard Business School, Cambridge, MA.

Kong, E. (2007). 'The Strategic Importance of Intellectual Capital in the Non-profit Sector', *Journal of Intellectual Capital*, 8 (4), 721–31.

Kujansivu, P. and Lönnqvist, A. (2007). 'Investigating the Value and Efficiency of Intellectual Capital', *Journal of Intellectual Capital*, 8 (2), 272–87.

Lev, B. (2000). 'Knowledge and Shareholder Value', available at: http://pages.stern.nyu.edu/~blev/knowledge&shareholdervalue.doc (accessed on 26 July 2010).

Lev, B. (2001). *Intangibles: Management, Measurement and Reporting*, Brookings Institution Press, Washington, DC.

Lönnqvist, A. (2004). 'Measurement of Intangible Success Factors: Case Studies on the Design, Implementation and Use of Measures' (Doctoral dissertation, Publication 475, Tampere University of Technology, Tampere).

Marr, B. and Adams, C. (2004). 'The Balanced Scorecard and Intangible Assets: Similar Ideas, Unaligned Concepts', *Measuring Business Excellence*, 8 (3), 18–27.

Marr, B. and Chatzkel, J. (2004). 'Intellectual Capital at the Crossroads', *Journal of Intellectual Capital*, 5 (2), 224–9.

Marr, B., Gray, D. and Neely, A. (2003). 'Why do Firms Measure Their Intellectual Capital?' *Journal of Intellectual Capital*, 4 (4), 441–64.

McGaughey, S. L. (2002). 'Strategic Interventions in Intellectual Asset Flows', *Academy of Management Review*, 27, 248–74.

Molnar, M. J. (2004). 'Executive Views on Intangible Assets: Insights from the Accenture/Economist Intelligence Unit Survey', Accenture Research Note.

Mouritsen, J., Larsen, H. T. and Bukh, P. N. (2005). 'Dealing with the Knowledge Economy: Intellectual Capital versus Balanced Scorecard, *Journal of Intellectual Capital*, 6 (1), 8–27.

Nakamura, L. (2001). 'Investing in Intangibles: Is A Trillion Dollars Missing from GDP?' *Business Review*, 4th Quarter.

Neely, A., Adams, C. and Kennerley, M. (2002). '*The Performance Prism: The Scorecard for Measuring and Managing Business Success*', Financial Times, Prentice Hall, London.

Peppard, J. and Rylander, A. (2001). 'Using An Intellectual Capital Perspective to Design and Implement A Growth Strategy: the Case of APiON', *European Management Journal*, 19 (5), 510–25.

Petty, R. and Cuganesan, S. (2005). 'Voluntary Disclosure of Intellectual Capital by Hong Kong Companies: Examining Size, Industry and Growth Effects Over Time', *Australian Accounting Review*, 36, 32–48.

Petty, R., Cuganesan, S., Finch, N. and Ford, G. (2009). 'Intellectual Capital and Valuation: Challenges in the Voluntary Disclosure of Value Drivers', *Journal of Finance and Accountancy*, 1, 1–7.

Porter, M. E. (1979). 'How Competitive Forces Shape Strategy', *Harvard Business Review*, 57 (2), 137–45.

Prahalad, C. K. and Ramaswamy, V. (2000). 'Co-opting Customer Competence', *Harvard Business Review*, 78 (1), 79–87.

Reilly, R. F. and Schweihs, R. P. (1998). *Valuing Intangible Assets*, McGraw-Hill, New York, NY.

Roos, J., Ross, G., Dragonetti, N. and Edvinsson, L. (1998). *Intellectual Capital: Navigating in the New Business Landscape*, Macmillan Business, London.

Rucci, A. J., Kirn, S. P. and Quinn, R. T. (1998). 'The Employee-Customer-Profit Chain at Sears', *Harvard Business Review*, 76 (1), 82–97.

Sánchez, P., Chaminade, C. and Olea, M. (2000). 'Management of Intangibles: An Attempt to Build A Theory', *Journal of Intellectual Capital*, 1 (4), 312–27.

Stewart, T. A. (1997). *Intellectual Capital: The New Wealth of Organisations*, New York, Bantam Doubleday Dell Publishing Group, Inc.

Subramaniam, M. and Youndt, M. A. (2005). 'The Influence of Intellectual Capital on the Types of Innovative Capabilities', *Academy of Management Journal*, 48 (3), 450–63.

Sullivan, P. H. (1998). *Profiting from Intellectual Capital: Extracting Value from Innovation*, John Wiley & Sons, New York, NY.

Sullivan, P. H. (2000). *Value-driven Intellectual Capital: How to Convert Intangible Corporate Assets into Market Value*, John Wiley & Sons, New York, NY.

Sveiby, K. E. (2001). *Methods for Measuring Intangible Assets*, available at http://www.sveiby.com/articles/IntangibleMethods.htm (accessed on 26 July 2010).

Teece, D. J., Pisano, G. and Shuen, A. (1997). 'Dynamic Capabilities and Strategic Management', *Strategic Management Journal*, 18 (7), 509–33.

Tseng, C. Y. and Goo, Y. J. (2005). 'Intellectual Capital and Corporate Value in An Emerging Economy: Empirical Study of Taiwanese Manufacturers', *R&D Management*, 38 (2), 187–201.

Von Krogh, G., Roos, J. and Klein, D. (1998). *Knowing in Firms: Understanding, Managing and Measuring Knowledge*, Sage Publications, London.

Wernerfelt, B. (1984). A Resource-based View of the Firm, *Strategic Management Journal*, 5 (2), 171–80.

Williams, M. (2000). 'Is A Company's Intellectual Capital Performance and Intellectual Capital Disclosure Practices Related? Evidence from Publicly-listed Companies from the FTSE 100' (Paper presented at McMasters Intellectual Capital Conference, Hamilton).

Wingren, T. (2004). 'Management Accounting in the New Economy: From 'Tangible and Production-focused' to 'Intangible and Knowledge-driven' MAS by integrating BSC and IC', *Managerial Finance*, 30 (8), 1–12.

Zander, U. and Kogut, B. (1995). 'Knowledge and the Speed of the Transfer and Imitation of Organisational Capabilities: An Empirical Test', *Organisation Science*, 6 (1), 76–92.

11
Strategic Performance Measurement Systems and Managerial Judgements

Mandy Man-sum Cheng

11.1 Introduction

The introduction of the Balanced Scorecard (BSC) by Kaplan and Norton in the early 1990s has put performance measurement system design firmly on many executives' agendas. A 2009 Bain & Co. survey of 1,430 international executives reported that the BSC ranks sixth among 25 popular management tools, with a global adoption rate of 53 per cent (Rigby and Bilodeau, 2009). Contemporary performance measurement systems (often referred to as *strategic* performance measurement systems), such as the BSC, have a number of distinguishing features. In particular, these systems: (1) contain a diverse range of performance measures that reflect the organisation's key strategic areas, and (2) illustrate the cause-and-effect linkages between operations, strategy and goals, and between various aspects of the value chain (Chenhall, 2005). Many professional and academic articles have been published on the benefits, design and implementation processes associated with various types of strategic performance measurement systems (e.g., the BSC, *Tableu de bord*, and the performance pyramid). The aim of this chapter is not to add to the extant literature comparing the merits of different performance measurement frameworks; rather, it takes a different, 'behavioural' perspective by focusing on how the design features of strategic performance measurement systems influence individual managers' judgements.

Specifically, this chapter reviews recent academic research in the field of *behavioural management accounting* – a stream of research that investigates how management accounting information and systems influence, and are influenced by, managers' behaviours, judgements and decisions. Understanding how the design of strategic performance measurement systems influences managers' decisions and judgements is important for at least two reasons. First, a 2008 Accenture study reports that 40 per cent of major corporate decisions are based on subjective judgements rather than specific quantitative techniques (Wailgum, 2009). The evaluation of subordinates' performance and the assessment of different strategic options using the BSC are two examples of decision-making scenarios that frequently involve some degree of subjective judgement. At the same time, business executives are aware that their judgement quality needs improvement: only 28 per cent of the 2,207 executives surveyed by McKinsey in 2009 believed that the quality of decisions in their companies was generally good, while 60 per cent said that bad decisions were just about as frequent as good decisions (Lovallo and Sibony, 2009). One can deduce from these figures that organisations cannot afford to ignore the human factors when evaluating the effectiveness of management accounting systems.

Second, a fundamental purpose of a strategic performance measurement system is to influence managerial decisions and behaviours, to maintain 'viable patterns of behaviours' (Dunk, 2001; Otley, 1999). This can be achieved either by motivating managers to 'do the right things' (to align the managers' interests with those of their stakeholders), or informing managers how to 'do things right' (to make high-quality judgements). Behavioural issues, including how managers react to and use information generated by their organisations' systems, are therefore central to understanding how the designs of strategic performance measurement systems can be improved.

This chapter has a couple of key objectives. First, it outlines the common decision biases and challenges associated with using strategic performance measurement systems for decision-making. Second, it provides some recommendations on how these biases and challenges can be overcome. In reviewing and synthesising findings in this area, this chapter is structured based on the two broad purposes of strategic performance measurement systems which are related to managerial decision-making: (1) using strategic performance measurement systems to *evaluate managerial performance*; and (2) using strategic performance measurement systems *to inform strategic choices*. Although most of the research in this area focuses on the BSC, the findings from these research studies can apply to other strategic performance measurement systems.

11.2   Using strategic performance measurement systems to evaluate managerial performance

The BSC was initially developed as a robust performance measurement system that integrates operational metrics and financial outcomes

(Kaplan, 2009). While Kaplan and Norton (1996) argue that the BSC is more than just a performance measurement system, and warn managers of the many risks associated with tying the BSC to executive compensation plans, evidence from research and from practice suggests that organisations do tend to use the BSC as a performance evaluation tool (e.g., Ittner *et al.*, 2003). This section reviews some research findings on the common decision biases and challenges when using the BSC to evaluate managerial

Table 11.1 Summary of common decision biases and challenges and recommendations

Common decision biases and challenges

The categorisation effect	Managers tend to seek relations between performance measures contained in the same category (e.g., those contained in the customer perspective of a BSC). This causes managers to assess the impact of these performance measures loosely as a 'whole', rather than seeing each performance measure as representing a specific and important performance aspect, such as a customer value parameter (in doing so, managers underweight some performance measures).
The common measures bias	Managers often over-rely on performance measures that are common to multiple divisions, and ignore unique performance measures. This is of concern because unique performance measures are more likely to reflect a business's strategy.
Consensus divergence in evaluations	When it comes to performance evaluation, there is often a low level of consensus between superiors, and between superiors and subordinates.

What can managers do?

Assisting managers to increase their cognitive effort	Adopt a disaggregated decision strategy (i.e., assess each performance measure of a BSC separately before aggregating the assessments to form an overall evaluation judgement).
	Hold managers accountable for their decision processes (rather than decision outcomes).
Improving task setting to reduce the required cognitive effort	Clear communication of strategic information to managers (e.g., via the strategy map, or incorporating narrative and graphical linkages on a BSC), and ensure that all performance measures are linked to a company's strategy.
	Improve managers' confidence in the reliability and relevance of the performance information (e.g., via an independent assurance process).

performance. Table 11.1 summarises three of the most common decision biases and challenges, and what managers can do to overcome them.

11.2.1 The scorecard categorisation effect on performance evaluation judgements

A key feature of the strategic performance measurement system is the grouping of a diverse set of performance measures into categories that represent an organisation's key performance areas. The classic BSC, introduced in Kaplan and Norton's (1996) business best-seller, *The Balanced Scorecard: Translating Strategy into Action*, structures performance measures into four generic categories (or 'perspectives'): financial, customer, internal business process, and learning and growth. While these categories are meant to represent a framework that allows managers to develop (and therefore monitor) appropriate performance measures for their organisations, research shows that the categorisation scheme can cause managers to pay less attention to performance measures contained within a single category.

Lipe and Salterio (2002) were the first study to demonstrate this effect on managers' performance evaluation judgements. They conducted an experiment where a group of MBA students assumed the role of a superior and were asked to evaluate two managers based on a diverse set of 20 performance measures and targets. The two managers being evaluated had performed similarly on all performance measures except for four customer-related measures. For these measures, one manager performed substantially better than the other. The researchers then compared the performance evaluation scores of MBA students who received the set of performance measures categorised based on the four BSC perspectives, against those MBA students who received the same measures as a list without any categorisation. They found that the evaluation scores of those MBA students who received categorised performance measures showed less discrimination between two managers than MBA students who received uncategorised performance measures. In other words, MBA students who received the categorised performance measures appeared to have significantly underweighted the four customer-related measures that were meant to differentiate the two managers. Their study suggests that the BSC categorisation scheme can 'prime' decision-makers to see all customer-related measures as closely related and represent the same underlying dimension, rather than seeing each performance measure as it is – a unique and important aspect of customer value.

A subsequent study by Liedtka *et al.* (2008) showed that the 'categorisation effect' is even worse when performance measures within a category have high variances, and when the decision-makers are ambiguity-intolerant (i.e., uncomfortable with processing ambiguous information). Similar categorisation effects were also observed by Kaplan and Wisner (2009), who found that adding a fifth perspective (an environmental perspective) to the classic four BSC categories resulted in managers underweighting various environmental measures, compared with embedding the same environmental measures in each of the existing four BSC categories. Overall, these studies suggest that the categorisation scheme in strategic performance measurement systems reduces the impact of individual measures on managers' performance evaluation judgements.

11.2.2 The effect of common measures bias on performance evaluation judgements

In addition to underweighting performance measures within a single category, researchers have also found that managers tend to over-rely on performance measures common to multiple divisions while ignoring each division's unique performance measures. This tendency is known as the common measures bias.

In their seminal experiment published in 2000, Lipe and Salterio asked MBA students to evaluate two managers based on the performance of their respective business units, *RadWear* and *WorkWear*. Both business units were in the retail industry but each adopted a very different strategy and targeted different customer segments. *RadWear* had a growth strategy and targeted teenagers with a strong brand offering. In contrast, *WorkWear* focused on selling basic business uniforms through catalogue orders. The divisional BSC for the two business units therefore shared some common performance measures (for example, return on sales and customer satisfaction rating), but each business unit also had its own unique performance measures ('average brand name per stores' was a performance measure unique to *RadWear*'s BSC, and 'catalogue orders filled with error' was a unique performance measure on *WorkWear*'s BSC).

Lipe and Salterio (2000) found that when evaluating these managers, MBA students placed more weight on measures that were common to both *RadWear* and *WorkWear*, and ignored the performance measures that were unique to each division. This finding is consistent with prior psychology research, which shows that when making comparative judgements, people rely much more on information common to all alternatives than information unique to an alternative, because common information is much easier to process (Slovic and MacPhillamy, 1974).

The common measures bias is particularly problematic when managers use strategic performance measurement systems to evaluate business unit performance, because unique performance measures are more often leading and non-financial indicators, while common measures tend to be financial, lagging indicators. Furthermore, unique performance measures are also more likely to directly reflect a business unit's strategy. Therefore, insufficient attention paid to unique performance measures by managers basically defeats the main advantage of these systems, which is to provide a balanced, comprehensive set of leading and lagging indicators that together reflect the cause-and-effect assumptions of a business unit's strategy.

While the experimental participants in Lipe and Salterio (2000) were novices to the BSC, subsequent replication by Dilla and Steinbart (2005a) showed that knowledgeable decision-makers also suffered from the common measures bias (although to a smaller extent). Similarly, Libby *et al.* (2004) found that specific work experience in the accounting and finance fields reduced, but could not eliminate, managers' common measures bias. Overall, the common measures bias appears to be a prevalent and robust cognitive bias.

11.2.3 Consensus issues in performance evaluation

One indicator of judgement quality is the degree of agreement between different evaluators, or between evaluators and those who are being evaluated (Keeping and Levi, 2000; Ashton, 1985). The former is important because a low level of consensus among superiors when evaluating the performance of their subordinates is indicative of arbitrary judgements and may be seen by subordinates as unfair. A lack of perceived fairness in turn can lead to lower organisational commitment, reduced job satisfaction and higher turnover intentions (e.g., Sholihin and Pike, 2009; Parker and Kohlmeyer, 2005). Consensus between superiors and subordinates is also critical because disagreements between the two parties can result in reduced satisfaction with the evaluation process and lower performance (e.g., Heidemeier and Moser, 2009).

Dilla and Steinbart (2005b) examined judgement consensus between evaluators when they were asked to evaluate two managers based on their respective BSC. The researchers found that the overall level of consensus was relatively low: the average consensus score was 0.528 (where 0 means no consensus at all and 1 means maximum consensus). The consensus scores did not improve even when the evaluators were given supplementary information displays, such as comparative tables or comparative bar charts.

Wong-on-Wing *et al.* (2007), on the other hand, examined the level of performance evaluation consensus between top managers and divisional managers. In their experiment, participants were asked to evaluate the manager of a poorly performing business division. The researchers designed a scenario which suggested that the division's strategy, recommended by an independent consultant, was potentially problematic. As expected, they found that experimental participants who assumed the role of top management rated the division's performance more harshly than those participants who assumed the role of divisional managers, because taking a top management perspective prevented the participants from taking into account the quality of the strategy being executed. That is, Wong-on-Wing *et al.* (2007) showed that top managers were more likely to attribute the poor performance to the ability of the divisional manager, rather than the quality of the strategy itself. This result demonstrates the existence of an attribution bias – a well-established psychological condition which suggests that an observer frequently attributes negative performance to the abilities and dispositions of the observed, rather than situational factors such as the business environment (or in this case, the quality of the strategy). Such misattributions can be damaging, as they may result in the continuation of a bad strategy, or the incorrect promotions of or sanctions to subordinates.

11.2.4 Implications of the research findings

In summary, prior research has shown that managers need to be aware of a number of cognitive biases and challenges when using strategic performance measurement systems to evaluate the performance of business units and subordinates. First, while the categorisation scheme of a strategic performance measurement system is meant to highlight the strategic criticality of a diverse set of performance measures, it can also lower the decision impact of individual performance measures. This effect is not restricted to the BSC, but extends to any strategic performance measurement systems that categorise their performance measures. As long as these categories are meaningful to the managers, it will cause managers to seek relations between performance measures and in doing so they may suffer from the categorisation effect.

Second, research finds that managers frequently exhibit the common measures bias. To the extent that all performance measures contained on a BSC are informative and reflect a division/manager's performance, underweighting certain performance measures, and in particular unique, strategically linked performance measures, reduces the quality of the evaluation judgements. Further, if subordinates realise that unique, strategically linked performance measures and targets are not properly integrated into *ex post* performance evaluation judgements, then it is unlikely that they will use these performance measures for *ex-ante* day-to-day action planning (Lipe and Salterio, 2000).

Finally, past research also shows divergence in performance evaluation judgements between superiors, as well as between superiors and subordinates. Such performance evaluation discrepancies can have a negative impact on morale and the general effectiveness of strategic performance measurement systems.

The decision biases and issues outlined earlier are not only restricted to judgements made under controlled laboratory conditions; various field studies and interviews with managers show that these are also common in practice. For example, Ittner *et al.* (2003) studied a large financial services firm that had implemented a bonus plan linked to the BSC. They found that when superiors were evaluating the branch managers and making bonus allocation judgements, they tended to ignore strategically linked performance measures that were predictive of future financial performance, and instead focused mostly on common, outcome-based performance measures such as revenue and customer satisfaction. Worse still, the subjective evaluation process caused great concern among the branch managers, as the performance measurement system was seen as both arbitrary and unfair.

The underlying cause of these decision biases can be traced to humans' limited cognitive capacities. In 1956, George Miller put forth his legendary 'magic seven, plus or minus two' proposition: people are generally only able to process 5–9 pieces of information simultaneously (Miller, 1956). In light of Miller's premise, one can see strategic performance measurement systems which contain a large number of performance measures represent a particularly complex decision context for managers (a BSC, for example, would typically contain around 16–28 performance measures and targets). An important question is what managers can do to improve their performance evaluation judgements. Being aware of the issues outlined in the earlier sections would be a useful first step, but awareness is often not sufficient to overcome cognitive biases and challenges. A number of recent research studies aimed at 'de-biasing' performance evaluation judgements provide some useful recommendations. These recommendations follow two approaches: (1) assisting managers to increase their cognitive effort; and (2) improving task setting to reduce the required cognitive effort. These recommendations are presented in the next sections.

11.2.5 Assisting managers to increase their cognitive effort

Faced with a large number of performance measures, the cognitively overloaded managers are likely to selectively process only some of these performance measures. Thus one way to overcome cognitive biases is to encourage managers to utilise decision strategies that facilitate greater and more effective cognitive effort. For example, Roberts *et al.* (2004) showed that a disaggregated decision strategy is a useful way to encourage superiors to utilise both common and unique performance measures. A disaggregated decision strategy involves first evaluating performance for each performance measure separately; then aggregating the separate judgements using pre-assigned weights. This decision strategy simplifies the complex performance evaluation judgement by breaking the evaluation process into smaller decisions; while the final aggregation process can ensure that all measures are considered in the overall performance evaluation judgement. In doing so, the disaggregated decision strategy reduces the cognitive demand at each decision step while increasing the overall effort exerted by managers to reach a higher quality judgement.

An alternative to prescribing a decision strategy is to motivate managers to exert greater cognitive effort through the use of accountability. Libby *et al.* (2004) showed that the act of holding managers accountable for their decision processes when making performance management judgements resulted in a lower level of common measures bias. Accountability refers to 'the implicit or explicit expectation that one may be called to justify one's beliefs, feelings and actions to others' (Lerner and Tetlock, 1999, p. 255). Psychological research has shown that people will put in more effort when they are accountable for their actions because they want to avoid looking inept or foolish. It is important, however, to focus on *process* accountability (i.e., accountability for decision processes, such as explaining how the performance evaluation judgement is reached) rather than *outcome* accountability (i.e., to be held accountable for decision outcomes, such as the subsequent performance of a subordinate). Outcome accountability may worsen cognitive biases as it tends to create stress and narrow attention spans. Further, the superiors/evaluators must be informed of the requirement of process accountability *before* their evaluation judgements; otherwise, it will lead to self-justification and will be ineffective in encouraging greater cognitive effort when completing their decision tasks.

11.2.6 Improving information quality and the decision context

Another approach to improving managers' judgement processes is to reduce the cognitive effort required in these evaluation tasks by improving the quality of information provided and the decision context. Several studies have demonstrated the importance of communicating information on the organisation's strategy to managers to create a richer decision context that informs their subsequent performance evaluation judgements. Banker *et al.* (2004) found that providing superiors with detailed strategy information about different business units directed their focus away from generic performance measures and towards the more important, strategically linked performance measures. However, this information alone did not prevent common measures bias from appearing in their judgements. Humphreys and Trotman (2011) showed that common measures bias can be eliminated only when managers are provided with both strategy information and performance measures that are fully linked to the organisation's strategy. This combination of strategy information and strategically linked measures helps managers to identify each measure's strategic context, thereby reducing the cognitive complexity of the task. This resulted in a 'balanced' judgement where managers incorporated both common and unique measures for each division. Wong-on-Wing *et al.* (2007) found that requiring the superior first to assess the quality of a business unit's strategy 'primed' the superior to consider the quality of the strategy when s/he then evaluated a subordinate's performance; as a result, this reduced the divergence of evaluation scores between superiors and subordinates.

Libby *et al.* (2004) suggested that managers might place less weight on some performance measures on the BSC because they saw these performance measures as less accurate or reliable. Non-financial measures (which also tend to be strategically linked unique measures) are often seen by managers as 'soft measures' compared to the more reliable 'hard' financial data. Libby *et al.* (2004) subsequently demonstrated that asking a chartered accounting firm to provide assurance of the reliability and relevance of a company's performance information improved perceived data quality and encouraged managers to use all of the performance measures contained in their BSC.

11.3 Using strategic performance measurement systems to inform strategic decisions

While the BSC was first developed as a performance measurement tool, it has evolved into a more complete management tool which can assist organisations to implement and evaluate their strategic actions. As a result, in their subsequent publications, Kaplan and Norton (2001, 2004) articulate more fully the importance of understanding the cause-and-effect linkages between strategic objectives and measures. For example, employees who are better trained in quality management tools are expected to lower their company's process time, which in turn will shorten customer lead time and enhance on-time delivery; better customer experience then drives revenue growth and ultimately improves shareholder returns (Kaplan, 2009). The ability to capture such causal linkages on the BSC (and the accompanying strategic map) has become known as the second key feature of a strategic performance measurement system. More recently, behavioural management accounting researchers have begun to examine how this feature of strategic performance measurement systems helps inform managers' strategic choices. Their findings are outlined in this section.

11.3.1   Managerial cognitions and strategic choices

The evaluation of strategic options is arguably even more challenging than the evaluation of managerial performance, because making strategic choices usually requires an understanding of the relationships among performance information, interpreting business intelligence, and predicting how various strategic actions will turn out in the future. Central to these cognitive tasks is a manager's mental model – a mental structure that supports understanding, reasoning and prediction (Markman and Gentner, 2001). This mental structure enables managers to observe important information, interpret and make sense of what they noticed, and ultimately guides strategic choices (Bogner and Barr, 2000).

However, research from both psychology and business disciplines shows that managers often do not possess a mental structure sophisticated enough to understand complex relationships (Luft and Shields, 2010; Markman and Genter, 2001), especially when it comes to interpreting the causal linkages between performance information and strategic outcomes. Therefore explicating a company's business model in the strategic performance measurement system becomes critical in guiding managers towards making desirable strategic choices.

Recently, Tayler (2010) investigated how managers interpret performance data which provided mixed support for a strategy. In Tayler's (2010) experimental scenario, MBA participants assumed the role of a manager reviewing the performance at a restaurant belonging to a fictitious pizza chain. The restaurant had launched a new strategic initiative, but subsequent performance information showed that the strategic initiative had questionable success – an improvement in customer perspective performance did not result in improved financial returns.

According to Kaplan and Norton (2004), this should trigger a re-think of whether the new strategy was appropriate. Tayler (2010), however, found that only managers who were not involved in the initial selection of the strategic initiative recognised the meaning of the performance information; managers who chose the strategic initiative in the first place focused selectively on the improvement of customer perspective performance, and subsequently recommended rolling out the strategic initiative across the entire pizza chain. The decisions of these managers were attributed to the motivated reasoning bias – the tendency of individuals to interpret information in a way that supports their prior preferences (Kunda, 1990). In the same study, Tayler (2010) showed that the motivated reasoning bias of managers could be overcome by visually presenting the BSC as a causal chain, and involving managers in the process of selecting the performance measures contained on the restaurant's BSC.

In addition to interpreting the relationships between performance information, managers also need to recognise weak but potentially important strategic signals in their business environment, and use this information to make timely strategic decisions. Day and Schoemaker (2006) called this managers' 'peripheral vision'. Cheng and Humphreys (2012) showed that the structural properties of strategic performance measurement systems (in particular, the explication of casual linkages in a strategy map) have important impacts on managers' ability to recognise and use relevant strategic information in their business environment. They argued that a strategy map encourages managers to form a cognitive representation based on the strategic themes presented in the strategy map, while the scorecard component of the BSC encourages managers to construct a cognitive representation based on the four BSC categories. Cheng and Humphreys (2012) demonstrated that the strategy map-based cognitive representation, with its focus on cause-and-effect linkages between strategic objectives, was more useful than a BSC-based cognitive representation in assisting managers to interpret the strategic relevance of external business information (e.g., changes in customer preferences), and to use this information to evaluate a company's strategy.

The illustration of causal linkages also helps articulate the intangible benefits of capital investment decisions. Cheng and Humphreys (2010) found that the inclusion of a strategy map in a capital investment proposal significantly increased its chances of being approved, as well as directing the proposal reviewer's attention towards longer-term benefits of the investment project.

11.3.2 Summary, implications and recommendations

Recent research on the effect of strategic performance measurement systems on managers' strategic choices generally points to the importance of explicitly illustrating a company's strategy, in particular the cause-and-effect assumptions underlying its business model. This can be achieved by incorporating visual links between performance measures and strategic objectives on a BSC, providing narrative information about the cause-and-effect assumptions, and/or using a strategy map. In practice, however, many organisations do not have a validated strategic business model that can be incorporated in their strategic performance measurement systems. Evidence suggests that managers often think that the link between performance measures and drivers are self-evident, and few organisations tried to validate the cause-and-effect linkages in their models (Ittner and Larcker, 2003). The studies reviewed in the previous section highlight that developing and validating a company's strategy map is critical, because it influences the way in which managers interpret internal and external information. Kaplan (2009) goes a step further and recommends that organisations should aim to move away from the simplistic linear assumptions behind the cause-and-effect relationships inherent in a basic BSC, and start to incorporate a greater degree of complexities in their business models, such as estimating the magnitude and time delays between improvements in leading performance measures (e.g., cycle time) and improvements in lagging performance measure (e.g., percentage on-time delivery). This next step, however, would require significant investment in information technology and statistical modelling systems.

11.4 Concluding remarks

An important assumption underlying innovations in strategic performance measurement system design is that these systems help align managers' behaviours and decisions with organisation goals; but systems designers and users often fail to take into account the behavioural factors. Human decision-makers have limited cognitive processing powers, which makes them susceptible to a variety of biases and errors. Recent advances in neuroscience suggest that cognitive biases and errors commonly found in business-related decision scenarios may even be 'hard wired' into people's brains (Dickhaut *et al.*, 2010). For example, fMRI scans show increased activation in specific parts of the brains whenever people are processing and comparing numbers (Dehaene *et al.*, 2010), which suggests that people may have difficulties processing multi-dimensional numerical stimuli, such as performance measures that are quantified in different units (Dickhaut *et al.*, 2010). Furthermore, neuroscientists have found that the brain distinguishes between high-quality information and ambiguous information when processing stimuli; the latter leads to lower mental activation of the *intraparietal sulcus* located in the parietal lobe (Dickhaut *et al.*, 2009). If non-financial measures are interpreted as less reliable and more ambiguous, then it is not surprising that managers tend to focus more on financial-based, outcome measures than non-financial, leading measures.

This chapter reviews and summarises recent research in behavioural management accounting which examines how the design of strategic performance measurement systems influence managers' judgements and decisions. The body of research shows that when managers use these systems to evaluate managerial performance and to inform strategic choices, they often suffer from a variety of cognitive biases and challenges, which ultimately can overshadow the advantages associated with recent innovations in performance management. As a result, organisations need to carefully supplement the implementation of strategic performance measurement systems with 'behavioural strategies' that can counteract some of these biases.

References

Ashton, A. H. (1985). 'Does Consensus Imply Accuracy in Accounting Studies of Decision-making?', *The Accounting Review*, 60 (2), 173–85.

Banker, R. D., Chang, H. and Pizzini, M. J. (2004). 'The Balanced Scorecard: Judgmental Effects of Performance Measures Linked to Strategy', *The Accounting Review*, 79 (1), 1–12.

Bogner, W. and Barr, P. (2000). 'Making Sense in Hypercompetitive Environments: A Cognitive Explanation for the Persistence of High Velocity Competition', *Organization Science*, 11 (2), 212–26.

Chenhall, R. (2005). 'Integrative Strategic Performance Measurement Systems, Strategic Alignment of Manufacturing, Learning and Strategic outcomes: An Exploratory Study', *Accounting, Organizations and Society*, 30, 395–422.

Cheng, M. M. and Humphreys, K. A. (2010). 'The Effect of Causal Chain Illustration on Managers' Assessment of Perceived Strategic Contribution and Willingness to Approve A Capital Investment' (Working paper, University of New South Wales, Sydney, Australia).

Cheng, M. M. and Humphreys, K. A. (2012) 'The Differential Improvement Effects of the Strategy Map and the Scorecard Perspectives on Managers' Strategic Judgments'. *The Accounting Review* (forthcoming).

Day, G. and Schoemaker, P. (2006). *Peripheral Vision: Detecting the Weak Signals That Will Make or Break Your Company*, Harvard Business School Press, Boston, Massachusetts.

Dehaene, S., Piazza, M., Pinel, P. and Cohen, L. (2003). 'Three Parietal Circuits for Number Processing', *Cognitive Neuropsychology*, 20 (3/4/5/6), 487–506.

Dickhaut, J. W., Basu, S., McCabe, K. A. and Waymire, G. B. (2009). 'Supplement to Neuroaccounting: Consilience between the Biological Evolved Brain and Culturally Evolved Accounting Principles' (SSRN Working Paper http://papers.ssrn.com/sol3/papers.cfm?abstract_id=1517432).

Dickhaut, J. W., Basu, S., McCabe, K. A. and Waymire, G.B. (2010). 'Neuroaccounting: Consilience between the Biological Evolved Brain and Culturally Evolved Accounting Principles', *Accounting Horizons*, 24 (2), 221–5.

Dilla, W. N. and Steinbart, P. J. (2005a). 'Relative Weighting of Common and Unique Balanced Scorecard Measures by Knowledgeable Decision-makers', *Behavioral Research in Accounting*, 17, 43–53.

Dilla, W. N. and Steinbart, P. J. (2005b). 'The Effects of Alternative Supplementary Display Formats on Balanced Scorecard Judgments', *International of Accounting Information Systems*, 6, 159–76.

Dunk, A. S. (2001). 'Behavioural Research in Management Accounting: The Past, Present and Future', *Advances in Accounting Behavioural Research* 4, 25–45.

Heidemeier, H. and Moser, K. (2009). 'Self-other Agreement in Job Performance Ratings: A Meta-analytical Test of A Process Model', *Journal of Applied Psychology*, 94 (2), 353–70.

Humphreys, K. A. and Trotman, K. T. (2011) 'The Balanced Scorecard: The Effect of Strategy Information on Performance Evaluation Judgments, *Journal of Management Accounting Research* (forthcoming).

Ittner, C. D. and Larcker, D. F. (2003). 'Coming Up Short on Non-financial Performance Measurement', *Harvard Business Review*, November, 88–95.

Ittner, C. D., Larcker, D. F. and Meyer, M. W. (2003). 'Subjectivity and the Weighting of Performance Measures: Evidence from A Balanced Scorecard, *The Accounting Review*, 78 (3), 725–58.

Kaplan, R. S. (2009). 'Conceptual Foundations of the Balanced Scorecard' in Chapman, C. S., Hopwood, A. G. and Shields, M. D., *Handbook of Management Accounting Research*, Elsevier Ltd.

Kaplan, R. S. and Norton, D. P. (1996). *The Balanced Scorecard: Translating Strategy into Action*, Harvard Business School Press, Boston, MA.

Kaplan, R. S. and Norton, D. P. (2001). *The Strategy-Focused Organization: How Balanced Scorecard Companies Thrive in the New Business Environment*, Harvard Business School Press, Boston, MA.

Kaplan, R. S. and Norton, D. P. (2004). *Strategy Maps: Converting Intangible Assets into Tangible Outcomes,* Harvard Business School Press, Boston, MA.

Kaplan, S. E. and Wisner, P. S. (2009). 'The Judgmental Effects of Management Communications and A Fifth Balanced Scorecard Category on Performance Evaluation,' *Behavioural Research in Accounting*, 21 (2), 37–56.

Keeping, L. M. and Levy, P. E. (2000). 'Performance Appraisal Reactions: Measurement, Modeling and Method Bias', *Journal of Applied Psychology*, 85, 708–23.

Kunda, Z. (1990). 'The Case for Motivated Reasoning', *Psychological Bulletin*, 108 (3), 480–98.

Lerner, J. S. and Tetlock, P. E. (1999). 'Accounting for the Effects of Accountability', *Psychological Bulletin* 125 (2), 255.

Libby, T., Salterio, S. E. and Webb, A. (2004). 'The Balanced Scorecard: The Effects of Assurance and Process Accountability on Managerial Judgment', *The Accounting Review*, 79 (4), 1075–94.

Liedtka, S. L., Church, B. K. and Ray, M. R. (2008). 'Performance Variability, Ambiguity Intolerance and Balanced Scorecard-based Performance Assessments', *Behavioural Research in Accounting*, 20 (2), 73–88.

Lipe, M. G. and Salterio, S. E. (2000). 'The Balanced Scorecard: Judgmental Effects of Common and Unique Performance Measures,' *The Accounting Review*, 75 (3), 283–98.

Lipe, M. G. and Salterio, S. E. (2002). 'A Note on the Judgmental Effects of the Balanced Scorecard's Information Organization', *Accounting, Organizations and Society*, 27 (6), 531–40.

Lovallo, D. and Sibony, O. (2010). 'The Case for Behavioural Strategy', *McKinsey Quarterly Issue*, 2, 30–43.

Luft, J. and Shields, M. D. (2010). 'Psychology Models of Management Accounting', *SSRN Working Paper* http://papers.ssrn.com/sol3/papers.cfm?abstract_id=1564180).

Markman, A. and Gentner, D. (2001). 'Thinking', *Annual Review of Psychology*, 52, 223–47.

Miller, G. A. (1956). 'The Magical Number Seven, Plus or Minus Two: Some Limits On Our Capacity for Processing Information', *Psychological Review*, 101 (2), 343–52.

Otley, D. (1999). 'Performance Management: A Framework for Management Control Systems Research', *Management Accounting Research*, 10, 363–82.

Parker, R. J. and Kohlmeyer III, J. M. (2005). 'Organizational Justice and Turnover in Public Accounting Firms: A Research Note', *Accounting, Organizations and Society*, 30 (4), 357–69.

Rigby, D. and Bilodeau, B. (2009). *Management Tools and Trends 2009*, Bain & Company.

Roberts, M. L., Albright, T. L. and Hibbets, A. R. (2004). 'Debiasing Balanced Scorecard Evaluations', *Behavioural Research in Accounting*, 16, 75–88.

Sholihin, M. and Pike, R. (2009). 'Fairness in Performance Evaluations and its Behavioural Consequences', *Accounting and Business Research*, 39 (4), 397–413.

Slovic, P. and MacPhillamy, D. (1974). 'Dimensional Commensurability and Cue Utilization in Comparative Judgment', *Organizational Behaviour and Human Performance*, 11, 172–94.

Tayler, W. B. (2010). 'The Balanced Scorecard As A Strategy-evaluation Tool: The Effects of Implementation Involvement and A Causal-chain Focus', *The Accounting Review*, 85 (3), 1095–117.

Wailgum, T. (2009). 'To Hell With Business Intelligence: 40 Percent of Execs Trust Gut', CIO.com (12 January 2009) http://advice.cio.com/thomas_wailgum/to_hell_with_business_intelligence_40_percent_of_execs_trust_gut?page=0%2C1, accessed 22 February 2010.

Wong-On-Wing, B., Guo, L., Li, W. and Yang, D. (2007). 'Reducing Conflict in Balanced Scorecard Evaluation', *Accounting, Organizations and Society*, 32, 363–77.

12
Non-Financial Indicators and Strategic Management Accounting

Gregory Wegmann and Evelyne Poincelot

12.1 What do we mean by 'strategic management accounting'?

For Anthony (1965, p. 17), management control is 'the set of accounting and financial verification tools based on predefined objectives'; in other words, a verification planning process. The conventional approach to management accounting discloses a tension among the processes of strategic management, management control and operational control. Johnson and Kaplan (1987) explain that coordination between these processes is difficult to obtain. The Strategic Management Accounting (now SMA) stream is a concept and set of practices that tries to solve this difficulty of coordination. It emerged during the 1970s and has been developed since (Schendel and Hofer, 1979; Horovitz, 1979). There has been a growing amount of research on this subject since the mid-1980s. The impact of Johnson and Kaplan's 1987 work *Relevance Lost* on management accounting tools is significant.

In a firm, an SMA instrument exists when it can connect strategic decisions to operational decisions. Under the SMA concept, we bring together work that focuses on marketing aspects (Roslender and Hart, 2003) and work on strategic dimensions (Shank and Govindarajan, 1989). Simmonds (1981) and Bromwich (1990) suggest using qualitative and external measures with three dimensions of analysis: the products and customers (their level of satisfaction, for instance) dimension, the competitive (penetration level) and the environmental. Shank and Govindarajan analyse the concept of cost drivers as the central notion of the SMA approach considering that 'Understanding cost behavior means understanding the complex interplay of the set of "cost drivers" at work in any given situation' (Shank, 1989, p. 55).

The main reasons for implementing an SMA tool, according to the academic literature, lie in the evolution of the environment. This is described in successive stages: stable and predictable, unstable and difficult to anticipate, and finally turbulent and unpredictable.

As a consequence, scholars explain that management accounting tools must include external and leading non-financial indicators and integrate them into the company's drive. These indicators need to be articulated with traditional internal financial indicators. SMA also receives considerable attention due to the increasing complexity of the decision-making process. The concept has been deepened over the years (Wilson, 1995) even if 'there is still no agreed comprehensive conceptual framework for what SMA is' (Tomkins and Carr, 1996, p. 165).

12.2   The influence of strategic management accounting on European management accounting theories

In France, three SMA types have been specified (Teller, 1999, pp. 40–1; Wegmann, 2009).

- An SMA restrictive approach. In this context, management accounting is a tool to decline the strategy and to control it. This is a lagging approach to control that does not justify a deeper analysis of strategic cost drivers. A few indicators to observe the competitive environment and to test the customers' expectations seem enough. It is useless to question the organisational architecture. This type of SMA does not need to increase knowledge about the firm's processes.
- An SMA medium approach. In this context, management accounting is a tool to validate strategic hypotheses. This is a leading perspective of strategic control which requires deeper analysis of strategic hypotheses. In fact, they are key success drivers that management accounting sets along the firm's value chain.
- An SMA-extended approach. In this context, management accounting is a fundamental part of the strategy design and leadership. This approach requires three conditions:
  1. *The strategy design and leadership must be strongly connected.*
  2. *The management control system must be interactive, in a similar way to the concept of interactive control designed by Simons (1995).* According to the strategic situation and the environmental uncertainties, the author explains that managers choose some management accounting tools that become interactive control ones, because they use them to articulate the strategic and

operational management processes and to put in evidence new strategic opportunities.

3. *The new strategies must emerge step by step.*

The SMA restrictive version fits more with a contractual type of management. It suggests a disciplinary approach (Agency and Transaction Costs theories) where the objectives of management accounting are (Jensen and Meckling, 1992; Brickley *et al.*, 1997):

- To reduce conflicts and provide control,
- To tie the strategy to the resources allocation,
- And to facilitate the firm's internal coherence.

The SMA medium and extended versions imply a more participative approach for employees' activities concerning the management accounting processes. From a theoretical point of view, this process refers to a knowledge-based approach of management, as developed by Argyris and Schön (1978) with their Organisational Learning Theory. In this context, value creation is the result of an increase in resources (Resource-based View approach; Penrose, 1959) and competencies (Core-Competencies theory; Hamel and Prahalad, 1990). Several French empirical studies (Bollecker, 2007) describe this kind of situation, in which management accountants are just counsellors of a process and employees are the designers of management accounting tools.

12.3   The influence of strategic management accounting on European management accounting tools

In Europe, since the SMA stream development, the majority of management accounting tools have gained a strategic dimension. The most famous in Europe are:

- Activity-Based Costing and Activity-Based Management (Cooper and Kaplan, 1999),
- Non financial measures and the Balanced Scorecard (Kaplan and Norton, 1996, 2004, 2006),
- The Beyond Budgeting Model (Hope and Fraser, 1999) or the Time-Driven ABC (Kaplan and Anderson, 2004).

All these managerial information tools originate from the USA and have a great impact on European academics and managers. This chapter examines the Balanced Scorecard and non-financial indicators. Hoffjan and Wömpener (2006, p. 248) have shown that several SMA tools are well-developed in the European firms (customer profitability analysis, target costing, ABC method, future costs and non-financial measures). In the same way, Cinquini and Tenucci (2006) have presented the results of an empirical study of medium-size Italian firms. They describe the 14 most-used SMA tools and explain that most of them integrate non-financial marketing and commercial measures (p. 14), sometimes inside a Balanced Scorecard.

The Balanced Scorecard (Kaplan and Norton, 1996, 2004, 2006) is a global managerial information system that intends to articulate a company's strategies with its operational control (see Figure 12.1). It groups together several financial and non-financial indicators that describe a company's strategy (leading indicators) and its performance (lagging indicators) (see Figure 12.2). There are many Executive Information Systems (EIS) concerning Management Accounting. For instance, in 2005 Microsoft developed the 'Microsoft Office Business Scorecard Manager'. Now, around one American company in two uses the Balanced Scorecard. A European survey (Jouenne *et al.*, 2005) showed that 41 per cent of the European companies questioned use a Balanced Scorecard.

All these tools help to correlate lagging indicators with leading ones so that a statistical link may be established between strategic management and control management.

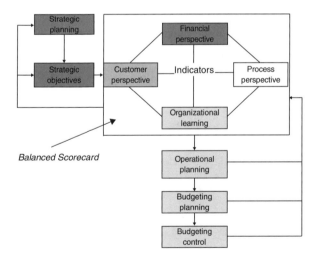

Figure 12.1 The Balanced Scorecard: a managerial information system tool

In many regards, the Balanced Scorecard has the characteristics of a SMA instrument:

- it deals with one of the organisation's process approaches;
- strategic and financial analyses are considered equally;
- the Balanced Scorecard aims to be a global corporate performance analysis tool (financial, customer, processes and innovation, and organisational learning analyses are combined); and more importantly,
- the goal of the non-financial indicators is to combine the planning and control decisions.

Technically, the purpose of the Balanced Scorecard is to establish a causal chain between the indicators. Kaplan and Norton (2004) call this the 'Strategy Map'. We can distinguish two types of indicators. The lagging indicators are historical and express past results. The leading indicators express the objectives of the firm and are prospective.

Figure 12.2 presents an extract from the Strategy Map of a French insurance company called 'MAIF'. The arrows show some possible correlations between several indicators: two leading indicators ('customer satisfaction index' and 'average waiting time when a customer phones') and three lagging ones ('market share growth', 'return on sales rate' and 'return on investment rate'). We can assume that when the 'average phoning waiting time' decreases the 'customer satisfaction index' will

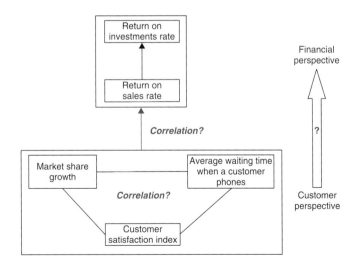

Figure 12.2   Extract from the strategy map of a French insurance company

increase, followed by 'market share'. If the correlations are validated, then the Strategy Map demonstrates a link between the operational management's objectives and the strategic ones.

Kaplan and Norton developed the Balanced Scorecard from a Contractual point of view. It is discipline-centred and hierarchically constructed, and the metrics insist on respecting the objectives. A traditional approach to formulating strategy (SWOT and Porter's models) is used and value creation is fundamentally based on shareholder satisfaction.

In Northern Europe, some very specific Balanced Scorecards called 'Intellectual Capital Scorecards' (Roos *et al.*, 1997) can be observed. They represent another type of Balanced Scorecard. The Navigator, conceived by the Swedish insurance company Skandia, is the most widely known Intellectual Capital Scorecard (Edvinsson and Malone, 1997). Although these instruments derive from the Balanced Scorecard, they have been conceived in the framework of the knowledge-based theories. They are more participative and the metrics insist on the development of knowledge and competencies. The classical strategic process is reversed (Grant, 1991, p. 116). First, it consists in carrying out an internal analysis to detect the strategic assets; then it measures and characterises the firm's skills and resources. In the end, the method suggests that an external analysis complete the process, including the identified resources and skills. Mintzberg and Waters (1985) name this trend 'the process strategy'. They explain (1985, p. 270) how the formulation originates within the processes. They are both deliberate and emergent.

12.4   Conclusion

In European countries, the evolution of managerial accounting information systems is influenced by Anglo-Saxon trends. In the recent years, the most famous have been the Balanced Scorecard and non-financial indicators. With this research, we analyse how French managers feel about it. Do they see the Balanced Scorecard as just a new trend or as a truly useful managerial information system?

In our investigation (see Poincelot and Wegmann, 2008, for the results), we demonstrate that there is a correlation between the choice of non-financial indicators and the motives behind them. As such, we demonstrate that the managers associate non-financial indicators with strategic objectives, which is the theoretical basis of the Balanced Scorecard. So we conclude that French managers think that non-financial indicators and the Balanced Scorecard are useful tools with which to drive their company.

References

Anthony, R. N. (1965). *Planning and Control Systems: A Framework for Analysis*, Harvard University Press, Cambridge.

Argyris, C. and Schön, D. (1978). *Organizational Learning: A Theory of Action Perspective*, Addison-Wesley, Reading Mass.

Bollecker, M. (2007). 'La Recherche sur les Contrôleurs de Gestion : état de L'art et Perspectives [Research on Management Accountants: State of the Art and Perspectives]', *Comptabilité Contrôle Audit*, 13 (1), 87–106.

Brickley, J. A., Clifford, W. S. Jr and Zimmerman, J. L. (1997). *Managerial Economics and Organizational Architecture*, Irwin, Chicago.

Bromwich, M. (1990). 'The Case for Strategic Management Accounting: The Role of Accounting Information for Strategy in Competitive Markets, *Accounting, Organizations and Society*, 15 (1–2), 127–46.

Cinquini, L. and Tenucci, A. (2006). 'Exploring the Relationship between Strategy and Strategic Management Accounting Techniques', Working Paper Series, Social Science Research Network.

Cooper, R. and Kaplan, R. S. (1999). *The Design of Cost Management Systems*, Prentice Hall, New Jersey.

Edvinsson, L. and Malone, M. S. (1997). *Intellectual Capital, Realizing Your Company's True Value by Finding Its Hidden Brainpower*, HarperBusiness, New York.

Grant, R. (1991). 'The Resource-Based Theory of Competitive Advantage: Implications for Strategy Formulation', *California Management Review*, 33 (3), 114–35.

Hamel, G. and Prahalad, C. K. (1990). 'The Core Competence of the Corporation', *Harvard Business Review*, 68 (3), 79–92.

Hoffjan, A. and Wömpener, A. (2006). 'Comparative Analysis of Strategic Management Accounting in German – and English – Language General Management Accounting Textbooks', *Schmalenbach Business Review*, 58, 234–58.

Hope, J. and Fraser, R. (1999). *The BBRT Guide to Managing Without Budgets*, Cam I Beyond Budgeting Round Table, V3.01, 8, December.

Jensen, M. C. and Meckling, W. H. (1992). 'Specific and General Knowledge, and Organisational Structure', in Werin, L. and Wijkander, H. (eds.), *Contract Economics*, Blackwell, Oxford, 251–74.

Johnson, T. H. and Kaplan, R. S. (1987). *Relevance Lost: The Rise and Fall of Management Accounting*, Harvard Business School Press, Boston.

Jouenne, L. *et al.* (2005). *Du Reporting au Pilotage : L'entreprise en alerte [From the Reporting to the Driving: The Company in Alert]*, Report, Unilog Management and IDC, Paris.

Kaplan, R. S. and Anderson, S. R. (2004). 'Time-Driven Activity Based Costing', *Harvard Business Review*, 82 (11), 131–8.

Kaplan, R. S. and Norton, D. P. (1996). *The Balanced Scorecard: Translating Strategy into Actions*, Harvard Business School Press, Boston.

Kaplan, R. S. and Norton, D. P. (2004). *Strategy Maps: Converting Intangible Assets into Tangible Outcomes*, Harvard Business School Press, Boston.

Kaplan, R. S. and Norton, D. P. (2006). *Alignment: Using the Balanced Scorecard to Create Corporate Synergies*, Harvard Business School Press, Boston.

Malhotra, N. (2004). *Etudes Marketing Avec SPSS [Marketing Studies with SPSS]*, 4th edition, Pearson Education France, Paris.

Mintzberg, H. and Waters, J.A. (1985). 'Of Strategies, Deliberate and Emergent', *Strategic Management Journal*, 6 (3), 257–72.

Penrose, E. (1959). *The Theory of the Growth of the Firm*, Oxford University Press, UK.

Poincelot, E. and Wegmann, G. (2008). 'Les motivations des managers utilisant des critères non financiers: une analyse empirique [What are the Motives of the Managers Using Non-Financial Indicators? An Empirical Study]', *Comptabilité Contrôle Audit*, 14 (1), 69–92. (for the English version: http://ideas.repec.org/p/dij/wpfarg/1060905.html).

Roos, J., Roos, G., Dragonetti, N. and Edvinsson, L. (1997). *Intellectual Capital: Navigating the Business Landscape*, MacMillan Business, England.

Roslender, R. and Hart, S. J. (2003). 'In Search of Strategic Management Accounting: Theoretical and Field Study Perspectives', *Management Accounting Research*, 14 (3), 255–79.

Schendel, D. E. and Hofer, C. W. (1979). *Strategic Management: A New View of Business Policy and Planning*, Little, Brown and Company, Boston.

Shank, J. K. (1989). 'Strategic Cost Management: New Wine or Just New Bottles?' *Journal of Management Accounting Research*, 1, Fall, 47–65.

Shank, J. and Govindarajan, V. (1989). *Strategic Cost Analysis: The Evolution from Managerial to Strategic Accounting*, Burn Ridge Inc, Illinois.

Simmonds, J. (1981). 'Strategic Management Accounting', *Management Accounting*, 59 (4), 26–9.

Simons, R. L. (1995). *Levers of Control*, Harvard Business School Press, Boston.

Teller, R. (1999). *Le contrôle de gestion – Pour un pilotage intégrant stratégie et finance [Management accounting: for a driving which integrates strategy and finance]*, Paris: Editions Management et Société.

Tomkins, C. and Carr, C. (eds.) (1996). 'Special Issue on Strategic Management Accounting', *Management Accounting Research*, 7 (2), 165–7.

Wegmann, G. (2009). 'The Activity-based Costing Method: Development and Applications', *The IUP Journal of Accounting Research and Audit Practices*, 8 (1), 7–22.

Wilson, R. M. (1995). 'Strategic Management Accounting', in Ashton, D. *et al.* (eds.), *Issues in Management Accounting*, 2nd edn, Prentice Hall, New York.

Zimmerman, J. L. (1997). *Accounting for Decision Making and Control*, 2nd edn, Irwin Mc Graw-Hill, Chicago.

13
Management Tools for Evaluating Performance and Value Creation in Sports Organisations

Angel Barajas

13.1 Introduction

Sport has the capacity to mobilise and bring together people at all levels. At the same time, sport is a fundamental pillar of a country's education system and essential for keeping its citizens healthy. More time and resources are being spent per capita on sporting activities. Many organisations use sport as a medium for increasing or reinforcing their productivity and innovation due to the positive effects of sport and recreational activities at work and on social behaviour, as well as on physical and mental health.

This boom in interest has increased the wealth of the leisure and sporting sectors of many countries, and this is underlined by the report of the European Council of Helsinki, where it is estimated that the number of direct or indirect employment positions created by sport increased by some 60 per cent in the 1990s (COM, 1999). Sport can be considered as a driver for job creation.

Taken together, these features mean that sport may be considered as a determining element in contemporary society to such an extent that it appears to be fundamentally integrated in the social and economic policies of the majority of developed countries' constitutions.

Some general characteristics of sport are as follows:

- The practice of sport by citizens as a spontaneous, selfless and playful activity, or towards educational or healthy ends.
- Sporting activity may be organised through association structures.
- Sporting events may serve as group phenomena for the masses, and are increasingly professionalised and commercialised.

It is perhaps unnecessary to remark that the important differences between these characteristics mean that each one requires specific treatment in each and every stage of development or planning, despite all forming part of the same sporting activity.

Nevertheless, in summary, we can conclude that there are three main 'commandments' for public administration of sporting matters:

- Promotion of the practice of sport and the structuring of how it functions.
- Appreciation and promotion of the sporting activity organised through association structures.
- Regulation of sporting events, which are increasingly consolidated as commercial, professional activities.

These three areas of sporting activity and their increasing complexity make it necessary to have tools or instruments available that allow the various governing agents to proceed with their task in a legitimate way, and to avoid, as far as possible, subjective considerations in decision-making. Many organisations related to sport are not structured as companies and are not obliged to present annual company accounts. This is not, however, an obstacle that prevents them from pursuing their activities with certain economic criteria.

Finally, regarding the objectives of sport investment, it is useful to establish a separation between direct objectives and those that may be considered indirect but which are increasingly acquiring more importance in today's society (promoting social integration, reducing drug addiction etc.). It is at this point of establishing objectives, direct and indirect, that the principal problem arises of how to evaluate them. For this reason, it is necessary to have the correct tools in order to measure the degree to which these objectives have been achieved.

It is in this context, and bearing in mind the documents of the AECA (1998, 2000), there is a need for evaluating the achievements of the social objectives that public administrations set when investing in sport. This leads to a search for control elements that can facilitate the pursuit and attainment of public objectives when administering costs in sport.

The next section explains how some management tools have been used for evaluating public initiatives mainly related to sport, and introduces best practices in management through a case study. Then, we explain the idea of linking the strategy map and Balanced Scorecard and how this can be adapted. Finally, we focus on the performance indicators. The chapter finishes with a summary.

13.2   Management tools for evaluating public initiatives

Throughout the process of programming and planning, it is necessary to have some type of indicator to evaluate and monitor the degree to which the set objectives are being met. Therefore the availability of such indicators is essential in both the private and public arenas.

The day-to-day business of any organisation is characterised by undertaking a growing number of activities with increasingly few economic resources. Therefore an evaluation of these initiatives is essential, designed to rationalise these few resources and apply them correctly through mechanisms that permit the measuring of results and, therefore, their improvement. In this sense, strategic maps, the Balanced Scorecard and performance indicators can be considered adequate instruments in the completion of these types of tasks. Therefore we propose an advance in the management of sport organisations through the adaptation of mechanisms considering the specific features of those particular organisations.

From the perspective of public investments in sports, the aim is to achieve adequate administration of the resources within the control of the public sector as a determining factor in satisfying the collective needs of citizens, and to determine the degree to which the objectives have been met (Prado and Garcia, 2004). Specifically, there is a clear need for an evaluation of public services, based on the established objectives.

In this area, among the first proposals were the GASB Indicators (Governmental Accounting Standards Board), for the preparation of annual management reports by boroughs in the USA, and the SEA Indicators (Service Efforts and Accomplishments) used by the ICMA (International City/County Management Association) in the continuous process of improvement in local government.

Similarly, in the UK, the Audit Commission set out in 1991 a series of indicators to evaluate civic management. As a result of these efforts, 2000 saw the publication of a report which, in light of the difficulties detected, stressed the usefulness of focusing on a series of key objectives, on the basis of which it is essential to frame the indicators towards operational levels (Audit Commission, 2000).

Other analogous experiences were those undertaken in Australia by the Steering Committee, an entity charged with gathering and analysing the management indicators of Australian public administrations and publishing them annually in the Report on Government Services; and the Canadian Comprehensive Auditing Foundation (2002) which publishes a similar report.

It is noteworthy to remark on the interesting study undertaken by the County Council of Barcelona on the Indicators of Civic Service Management, which started in 1983 and continues today with success.

Concentrating specifically on the application of a Balanced Scorecard in the public arena as a tool that, emulating the private sector, allows the measurement of performance, we uncover a growing reality in developed countries. In fact, it is already possible to find references in the literature that record practical experiences. Specifically, Kloot and Martin (2000) analysed the performance measurement systems in the Australian administration using the four dimensions of the Balanced Scorecard, while Cavalluzo and Ittner (2004) performed a similar analysis in Europe.

Of all the experiences in the public context, it is probably in the health sector that most initiatives can be found – see, for example, Forgione (1997), Pink (2001) or Voelker *et al.* (2001). Similarly, there are various initiatives using a Balanced Scorecard as a management system in certain local authorities. For example, this tool was implemented in Charlotte, North Carolina (Eagle, 2004) and Brisbane, Australia (Willett, 2003).

13.3 Best practices in sports organisations

Investment in sporting activities has the same needs as those of any other public or private investment. These needs present specific characteristics that appear at the time when the objectives and measurement tools for that particular activity are established.

Any organisation should know exactly what its mission is and what it would like to be in coming years. Once the organisation's mission and vision are clear it is time to define the strategy that will follow. The strategy will be a consequence of the mission and the analysis of the strengths, weaknesses, opportunities and threats (SWOT) faced by the organisation. Then, the mission has to be developed into outcomes with their own objectives, taking into account the programmes, areas and agents that will be involved in them. Each outcome should be designed with key performance indicators to measure whether its goals have been achieved.

On the other hand, the strategic plan should include a monitoring process considering the expected outcome, the outcome indicator, the data source and a reporting plan (with timing and models). Moreover, a benchmark programme to compare the results from other organisations or within the same organisation among different periods or areas would be convenient.

This process may be given shape through a strategy map, a Balanced Scorecard and a different matrix of key performance indicators, although no single method works best. Each organisation has to decide how it is going to design and work with these or other tools.

Indeed, when talking about public investments, the tracking and evaluation of public structural operations are currently a legal requirement. Nevertheless, the method of achieving these tasks depends on the nature and content of the operation in question, while the final objective is to determine the degree of effectiveness of the operation's execution and the resources used, through indicators defined at an appropriate level.

Independently of the chosen indicators, they should permit the treatment of five fundamental aspects to consider at the time of investing in the sporting sector. The parameters to analyse are the following: pertinence, efficacy, efficiency, utility and durability. **Pertinence** is the opportunity or convenience of carrying out a foreseen action; that is to say, whether or not it is appropriate. Regarding efficacy and efficiency, both are concerned with the ability to reach those planned objectives with the investment available. The difference between them lies in the fact that **efficacy** is about the fulfilment (or not) of objectives, while **efficiency** focuses more on the optimisation of the available resources (including time). **Utility** refers to the advantage or convenience gained by the investment, while **durability** brings the perspective of the duration or permanence in the mid- or long term.

13.3.1   Best practices in sport: the Sport England model

The Sport England Strategy 2008–2011(Sport England, 2008) offers a useful case study demonstrating good practice for sport management in England. This document is used as a reference. As a previous step, Sport England set the referential framework from the government targets relevant to Sport England. According to Appendix A of the quoted document, these are to:

- increase the percentage of adults who participate in culture or sport and active recreation (at national, departmental and local levels),
- increase participation in sport and active recreation among 2 million people – of which 1 million will be via sport,
- deliver a successful Olympic Games and Paralympic Games and get more children and young people taking part in high-quality physical education and sport.

The government established those targets because it considers that sport plays a major role in achieving social and economic benefits.

Once the context is clear, the organisation may study the challenges it has to face and can define its mission. Sport England identifies its mission as 'Creation of A World-Leading Community Sports System' which will ensure that:

(a) a growing number of people practise sport,
(b) the early identification of talented people in order to progress to elite level, and
(c) everyone who plays sport has a good experience.

This mission is in line with the shared goal of the Government and National Governing Bodies (NGBs) of 'maximising English sporting success in all its forms' but 'overall creating a vibrant sporting culture in England'.

The mission and general goal will not be useful if the agents involved in the programme are not clear. So, the Sport England document defines who is going to develop the strategy, in this case the Youth Sport Trust, UK Sports and the NGBs. The role of each agent has to be visibly demarcated in order to follow the outcomes.

The strategy includes a benchmark with the UK Sport's Mission 2012 and monitoring is contemplated that compares performance against outcomes. There is a clear set of measurable achievements to pursue and deliver. Point 21 of the document states that Sport England is committed to deliver:

- 1 million people doing more sport by 2012–13.
- A reduction in post-16 drop-off in at least five sports by 25 per cent by 2012–13.
- A quantifiable increase in satisfaction.
- Improved talent development systems in at least 25 sports.
- A major contribution to the delivery of the Five Hour Sport Offer.

It is worth remarking that these achievements have some relevant characteristics. They are general because they are related to the global strategy of Sport England. They are related to the challenges that the organisation understands that community sport is facing, namely increasing participation in sport, bringing down the drop-off age (to age 16) and developing talent. They are measurable. Even in more vague cases, the document specifies that they should develop a new satisfaction baseline from which active people will ascertain their satisfaction with the quality of their experience.

Strategy has to become reality. It implies a plan of action. This plan should be linked to strategy and should develop programmes that allow the organisation to reach its goals and mission. Each programme will have areas of expected results defined by individual performance measurements. Defining the priority areas and the agents involved is also relevant.

In Sport England's case, they defined three key outcomes linked with the challenges previously quoted and developed these with their correspondent key performance measurements. The first outcome is excellence, related to talent; the second is sustainability, linked with avoiding drop-off; and the third is growth, corresponding to increased participation.

Each outcome is then attributed to the defined priority areas with its specific performance measures. The measures have to fit with the nature of the expected results. For example, the Efficiency Programme has to achieve the performance measure of an agreed reduction in operating costs.

The next step is the development of each programme – related to the three outcomes in this case – with the way in which they are expected to be carried out and the key performance indicators. Now, logically, the indicators should be more specific and less general, but easily measurable. Some programmes will need more detailed KPIs.

With regard to funding, it may be useful to determine the distribution among the different programmes and actions in order to follow up on the degree of financial success. Ratios linking cost (or investments) and results (degree of realisation) can be created.

Finally, the strategy plan would include the monitoring schedule, which should consider the outcomes, their indicators, the data source (surveys or other sources), and how, when and whom to report to.

13.3.2   Strategy map linked to balanced scorecard: soccer club proposition

In introducing best practices for sports organisation management, an important step forward would be to work with the Balanced Scorecard (BSC). Originally proposed by Kaplan and Norton (1996), it represents a tool that translates the mission and vision of a particular organisation into a wide collection of metrics and indicators that subsequently offer the frame for controlling and implementing the strategy.

The BSC should include the different perspectives (traditionally four: financial, customer, internal management and learning and growth, but each organisation should group in what it considers high-level strategic areas).

How a strategic map may be related to a BSC is demonstrated using the case of a soccer club. Figure 13.1 will be the reference for this section. It has been built taking into account the paper by Urrutia *et al.* (2006) and adapted to the needs of this chapter.

Strategy mapping is a method to turn the complex strategic plan into a roadmap for the plan's successful execution. The strategy map is a simple and visual representation of key elements in the strategic plan. It helps to group the organisation's highest-level objectives by areas, or 'perspectives'. Cause-and-effect relationships included on it contribute to improve the use of the BSC and help to execute the strategy effectively. The map could also include the objectives for the desired outcomes (we are not going to introduce them in the case study for clarity reasons).

This strategy map has been built taking into account the traditional perspectives in BSC. Each perspective may be identified with a different shade of grey in the figure. First, at the top of the map, the mission and vision of the club appears. So, the board of this club considers that it should be the best club in the world. This general objective is the key to designing the organisation's whole strategy. All the perspectives, which include the different areas, should point to the execution of that mission.

In summary, this affirms that the club will be the best if it gets financial stability after creating a strong brand and having sporting success. The advantage of this map is that it shows how the different elements need to work to realise the organisation's vision.

We can see that improving the scouting system of the club (inside the internal management perspective), for example, will drive the development of talent at the grassroots (learning and growth perspective), which will help to create a more competitive team and achieve a better sporting performance, while reducing costs (financial perspective).

Recruiting the best players and coaches may be a fundamental pillar in the internal management perspective. It will create value because it helps to improve sporting performance throughout, creating a competitive team. Even failing in that purpose, it would be useful in attracting supporters and interest from broadcasting corporations, as well as promoting the club's international presence (customer perspective). All these items will be drivers for creating a powerful brand which will contribute to increased revenues (financial perspective) and at the same time reinforce the club's position to become 'the best in the world'.

It is worth noting that European soccer clubs have certain specific features that influence the financial sphere. Some clubs still remain

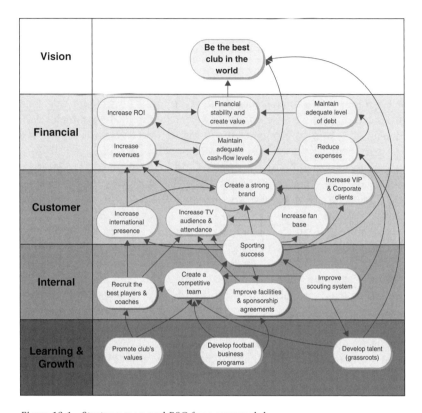

Figure 13.1   Strategy map and BSC for a soccer club

as members' clubs, which means that profits and returns are not so relevant. Sloane (1971) states that in England, instead of maximising profit, clubs maximise utility. Along those lines, Morrow (1999) similarly reasons that the objective for a soccer club is to get the best sporting performance instead of just fulfilling some financial restrictions. It implies that perhaps increasing return on investment or creating economic value to shareholders will not be an objective for many soccer clubs. Financial stability and keeping the right level of debt would become more relevant.

To conclude this section, it is worth noting the idea of linking the strategy map to the BSC as it helps to make it a more operative tool. In the following sections, the BSC will be applied to public investments in sport and sports organisations and expounded in greater detail.

13.3.3　Balanced Scorecard adaptation to public investment in sport

The Balanced Scorecard, when adapted to the specific circumstances of public investment, is a useful tool that provides a combined overview of the performance of public investment or of a public entity running sports facilities or events.

Figure 13.2 captures the basic structure of the Balanced Scorecard along with the modifications necessary for its use by public entities or for the evaluation of investment made by public institutions in sport. It should be highlighted that the main modification necessary can be found within the Financial Perspective box, given that performance for shareholders must be replaced by a focus on the analysis of the performance of the public funds employed in the sports initiative. Indeed, it is the taxpayers who experience a level of satisfaction from the resources they contribute to public authorities for spending, in this case, on sport.

Rodríguez *et al.* (2006) proposed a more specific approach to the financial perspective. They suggested that the Granada Municipal Agency Body of Sports set increased financial stability and balance as their financial objective. Logically, typical criteria used by companies, such as an increase in financial performance, become redundant in this area.

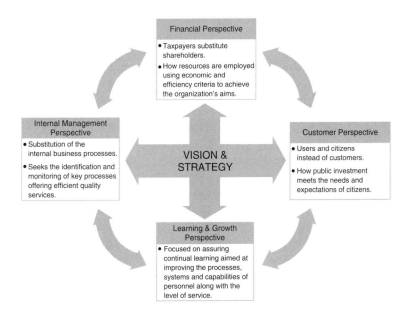

Figure 13.2　Adaptation of the Balanced Scorecard to public investment

In terms of the customer perspective, our model is very similar to a company's attitude towards its customers. However, public investment in sport should also consider those who benefit from the services, not from a corporate perspective, but rather from one of helping citizens. As such, it becomes necessary to think more in terms of users, instead of customers. Moreover, the potential satisfaction of citizens who do not make use of the facilities or participate in events must be considered as well. Rodríguez *et al.* (2006) propose the creation of a high-quality sports service image and an increase in customer base as the strategic objectives from this perspective. We believe this falls short, since it fails to consider the benefit that investment in sport supposes for the population in general.

The internal business processes perspective is replaced by an internal management perspective which runs parallel to the way companies work. It is aimed at identifying the key processes through which public money spent on sport is translated into high-quality, efficient services. Clearly, it is not enough merely to identify these processes; we must then go on to monitor them in order to achieve the desired results.

One point which may be considered key for internal management is better coordination of sports activities promoted by the public authorities, as well as cooperation with other institutions organising sports competitions. An example of how this could be done would be designing an events calendar aimed at increasing the use of the sports facilities.

Finally, the learning and growth perspective is very similar to that found in the Balanced Scorecard of a company. One of the key aspects is the continual improvement in employee training, not only in technical areas but also in terms of economic efficiency.

13.3.4   Balanced Scorecard adaptation to sports organisations

The Balanced Scorecard is more a concept than a tool. It means that it can and should be adapted to each particular organisation. The specific components included in its design should help to ensure that the Balanced Scorecard is essentially tied to the organisation's critical strategic needs. We have already done this in the preceding section considering public investments in sport. In this section, we propose a particular adaptation for sport clubs considering their key business elements. We also show a step forward in the practices of managerial accounting. The Balanced Scorecard is not only a way of transforming the strategic plan into a real tool for managing the organisation on a daily basis. It helps planners identify what should be done, who should do it, which would be the objectives to reach and how to measure the performance.

It enables executives to execute their strategies and have a clear idea of the success.

Figure 13.3 shows an example of how a Balanced Scorecard can be adapted to a sport club. It has been developed from the proposition of Urrutia *et al.* (2006). We want to remark here on how the different perspectives are related to the mission directly or indirectly. They may also have relationships between them. Moreover, it is important that each perspective has to answer a specific question, which is the reason for including that perspective. As supporters are a key element for a professional sport club, it would be convenient to introduce this perspective in the BSC. The organisation would then know how to reach supporters in order to achieve its mission. This is the question driving this perspective. Then, defining the BSC, it is also necessary to establish which will be the key areas in that perspective in order to demonstrate to the supporters the way that the club could develop its mission (for example, becoming the best soccer club in the world).

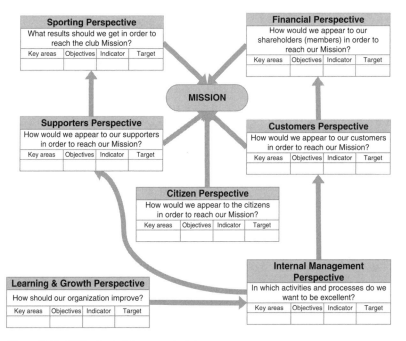

Figure 13.3 BSC adapted to a sport club

The key areas would have clear objectives to develop. It should be defined with a programme of activities in order to achieve it. Each objective needs a target to reach. Finally, the system would be worthless if it is not measurable. So, from the start, the BSC needs to establish clearly the indicators that the club is going to use for monitoring performance.

If the BSC is designed only for top-level management it will not drive results. A framework of linked BSC organised in a cascade from top to bottom and across the organisation will be a really helpful tool of managerial accounting. With this conception, the managers will have a clear idea of how objectives and measures affect all the areas of the organization, horizontally and vertically. So with clear objectives and the right indicators compared with the target, managers will easily identify problems when they can still be addressed.

13.3.5   Developing performance indicators

Performance indicators are key elements in the context of BSC and best practices in organisations. For that reason, we concentrate our attention on them in the present section.

When an organisation faces the task of developing an adequate set of performance indicators, it needs to establish which aspects it needs those indicators to focus on and which factors need to be measured. The indicators must be sufficient at all levels, bearing in mind the key objectives and evaluating whether they are achieved. They need to be oriented towards evaluating the factors that really indicate the performance obtained in accordance with the proposed targets and objectives. Furthermore, it is vital to obtain a balanced set of indicators that truly reflect the performance of the activity, rather than an endless set of indicators that provide no clear idea.

The performance dimensions to measure can provide an appropriate selection of indicators. Those dimensions, and the elements to consider in order to be able to determine the dimensions, are summarised in Figure 13.4. Following the Audit Commission (2000), we can affirm that the dimensions to consider are economy, efficiency and effectiveness, as well as the cost of that effectiveness. The elements necessary to obtain them are the cost or necessary investment, the human and material resources employed, the products or services obtained, the global result of the activity, and the value that it is expected to achieve.

The indicators that analyse the **economic** nature of investment in sport will measure whether the best quality material and human resources have been obtained in the greatest quantity and at the lowest cost possible,

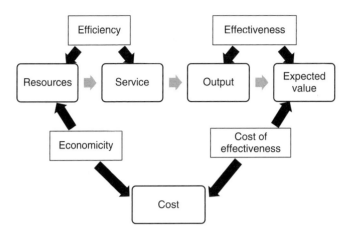

Figure 13.4 Elements to consider in performance analysis

or, if given a fixed cost budget, whether the best resources have been obtained; for example, whether the construction of a sports hall has been achieved at the lowest possible cost while still meeting certain minimum quality requirements. **Efficiency** measures the achievement of the maximum service or quantity of product for the set of resources available for this end. This type of indicator could be, for example, the cost per user of a sporting facility or the number of employees per user. The **effectiveness** measures the degree to which the proposed objectives have been achieved, by comparing the expected value with the value obtained. The indicators will be, for example, a percentage of the facility's occupation over the time available, or its capacity. Finally, we can measure the **cost effectiveness** by relating the money invested or spent to the degree to which the objective has been realised.

As noted above, working with indicators should be concentrated on a reduced group of key indicators and not on a large number of them. Dealing with many indicators at the same time can render the tool inoperable. It is for this reason that Bauer (2004) suggests finding the value indicators which can be classified in categories of indicators within the BSC.

During the selection and later classification of the indicators into corresponding perspectives, it must be borne in mind that the indicators to be employed need to be standardised. This process requires a standardisation of measurements in order to facilitate the search for common and comparable elements. Standardisation is achieved by establishing the measurements on a similar basis.

The right level of importance must also be allocated to the indicators in such a way that the data are calculated using meaningful, derived measurements that clearly reflect the effect of the value indicators. The indicators can be designed in the following ways:

- **Direct**: data values are unprocessed and measured directly. They may be in units or monetary terms, for a single event or for the whole season; in the last case averages may also be used. Examples include the level of sales (where an entrance fee is charged to use the facilities), number of spectators attending one match, or in monetary terms, income from match day tickets at a particular match or the average for the season.
- **Percentage**: useful for comparing changes in performance of a value relative to the same value at a different time or in different places or compared to an objective; for example, the percentage of variation in the average attendance to home matches from one year to the next or the percentage of variation in the attendance to the different competitions in which a club is involved (league, cup, international competitions).
- **Simple ratio**: relation by quotient between two amounts; for example, points gained in league competition per euro expended on players, revenues from stadium per employee working at the stadium etc.
- **Rate**: combination of separate measures which together give a general indication of performance; for example, the growth in number of users of a facility with respect to the increase in users of a particular type of sports activity in a centre.
- **Compound average**: sum of the weighted averages of various similar measurements which gives a general composite indicator of performance. For example, user satisfaction can be established from the weighted average of questionnaire results, the number of complaints and the degree of loyalty of the user.

In addition, the performance indicators should be considered within a specific approach. That is, considering the possible perspectives that should balance the information to be extracted from them. The time focus should also be looked at – whether we are interested in the long or short term; whether the orientation is strategic or tactical; whether we want information based on prospective or real data; whether we are analysing a process or a result; and whether the aim is to plan or to monitor.

When selecting indicators it is important to ensure that not all of them are short-term, quantitative, tangible and based on collected data. These are the easiest to identify but, in the end, if we limit ourselves to these we will fail to achieve the level of utility we are pursuing. Finally, the task of measuring and evaluating carried out based on the indicators and their integration into the BSC will be in vain if it does not lead to an improvement in the products and services provided by the sports organisations. As such, the dynamic application of these indicators should be brought into play.

13.4 Summary

Having considered the points made throughout this chapter, in summary, it is useful to extract a series of conclusions. Firstly, we propose modifying tools commonly used in business to meet the needs of evaluating investment in sport and we suggest how to adapt them in sports organisations.

Specifically, a process that begins building a strategy map is suggested. The map should be related to the BSC and its perspectives. Then the BSC has to fit the needs of sports organisations. The chosen perspectives should consider the key question to answer in order to contribute to the organisational mission. Clear objectives, with their targets and indicators must be set. We do not need a large array of indicators; it is more important that they are 'key' indicators. This was noted by the *Leisure Industries Research Centre* at Sheffield Hallam University in their report on performance measures for sport development (LIRC, 2003).

The indicators must be placed within a wider context, based on consideration of the user levels of the information given. The series of indicators contemplated must include economy, efficiency and effectiveness, from the resources themselves to the expected value to be obtained from them. The cost of this effectiveness must also be considered.

The use of indicators becomes even more enriching where the causalities are considered; that is, the cause-and-effect relationship between the main areas of activity. The strategy map will help to establish those relationships.

Finally, we highlight the need to implement an evaluation system, based on indicators, to carry out a comparative analysis aimed at uncovering differences between homogeneous benchmarks, finding the origin of these differences and, based on the data, assisting in formulating suggestions for improvement.

References

AECA (1998). 'Indicadores Para La Gestión Empresarial', Documento n. 17, Asociación Española de Contabilidad y Administración de Empresas, Madrid.

AECA (2000). 'Indicadores de Gestión Para Las Entidades Públicas', Documento n.16, Asociación Española de Contabilidad y Administración de Empresas, Madrid.

Audit Commission (2000). *On Target. The Practice of Performance Indicators*, Ministry of Design, Bath.

Bauer, K. (2004). 'Key Performance Indicators: The Multiple Dimensions', *DM Review*, October.

Canadian Comprehensive Auditing Foundation (2002). *Public Performance Reporting: Reporting Principles*.

Cavalluzzo, K. S. and Ittner, Ch. D. (2004). 'Implementing Performance Measurement Innovations: Evidence from Government', *Accounting, Organizations and Society*, 29, 243–67.

COM (1999). *The Helsinki Report on Sport,* Report from the Commission to the European Council (COM (1999) 644 final, Brussels, 10 December).

Eagle, K. (2004). 'Translating Strategy Public Sector Applications of the Balanced Scorecard: The Origins and Evolution of Charlotte's Corporate Scorecard', *Government Finance Review*, Virginia Tech's Center for Public Administration and Police, 19–22.

Forgione, D. A. (1997). 'Health Care Financial and Quality Measures: International Call for A "Balanced Scorecard" Approach', *Journal of Health Care Finance*, 24 (1), 55.

Kaplan, R. and Norton, D. (1996). *The Balanced Scorecard: Translating Strategy into Action*, Harvard Business School Press, Boston.

Kloot, L. and Martin, J. (2000). 'Strategic Performance Management: A Balanced Approach to Performance Management Issues', *Local Government in Management Accounting Research*, 11 (2), June.

LIRC (2003). *Performance Measurement for the Development of Sport: Final Report*, Leisure Industries Research Centre, Sheffield Hallam University.

Morrow, S. (1999). *The New Business of Football: Accountability and Finance in Football*, Palgrave Macmillan, Basingstoke.

Pink, G. H. (2001). 'Creating A Balanced Scorecard for A Hospital System', *Journal of Health Care Finance*, 27 (3), 1.

Prado, J.M. and García, I. M. (2004). 'Los Indicadores de Gestión en el Ambito Municipal: Implantación, Evolución y Tendencias', *Revista Iberoamericana de Contabilidad de Gestión*, n. 4, 149–80.

Rodríguez, M. P., Ortiz, D. and López, A. (2006). 'Balancing Sports Scorecards: In Spain, the Local Granada Government Uses the Balanced Scorecard to Help Manage Sports Programs', *The Public Manager*, Summer.

Sloane, P. (1971). 'The Football Club As A Utility Maximizer', *Scottish Journal of Political Economy*, 17, 121–46.

Sport England (2008). *Sport England Strategy 2008–2011,* Sport England, London. Available at: http://www.sportengland.org/.

Urrutia, I., Kase, K., Martí, C. and Opazo, M. (2006). 'El Mapa Estratégico del Real Madrid: el arte de Construir Una Marca', *Estrategia Financiera,* 231, Septiembre, 10–17.

Voelker, D. E., Rakich, J. S. and French, G. R. (2001). 'The Balanced Scorecard in Healthcare Organizations: A Performance Measurement and Strategic Planning Methodology', *Hospital Topics*, 79(3).

Willett. R. (2003). *Establishing and Assessing Criteria for Judgement of Effectiveness of the Balanced Scorecard in A Large Australian Local Government Authority* (Working Paper No. 2003-013), Queensland University.

Part IV
Public Sector Management

14
Measuring Performance in Government and Non-Profit Organisations: The Role of the Balanced Scorecard

Zahirul Hoque

14.1 Introduction

Organisations, regardless of their ownership orientation, need to develop measures or indicators to assess their performance. These measures, within a performance measurement system (PMS), are also expected to guide business managers' decisions, including employee incentive or reward schemes. Through the PMS, the organisation communicates how it wishes its employees to behave and how this behaviour will be judged and evaluated. Recently, government organisations have also opted for a private-sector style PMS where emphasis has been placed on indicators or measures oriented towards financial as well as non-financial aspects of government activities. Such an orientation has been triggered by governments' recent reform programmes for the public sector. This chapter reports on how government departments and non-profit organisations will benefit from implementing a private-sector style PMS such as the Balanced Scorecard for improving organisational effectiveness. In so doing, the chapter uses some empirical evidence from Australia as examples.

The remainder of this chapter is organised in the following manner. In Section 14.2, the recent reforms in the Australian public sector are outlined, with particular emphasis on the recently introduced 'output–outcome' framework. In Section 14.3, a brief introduction to the Balanced Scorecard is presented. Section 14.4 discusses the application of the Balanced Scorecard in public and non-profit sectors while the Section 14.5 presents some empirical findings on the implementation of the Balanced Scorecard in government organisations. Section, 14.6 concludes the chapter.

14.2   Public sector reforms in the Australian public sector

Today's competitive business environment encompasses fierce global competition, advancing technology and increased customer awareness, and traditional measures of performance, such as return on assets, return on investment, operating income and earnings per share, are deemed to be inadequate for assessing business performance. These traditional measures are likely to provide little useful information to aid decision-makers in their attempts to assess performance, which could be a function of many controllable and uncontrollable organisational, social and environmental factors. A major concern with traditional performance measures is that these measures focus on results largely internal to the firm (Herawaty and Hoque, 2007; Hoque and James, 2000; Kaplan and Norton, 1992, 1993, 1996).

The imperative for improved performance measures cannot be ignored given today's reforms in the public sector, which focus on private sector-style management including accounting. Once new organisational forms are introduced, major accounting changes are required, as the interaction between organisational processes and accounting is essential to ensure that business processes become more effective. Recent performance measurement literature suggests that performance measures which focus purely on financial criteria will not reflect the new business environment. The Australian government recently introduced accrual accounting and output–outcomes-based performance management systems. It has been suggested that new performance measures, if devised strategically, will profoundly influence organisational performance. Public sector scholars suggest that more attention now needs to be placed on generating suitable performance measures to be a successful organisation, given today's 'new' public sector environment.

In the public sector accounting literature, such a new public sector environment is commonly referred to as New Public Management (NPM). The public sector has seen a shift in focus from adherence to formalised procedures to an emphasis on full costing and resource allocation and goal achievement (Hood, 1995). NPM encompasses several ideals, including accountability for results; the separation of commercial and non-commercial business activities; an emphasis on improved financial reporting, monitoring and accountability; an increase in the contracting out of business activities using specific contracts for short-term work; the mimicking of private sector management practices, such as the introduction of corporate plans, mission statements and strategic plans; a shift in preference from non-monetary incentives to monetary incentives; and an emphasis on cost-cutting and efficiency (For a detailed review of the literature pertaining to NPM see Hood, 1991, 1995; Hood and Peters, 2004; see also Moll and Hoque, 2008).

As the new public sector environment focuses on the introduction of market disciplines in government entities which are characterised by possible full cost pricing, commercialisation or corporatisation, in conjunction with the standing service focus, governments are now required to be more accountable to profit elements (Broadbent and Guthrie, 1992; Guthrie *et al.*, 1999). In short, this means that government entities are now required to become more accountable for the use of publicly generated funds. It is therefore imperative that the PMS reflects these structural and cultural changes (Broadbent and Guthrie, 1992). As a result of the current focus on this new public sector environment, government decision makers now seem to be aware that if they are to fulfil their organisation's strategic and operational plans, they should adopt a more contemporary or 'balanced' approach to assessing organisational performance by considering financial and non-financial performance measures (Hoque and Adams, 2008). The BSC approach suggests building a more extensive and linked set of measures for appraising and directing corporate and agency performance, influenced largely by Kaplan and Norton's work.

14.3   Kaplan and Norton's Balanced Scorecard

The Balanced Scorecard links performance measures with four distinct components or perspectives.

First, the financial perspective focuses on financial profitability or outcomes. This includes measures such as cash flow, quarterly sales growth and operating income by division, increased market share and return on equity.

Secondly, the customer perspective encompasses customer satisfaction, measured through market share, customer response time, on time performance, product or service reliability, percentage of sales from new products, percentage of sales from established products, on time delivery, share of key accounts purchases, ranking by key accounts and number of cooperative engineering efforts.

Thirdly, the internal business process perspective focuses on quality, time and efficiency measures, direct materials efficiency variances, effect yield, manufacturing lead time, head count and inventory, number of new patents, number of new product launches, process time to market and time to develop next generation.

Finally, the learning and growth perspective focuses on employee learning and growth measurement through employee satisfaction, employee retention, employee education and training, employee capabilities etc.

The three non-financial perspectives signal to employees the areas that top management view as critical to the company's success (Kaplan and Norton, 1992, 1996).

Companies worldwide have already adopted the Balanced Scorecard, demonstrating that the BSC meets several managerial needs. Firstly, they suggest, the scorecard brings together in one report many miscellaneous elements of a company's competitive plan, that is, customer orientation, improving response time, quality, promoting teamwork and encouraging shorter product launch times, as well as looking to the long term. Kaplan and Norton (1992, 1996, 2001) suggest that the BSC guards against sub-optimisation, in other words, by forcing top management to think about all the important operational measures together, the BSC enables them to see whether improvement in one area has been achieved at the expense of another area. By utilising the BSC, firms can establish management goals and managers can adapt their actions and behaviour as necessary to accomplish those goals. The measures are, according to Kaplan and Norton (1992), 'designed to pull people toward the overall vision'.

In a later paper, Kaplan and Norton (1993) suggested that 'different market situations, product strategies, and competitive environments require different scorecards' and that business units will create their scorecard to match their strategy, mission, technology and culture. Research has produced some evidence to confirm this idea (e.g., Hoque and James, 2000).

In their 1996 book, Kaplan and Norton demonstrate how the balanced scorecard can help in translating strategy into actions. Traditional performance measures are deficient in linking long-term strategy and goals with firm performance measures. Most traditional operational and control systems are designed around financial measures and targets, which do not promote progress in achieving long-term strategic objectives. To achieve long-term success, performance measures must be based on the firms' vision and strategic objectives. These strategic objectives must be expressed in such a way as to enable management to make relevant and reliable decisions that will drive success (Kaplan and Norton, 1996, 2001).

14.4 Balanced Scorecards for public sector and non-profit organisations

Prior research (for example, see Herawaty and Hoque, 2007; Hoque *et al.*, 2004; Modell, 2001, 2005; Moll and Hoque, 2008; Ryan and Walsh, 2004; Sharma and Wanna, 2005; Vickers and Kouzmin, 2001) has shown how NPM ideals have brought about significant changes to the processes of performance measurement of public sector organisations.

In relation to the public sector and non-profit organisations, Niven (2003) suggests that strategy allows an organisation to determine what it shouldn't do as much as what it should do. He makes the point that government organisations attempt to be everything and pander to everyone, rather than being assertive about their mission. Niven argues that many benefits arise when an organisation develops and commits to executing a strategy. These benefits may include promotion of strategic thought and action; improved decision-making; and enhanced performance. Further, Niven argues that if the organisation was to seriously consider adopting the balanced scorecard, then it would need to redefine its stakeholders and re-analyse its strengths, weaknesses, opportunities and threats. Niven states that a balance needs to be struck between what customers want from the organisation and what the organisation needs from its customers. Niven also stresses the point that discussion, generation of ideas and documenting strategy is not the key, execution is. The scorecard provides the framework to move from a 'deciding' phase to a 'doing' phase.

For public sector or non-profit organisations, Niven describes three types of performance measures:

- **Input measures:** Tracking of programme inputs such as staff time and budgetary resources
- **Output measures:** Tracking the number of people served, services provided, or units produced by a programme or service
- **Outcome measures:** Whether the target population is any better off.

The above suggests that inputs and outputs focus internally on the programme or service, whereas outcomes focus on the results of the programme relating to how it operates and what it achieves. Niven states that the balanced scorecard should contain a mix of lagging and leading performance measures. Lag refers to historical measures and lead refers to the future measures. A mix of lagging and leading measures will allow a balance of what has been achieved and what is to be achieved.

Niven (2003), however, lists the top 10 Balanced Scorecard issues which require addressing before its implementation:

- No executive sponsorship;
- Lack of BSC education and training;
- No strategy;
- No objectives for the balanced scorecard programme;
- Timing;
- Consistent management practices;
- No new measures;
- Terminology;
- Lack of cascading targets;
- Premature links to management processes.

It is recognised that the organisation would be better off with a holistic management strategy, and that the balanced scorecard offers a fundamentally logical and suitable strategy (Kaplan and Norton, 1996; Niven, 2003). Kaplan and Grossman (2010), referring to charitable foundations such as the Bill & Melinda Gates Foundation, suggest that '...the new foundations are transferring successful private sector practices into assessing the returns from their spending in the non-profit sector'. Other research (e.g., Hoque and Rossingh, 2006) has also found an extensive use of the Balanced Scorecard type performance management model in non-profit organisation. Further, Hoque and Rossingh (2006) found that the process of implementing the balanced scorecard within a non-profit charity was time-consuming and intensive exercise. They suggest that it can be looked upon as an opportunity to consolidate the organisation and bring the fragments together and push the cooperative spirit. A consolidation process using the BSC will allow the organisation to progress and prosper in the future and achieve growth and sustainability (Hoque and Rossingh, 2006).

14.5   Balanced Scorecard practice: Australian empirical findings

Hoque and Adams (2008) examined the extent of BSC implementation in a sample of Australian government departments. Their results indicate that BSC measurement systems were implemented, to a large or very great extent, in the departments in the areas of output measures (63.0 per cent; mean 3.57); and process efficiency/quality measures (47.8 per cent; mean 3.26). BSC measures typically implemented to little or no extent were in the areas of employee learning and growth measures (65.2 per cent; mean 2.20), and input measures (37.8 per cent; mean 2.89).

Hoque and Adams (2008) also found that BSC performance measures were least often used for punishment or reward of staff (85.7 per cent; mean 1.50). The most common reason for adopting BSC performance measures to a large or very great extent was to measure programme performance (53.3 per cent; mean 3.53), and to manage an activity or programme (53.3 per cent; mean 3.36). Their data also indicate that 58.7 per cent of the responding departments tend to use BSC measures to satisfy external legislative requirements such as government regulation and policy. Interestingly, their findings demonstrate the limited use of BSC measures to satisfy community expectations, social responsibility goals, environmental goals and professional associations (means range between 1.40 and 2.80).

In another study, Hoque (2008), using a case study methodology, documented the incidence of performance measurement and reporting practices of four government agencies in Australia. In his four cases, the government's reform policy and working for outcomes framework played an important part in shaping their performance measurement and reporting systems. Further, Hoque's findings revealed a clear linkage between the organisation's outputs–outcomes framework and perform-ance measurement and reporting practice.

In a related study, Herawaty and Hoque (2007) present a report on per-formance practices in Australian government departments. They suggest that the public sector operates in commercial as well as social economic contexts. As a result, they found that in their annual reports Australian government departments disclose discussion not only on financial per-formance but also on non-financial performance.

14.6 Conclusion

This chapter suggests that measuring the economy, efficiency, effectiveness and competence of today's public sector and non-profit organisations is crucial. The balanced scorecard plays an important role in promoting these goals in government and non-profit organisations because performance measures through the BSC are relevant when government and non-profit agencies are faced with diminishing resources and rising demand for qual-ity services and transparency. However, it is important to understand how social, economic and political structures within government and non-profit organisations are paramount to understanding performance measurement processes in these organisations. Further, the process of implementing the balanced scorecard is a time-consuming and intensive exercise. With consolidation and an interactive process, using networks among organisational actors, the BSC will allow government and non-profit organisations to progress and prosper in the future and achieve growth and sustainability.

References

Broadbent, J. and Guthrie, J. (1992). 'Changes in Public Sector: A Review of Recent "Alternative" Accounting Research', *Accounting Auditing and Accountability Journal*, 5 (2), 3–31.

Guthrie, J., Olson, O. and Humphrey, C. (1999). 'Debating Developments in New Public Management: The Limits of Global Theorising and Some New Ways Forward', *Financial Accountability and Management*, 15 (3), 209–28.

Herawaty, M. and Hoque, Z. (2007). 'Disclosure in the Annual Reports of Australian Government Departments: A Research Note', *Journal of Accounting & Organizational Change*, 3 (2), 147–68.

Hood, C. (1991). 'A Public Management for All Seasons', *Public Administration*, 69 (1), 3–19.

Hood, C. (1995). 'The 'New Public Management' in the 1980s: Variations on a Theme', *Accounting, Organizations and Society*, 20 (2/3), 93–109.

Hood, C. and Peters, G. (2004). 'The Middle Ageing of New Public Management: Into An Age of Paradox?' *Journal of Public Administration Research and Theory*, 14, 267–82.

Hoque, Z. (2008). 'Measuring and Reporting Public Sector Outcomes: Exploratory Evidence from Australia', *International Journal of Public Sector Management*, 21 (5), 468.

Hoque, Z. and Adams, C. (2008). 'Measuring Public Sector Performance: A Study of Government Departments in Australia', *CPA Australia Monograph*, Melbourne, March 2008.

Hoque, Z. and James, W. (2000). 'Linking the Balanced Scorecard Measures to Size and Market Factors: Impact on Organizational Performance', *Journal of Management Accounting Research* (12), 1–17.

Hoque, Z. and Moll, J. (2001). 'Public Sector Reform: Implications for Accounting, Accountability and Performance of State-owned Entities – an Australian Perspective', *International Journal of Public Sector Management*, 14 (4), 304–26.

Hoque, Z. and Rossingh, B. (2006). 'Radical Change and Management Control in A Not-for-profit Organisation: A Case Study Using Grounded Theory Approach in Conjunction with Institutional Theory of Change' (Paper presented at the *Interdisciplinary Perspectives on Accounting* (IPA) Conference in Cardiff, UK, July 2006).

Hoque, Z., Arends, S. and Alexander, R. (2004). 'Policing the Police Service: A Case Study of the Rise of "New Public Management" within an Australian Police Service', *Accounting, Auditing & Accountability Journal*, 17 (1), 59–84.

Kaplan, R. S. and Grossman, A. S. (2010). 'An Emerging Capital Market for Non-profits' (Keynote paper presented at the Second Global Accounting and Organisational Change Research Conference held in Babson College, Wellesley, MA, USA).

Kaplan, R. S. and Norton, D. P. (1992). 'The Balanced Scorecard – Measures that Drive Performance', *Harvard Business Review*, January–February, 71–9.

Kaplan, R. S. and Norton, D. P. (1993). 'Putting the Balanced Scorecard to Work', *Harvard Business Review*, September–October, 134–47.

Kaplan, R. S. and Norton, D. P. (1996). *The Balanced Scorecard: Translating Strategy into Action*, Harvard Business School Press, Boston, MA.

Kaplan, R. S. and Norton, D. P. (2001). 'Transforming the Balanced Scorecard from Performance Measurement to Strategic Management: Part I', *Accounting Horizons*, 15 (1), 87–104.

Modell, S. (2001). 'Performance Measurement and Institutional Processes: A Study of Managerial Responses to Public Sector Reform', *Management Accounting Research*, 12, 437–64.

Modell, S. (2005). 'Performance Management in the Public Sector: Past Experiences, Current Practices and Future Challenges', *Australian Accounting Review*, 15 (3), 56–66.

Moll, J. and Hoque, Z. (2008). 'New Organisational Forms and Accounting Innovation: The Specifier/Provider Model in the Australian Public Sector', *Journal of Accounting and Organizational Change*, 4 (3), 243.

Niven, P. R. (2003). *Balanced Scorecard: Step by Step: For Government and Non-profit Agencies*, John Wiley & Sons, Hoboken, New Jersey.

Ryan, C. and Walsh, P. (2004). 'Collaboration of Public Sector Agencies: Reporting and Accountability Challenges', *International Journal of Public Sector Management*, 17 (7), 621–31.

Vickers, M. and Kouzmin, A. (2001). 'New Managerialism and Australian Police Organizations', *The International Journal of Public Sector Management*, 14 (1), 7–26.

Wanna, J. and Sharma, B. (2005). 'Performance Measures, Measurement and Reporting in Government Organisations', *International Journal of Business Performance Management*, 7 (3), 320–33.

15
Performance Measurement in the Public Sector: Evaluating Performance Measurement and Reporting in Health

Suresh Cuganesan and Julie Foreman

15.1 Introduction: new public management and management accounting

Considerable research attention has focused on the influence and impact of New Public Management (NPM) for management accounting practice. Performance measurement and reporting as a key aspect of management accounting and a central theme within NPM (Hood, 1991, 1995) is the major focus of this chapter. The extent to which 'explicit formal measurable standards and measures of performance and success' (Hood, 1995, p. 96), as well as broader public sector performance measurement approaches have delivered sought-after effectiveness, efficiency and accountability gains has been the subject of a number of theoretical discussions and empirical examinations of the quality of measures and performance frameworks in practice (Ittner and Larcker, 1998; Lapsley, 2008; Lee, 2008). Generally, research to date emphasises that the objective of enhanced accountability through improved measures of efficiency and effectiveness has not been delivered in practice (Broadbent and Guthrie, 1998, 2008; Modell, 2004). Considerable opportunities for improvement exist, but these must be based on evaluations of current practice in public sector performance measurement.

This chapter reviews prior research on public sector performance measurement. It then presents selective evidence on the state of play using performance measurement and reporting in a case study of the Australian health sector. The health sector is used as a case study as performance measurement practice is continuously under scrutiny globally (OECD, 2002). Furthermore, funding is increasingly tied to the achievement of performance measurement targets. This makes well-designed performance measurement systems imperative. To date, however, evaluations of practice have been limited.

15.2 A review of public sector performance measurement research

Since initial academic theorising and research about public sector performance measurement almost two decades ago (Hood, 1991, 1995; Osborne and Gaebler, 1992; Pollitt, 1993), NPM research has expanded upon a number of observations of practice and underlying theoretical explanations. More generally this research has focused on examining 'ideal' theoretical frameworks against actual practice under NPM conditions. Critical reflections of theory and practice on its actual manifestations, foreseen and unforeseen, have been important contributions in this regard (Adcroft and Willis, 2005; Guthrie, 1998; Guthrie *et al.*, 2003).

Performance measurement in the public sector has been central to NPM initiatives designed to enhance agency efficiency, effectiveness and accountability (Hood, 1991). However, the movement by the public sector at large from input-based metrics to metrics grounded within a clear vision of agency efficiency and effectiveness in service delivery has been problematic. Studies in developing and implementing performance measurement systems and associated challenges are well established (see Carlin, 2005; Carnegie and West, 2005; Guthrie, 1994; Guthrie and Parker, 1998; Kloot and Martin, 2000; Lee, 2008; Modell, 2004; O'Faircheallaigh *et al.*, 1999; Walker, 2001, 2002). These find that agencies often establish broad performance measures of little relevance to their objectives; there is a reliance on financial measures that are inappropriate to the public sector or that result in a pre-occupation with efficiency; and there is a high turnover of performance measures and the quantitative measurement of outcomes that only emerge over the long term and which cannot be linked back to specific agencies and their outputs.

Recent research has focused on the perspectives of performance measurement reporting in terms of perceived usefulness of metrics (Lee, 2008; van Dooran, 2004) and the value to be derived by users (Bogt, 2004; Mack and Ryan, 2007). These perspectives present initial views on the influences and challenges confronting modern-day public sector entities in their design, implementation and reporting of performance measures. For example, Lee (2008) found that of the Australian public service managers surveyed, participants viewed measures on outputs (namely the goods and services delivered) and outcomes (namely the impact of such outputs) as being typically 'underdeveloped' and 'under-reported'.

Thus an in-depth examination of what Lapsley (2008) refers to as an area that consumes considerable effort in practice, that is the performance measurement design process, is still warranted. Contemporary public sector management reforms call for improvements in both financial and non-financial reporting frameworks. If performance measurement and reporting practice are to improve, then it is important that examinations of practice are conducted.

The next section presents a selective examination of performance measurement in the public health sector. Total global expenditure on health exceeds US$4.1 trillion dollars per year (World Health Organization, 2007). A significant proportion of this is in the public health system. Hence the ability to evaluate efficiency and effectiveness through well-designed performance measurement systems is critical.

15.3   Performance measurement for the public health sector

In this section recent research is reviewed first. Then actual practice in Australian health sector performance measurement and reporting is evaluated. A final sub-section presents commentary on the case study.

15.3.1   Research findings on public health performance measurement and reporting

The current approaches to performance measurement within the health sector reflect an evolution aligned to the adoption of private sector management philosophies. The intended focus of performance measurement has shifted from a focus on personnel costs, cost control and activity, to accountability and clinical quality. Over time, there has been increased reporting by hospitals and delivery units with the provision of government funding often tied to the achievement of particular service delivery 'targets'. While this inevitably creates incentives for 'gaming' (Greener, 2005; Mannion *et al.* 2007), it also makes it imperative that performance measurement frameworks are well designed. However, a number of studies of performance measurement in healthcare suggest this is far from the case.

Dey *et al.* (2008) suggest that current performance measures do not include planning, implementing and evaluating frameworks to improve measures. Adcroft and Willis (2005) argue that problems include a segregated rather than holistic approach where only individual departments are assessed, independent of each other. The author suggests that this can lead to improved waiting lists times but poorer health. Inappropriate targets may be established for impression management rather than real improvement. Samuel *et al.* (2005) suggest there are considerable tensions between clinicians and business managers and that much of this arises from the quality of care versus cost-effectiveness debate. Styles and Koprowski (2008) suggest that despite the calls for greater accountability and transparency (from regulators, professionals and academics), the 100 most technically competent US hospitals fail to provide adequate accounting details to stakeholders through websites. The authors suggest that data is often completely absent (only 37 per cent provide any), or that when data is provided, for example in annual reports, it is not useful to the community as it is poorly highlighted or presented in too aggregate a form. Therefore there is little communication with the community to which hospitals are accountable.

Turning to Australia, which is the focus of this chapter, Charles and Kelly (2008) comment on a 2007 study conducted by Deloitte which reveals that Australian hospitals engage in less public reporting than hospitals in other countries. Results indicated that improvements are observable where there is increased reporting of outcomes. Countries other than Australia tend to analyse quality and safety indicators and publish this information. However, Australian data on patient safety, intervention effectiveness or continuity of care are not currently published. The authors suggest there is insufficient information in Australia for policymakers to assess the efficiency and effectiveness of current performance measurement systems. They call for government leadership in defining indicators and for comparable and transparent public data sets for policy makers.

15.3.2 Performance measurement and reporting in health: an evaluation of Australian practice

The Australian health system operates within a multi-regulatory federal context where its funding is primarily provided by the Australian Commonwealth and individual State and Territory governments. These jointly contribute 93 per cent of the recurrent expenditure for the public hospital system and represents 40.8 per cent of the overall expenditure on health (SCRGSP, 2009). The sector produces comprehensive performance reports and statistics required by the Commonwealth and/or State or Territory governments.

There are several influencing factors behind any State Government's or individual hospital's reporting on health performance, and these are

224 Performance Measurement in the Public Sector

representative of their funding sources. A useful analytical framework to examine and evaluate current performance measurement and reporting in Australian Health is provided by the Productivity Commission of Australia. Commencing in 1995, it has developed a Reporting Framework and has continuously refined it. In the 2009 report, the framework key performance areas had expanded to three: Effectiveness, Efficiency and Equity. Effectiveness reports on four criteria (Access, Quality, Appropriateness and Sustainability), while Efficiency encompasses Recurrent Cost, Total Cost and Relative Stay Index.

The State Government of Victoria, along with the other States of Australia, has constitutional responsibility for the provision of health care within public hospitals. The key department is the Victorian Department of Health, which was created from pre-existing agencies in August 2009. Its strategic priorities are (see State of Victoria, Department of Health, 2010):

• improving health service performance
• reforming our response to mental health and drug and alcohol services to meet client needs
• strengthening prevention and health promotion
• developing our health service system and organisation
• responding to an ageing population
• reducing health inequalities.

In terms of reporting obligations and discharging its accountability, the Department of Health produces external performance reports. The most comprehensive data is presented in the Department of Health (formerly part of the Department of Human Services) *Annual Report* which includes the major outputs or deliverables for the financial year in accordance with financial management legislation operating at the state government level, as well as the *Your Hospitals* report, which presents both an aggregate report on total public hospital outputs with narrative highlighting specific hospital performance and a disaggregated snapshot of key outputs for each individual hospital.

In relation to funding, key dimensions of a hospital's performance were agreed in the Australian Health Care Agreements Performance Report effective 2004–2008, which was extended to 2009. These agreements are between the Australian Government and each state and territory, and are the means through which the Australian Government funds the public health system. Key reportable measures include patient numbers; hospital costs and funding; waiting times for elective surgery; and waiting times for emergency departments by triage category.

The following tables (15.1–15.6) present a snapshot of data categories and measures contained within the two reports.[1] Each table shows the alignment of performance measures across the two reporting mechanisms and the extent to which actual performance against established targets is reported. The latter is important, as it enables information users to judge performance against the reported upon criteria and compare this across different aspects of the health system.

15.3.2 Evaluation and discussion

This chapter acknowledges the considerable work undertaken by various authorities in improving the performance measurement system of the public health sector in Australia at both Commonwealth and State and territory levels. The result of these endeavours, however, does not subscribe to a common framework even within the State and therefore compromises comparability, rigorous analysis and the opportunity for adopting best practice. This chapter presents a brief picture of selective aspects of public hospital performance reports within the Department of Human Services (now Department of Health).

The key points of alignment between the two reports are with the timeliness of elective surgery admissions and the responsiveness to emergency presentations. Where targets were included in the *Your Hospitals* report, they aligned identically to the targets in the Annual Report. However,

Table 15.1 Quantity of admitted services

Measure	Annual report		*Your Hospitals* report	
	Performance measure reported?	Actual to target reported?	Performance measure reported?	Actual to target reported?
Palliative care bed days	Y	Y	N	N
Sub-acute bed days	Y	Y	N	N
Total separations	Y	Y	Y	N
WIES	Y	Y	N	N

Source: Victorian Government Department of Human Services Annual Report (2009); Department of Human Services *Your Hospitals* report July 2008–June 2009.

Explanation: The measures presented in Table 15.1 indicate the number of inpatient episodes of care delivered by all public hospitals within Victoria. The indicators are measured in bed days in recognition of duration of stay rather than patient numbers. Separations are incidents of admitted care. Weighted Inlier Equivalent Separation (WIES) is a measure which represents the weighted cost of an episode of care where the weighting represents the diagnosis-related group classification and the length of stay.

Table 15.2 Quality of admitted services

Measure	Annual report		*Your Hospitals* report	
	Performance measure reported?	Actual to target reported?	Performance measure reported?	Actual to target reported?
Major trauma patients transferred to a major trauma service	Y	Y	N	N
Hospitals meeting externally audited cleaning	Y	Y	Selected hospitals only	N
Public hospital accreditation	Y	Y	N	N
Patient satisfaction	N	N	Y	N

Source: Victorian Government Department of Human Services Annual Report (2009); Department of Human Services *Your Hospitals* report July 2008–June 2009.
Explanation: The above measures relate to appropriateness of the service delivered and recognition of the need to ensure infection control to minimise hospital-acquired infections. VICNISS is the Victorian Hospital Acquired Infection Surveillance System and all Victorian hospitals are required to participate according to the 100 per cent target within the Annual Report.

Table 15.3 Timeliness of service provision

Measure	Annual report		*Your Hospitals* report	
	Performance measure reported?	Actual to target reported?	Performance measure reported?	Actual to target reported?
Emergency patients transferred to ward within 8 hours	Y	Y	Y	Y
Category 3 elective surgery admissions less than 365 days	Y	Y	Y	Y
Category 2 elective surgery admissions within 90 days	Y	Y	Y	Y
Category 1 elective surgery admissions within 30 days	Y	Y	Y	Y

Source: Victorian Government Department of Human Services annual Report (2009); Department of Human Services Your Hospitals Report July 2008–June 2009.
Explanation: These measures relate to the efficiency of performing clinical services and are assessed against well-established and nationally agreed clinical benchmarks.

Table 15.4 Cost of service provision

Measure	Annual report		*Your Hospitals* report	
	Performance measure reported?	Actual to target reported?	Performance measure reported?	Actual to target reported?
Total output cost	Y	Y	N	N

Source: Victorian Government Department of Human Services Annual Report (2009); Department of Human Services Your Hospitals Report July 2008–June 2009.
Explanation: There is no explanatory note in the Annual Report as to how this figured is derived.

Table 15.5 Timeliness of provision of emergency services

Measure	Annual report		*Your Hospitals* report	
	Performance measure reported?	Actual to target reported?	Performance measure reported?	Actual to target reported?
Emergency category 1 treated immediately	Y	Y	Y	Y
Emergency category 2 treated within 10 minutes	Y	Y	Y	Y
Emergency category 3 treated within 30 minutes	Y	Y	Y	Y
Non-admitted emergency patients with a length of stay over 4 hours	Y	Y	Y	Y

Source: Victorian Government Department of Human Services Annual Report (2009); Department of Human Services *Your Hospitals* Report July 2008–June 2009.
Explanation: These measures report the clinical efficiency of meeting nationally agreed triage benchmarks for emergency presentations.

waiting list measures were found to be manipulated in one hospital and instigated a focus on data integrity, with the Government commissioning ongoing spot audits of hospitals and requiring health services to report on data integrity in their annual reports (Paxton Partners, 2009).

However, there are significant differences in the measures reported.[2] The *Your Hospitals* report aggregates admissions, ignores the clinical approach to determining quality and opts for measures on patient satisfaction instead. While funding is reported in the *Your Hospitals* report, the total cost of services and cost of categories of service are not

Table 15.6 Critical care services

Measure	Annual report		*Your Hospitals* report	
	Performance measure reported?	Actual to target reported?	Performance measure reported?	Actual to target reported?
Average daily hours of care in intensive care units	N	N	Y	N
Babies admitted to neonatal intensive care or special care nurseries	N	N	Y	N

Source: Victorian Government Department of Human Services Annual Report (2009); Department of Human Services Your Hospitals Report July 2008–June 2009.
Explanation: These measures report the complexity of critical services based on hours within areas of intensive care.

reported. There were several measures in the *Your Hospitals* report which were excluded from the Annual Report, including Patient Satisfaction and category 4 and 5 elective surgery admissions.

There was no systematic quantitative reporting of infection control in the *Your Hospital* report. Hospital cleanliness and accreditation were also a key omission from both the aggregate and individual hospital reports in the *Your Hospitals* report. The presentation of data is significantly different in the two reports but could be justified by a focus on relevance to its audience. The *Your Hospitals* report presents a trend analysis but only includes targets in the measures that are required to conform to agreed benchmarks.

While the Annual Report is compliant with the Victorian Government's *Financial Management Act 1994*, as attested by the Victorian Auditor-General (Victorian Government Department of Human Services, 2009), neither report conforms to the State Government Reporting Framework nor addresses requirements from the Department of Treasury and Finance to move to a focus on outcomes (Victorian Auditor-General's Office, 2010).

The failure to include comprehensive targets, quality measures of concern to the public and cost in the most accessible report, *Your Hospitals*, evidences a failure to provide a transparent picture of the state of the hospital system and the relative efficiency and effectiveness of individual hospitals. The inclusion of key measures within the Department's

Annual Report and measures reported nationally by the Productivity Commission prompts the question as to why these significant measures are not readily accessible to the public.

Overall, neither report aligns to the broader reporting frameworks for public sector performance reporting and, along with other State departments, there is no basis for direct comparability nationally. This compromises the ability to benchmark 'best practice' and provide a consistent basis for allocation of funds.

15.4 Chapter summary

Significant effort has been dedicated to establishing performance measurement frameworks for the public sector. However, research to date highlights several deficiencies in practice. Reform efforts need to be founded upon evaluations of practice that identify 'system gaps'. This chapter presents a review of performance measurement system research and conducts a selective evaluation of practice in the public health sector using the state of Victoria in Australia as a case study. In highlighting deficiencies in practice, the chapter illustrates the challenges and opportunities for management accounting practice in designing appropriate performance measurement systems that enable evaluations of efficiency, effectiveness and value for money in the public sector, and which facilitate government agencies discharging their accountability to the community.

Notes

1. The Annual Report reported a total of 34 aggregate measures under Acute Health and Emergency Services. The *Your Hospitals* report presented 37 aggregate measures within these categories. Measures for Mental Health and Dental Services reported in the *Your Hospitals* report were excluded from the analysis and only measures representative of Acute Health and Emergency Services were used. Disaggregated measures in the *Your Hospitals* report, such as admissions by clinical category, were also excluded to enable comparison on key aggregate measures.
2. It is acknowledged that the annual report will have a greater level of detail while the *Your Hospitals* report is conscious of its wider lay audience and uses a non-technical approach.

References

Adcroft, A. and Willis, R. (2005). 'The (un)intended Outcome of Public Sector Performance Measurement', *The International Journal of Public Sector Management*, 18 (4–5), 386–400.

Bogt, H. J. Ter (2004). 'Politicians in Search of Performance Information? Survey Research on Dutch Alderman's Use of Performance Information', *Financial Accountability and Management*, 20 (3), 221–52.

Broadbent, J. and Guthrie, J. (2008). 'Public Sector to Public Services: 20 years of "Contextual" Accounting Research', *Accounting, Auditing & Accountability Journal*, 21 (2), 129–69.

Carlin, T. (2005). 'Debating the Impact of Accrual Accounting and Reporting in the Public Sector', *Financial Accountability and Management*, 21 (3), 309–36.

Carnegie, G. and West, B. (2005). 'Making Accounting Accountable in the Public Sector', *Critical Perspectives on Accounting*, 16, 905–28.

Charles, D. and Kelly, M. (2008). 'Evaluating Australia's Health Outcomes', *The Melbourne Review*, 4 (1), 49–56.

Dey, P. K., Hariharan, S. and Despic, O. (2008). 'Managing Healthcare Performance in Analytical Framework', *Benchmarking: An International Journal*, 15 (4), 444–68.

Greener, I. (2005). 'Introduction to the Special Edition On Health Care Financing', *Public Finance and Management*, 5 (4), 486–91.

Guthrie, J. (1994). 'Performance Indicators in the Australian Public Sector', in Buschor, E. and Schedler, K. (eds), *Perspectives on Performance Measurement in Public Sector Accounting*, Paul Haupt, Berne.

Guthrie, J. (1998). 'Applications of Accrual Accounting in the Australian Public Sector – Rhetoric or Reality?', *Financial Accountability and Management*, 14 (1), 1–19.

Guthrie, J. and Parker, L.D. (1998). 'Managerialism and Marketisation in Financial Management Change in Australia', in Olson, O., Guthrie, J. and Humphrey, C. (eds.), *Global Warning! Debating International Developments in New Public Financial Management*, Cappelen Akademisk Forlag, Oslo.

Guthrie, J., Parker, L. D. and English, L. (2003). 'A Review of New Public Management Change in Australia', *Australian Accounting Review*, 13 (2), 3–9.

Hood, C. (1991). 'A Public Management for All Seasons?', *Public Administration*, 69 (1), 3–19.

Hood, C. (1995). 'The "New Public Management" in the 1980s: Variations on a Theme', *Accounting, Organizations and Society*, 20 (2–3), 93–109.

Ittner, C. D. and Larcker, D. F. (1998). 'Innovations in Performance Measurement: Trends and Research Implications', *Journal of Management Accounting Research*, 10, 205–38.

Jansen, E. P. (2008). 'New Public Management: Perspectives on Performance and the Use of Performance Information', *Financial Accountability and Management*, 24 (2), 169–191.

Kloot, L. and Martin, J. (2000). 'Strategic Performance Management: A Balanced Approach to Performance Management Issues in Local Government', *Management Accounting Research*, 11 (2), 231–51.

Lapsley, I. (2008). 'The NPM Agenda: Back to the Future', *Financial Accountability and Management*, 24 (1), 77–96.

Lee, J. (2008). 'Preparing Performance Information in the Public Sector: An Australian Perspective', *Financial Accountability and Management*, 24 (2), 117–49.

Mack, J. and Ryan, C. (2007). 'Is There An Audience for Public Sector Annual Reports: Australian Evidence?', *The International Journal of Public Sector Management*, 20 (2), 134–146.

Mannion, R., Goddard, M. and Bate, A. (2007). 'Aligning Incentives and Motivations in Health Care: The Case of Earned Autonomy', *Financial Accountability & Management*, 23 (4), November, 401–20.

Modell, S. (2004). 'Performance Measurement Myths in the Public Sector: A Research Note', *Financial Accountability and Management*, 20 (1), 39–55.

O'Faircheallaigh, C., Wanna, J. and Weller, P. (1999). *Public Sector Management in Australia*, 2nd edn, Macmillan, South Yarra.

Organisation for Economic Co-operation and Development (OECD). *Measuring Up: Improving Health System Performance in OECD Countries*, OECD Publishing, Paris.

Osborne, A. and Gaebler, T. (1992). *Reinventing Government: How the Entrepreneur Spirit is Transforming the Public Sector*, Addison-Wesley, Reading, Massachusetts.

Paxton Partners (2009). *Elective Surgery Waiting List Audit – Royal Woman's Hospital*, Department of Human Services.

Pollitt, C. (1993). *Managerialism and the Public Services: The Anglo-American Experience*, 2nd edn, Blackwell, Oxford.

Samuel, S., Dirsmith, M. W. and McElroy, B. (2004). 'Monetised Medicine: From the Physical to the Fiscal', *Accounting, Organizations and Society*, 30, 249–78.

State of Victoria, Department of Health (2010). *Your Hospitals: A Report on Victoria's Public Hospitals July 2009 to June 2010*, Hospital and Health Service Performance. Division, Victorian Department of Health, Melbourne.

Steering Committee for the Review of Government Service Provision (SCRGSP). *Report on Government Services 2009*, Productivity Commission, Canberra.

Styles, A. K. and Koprowski, W. (2008). 'The Disclosure of Financial Information Via the Internet by the 100 "Most Wired" Healthcare Systems', *Journal of Public Budgeting, Accounting and Financial Management*, 20 (3), 387–404.

van Dooran, W. (2004). 'What Makes Organisations Measure? Hypotheses on the Causes and Conditions for Performance Measurement', *Financial Accountability and Management*, 21 (3), 363–83.

Victorian Auditor-General's Office (2010). *Performance Reporting by Departments*, Victorian Government Printer, PP No 293, Melbourne.

Victorian Government Department of Human Services (2009). *Annual Report*, Melbourne.

Walker, R. G. (2001). 'Reporting on Service Efforts and Accomplishments on a 'Whole of Government Basis', *Australian Accounting Review*, 11 (3), 4–16.

Walker, R. G. (2002). 'Are Annual Reports of Government Agencies Really 'General Purpose' If They Do Not Include Performance Indicators?', *Australian Accounting Review*, 12 (1), 43–5.

World Health Organization (2007). 'Spending on Health: A Global Overview', *Fact Sheet No 319*, available at http://www.who.int/mediacentre/factsheets/fs319.pdf (accessed September 2010).

16
The Balanced Scorecard as a Performance Management Tool for Museums

Toomas Haldma and Kertu Lääts

16.1 Introduction

This chapter examines the impact of the design and implementation of the BSC concept on the development of performance measurement and management of museums. The main focus relies on the BSC design and the elements of implementation that enable the communication of strategy between the management of an organisation and its different departments. These issues are discussed based on the experiences of a central museum in Estonia.

During the last decade an almost worldwide reform of the public sector has taken place. In response to increasing concerns with the legitimacy and efficiency of public spending, New Public Management (NPM) has become the leading philosophy of those reforms in many countries, including Estonia. NPM will encourage the public sector to adopt private sector management techniques (Hood, 1995), as well as to develop performance measurement in order to monitor the degree of efficiency and effectiveness with which public services are delivered, and to evaluate the financial consequences of management decisions. The public sector reform will also modify the traditional channels of accountability. Conventional management accounting and perform-ance management, based on financial measurement, has lost relevance (Johnson and Kaplan, 1987), and the balanced scorecard (BSC) concept was developed as a solution to update performance measurement and management (Kaplan and Norton, 1992) in business and in public sector organisations.

The end of the 1980s and the beginning of the 1990s was a period of critical economic, social and political change in Estonia and other Eastern European countries. Estonia, a small country, has been described as having undergone a rapid and rather successful transformation from a planned to a market economy, starting with the separation from the Soviet Union and re-establishment of the Estonian Republic in 1991, and continuing with the development of market economy structures, acceptance into the European Union in 2004 and the introduction of the euro currency in 2011. Following these dramatic shifts in the social and environmental landscape, both financial and management reform were implemented in the country's local and central government systems. These changes have also affected the nature and practice of accounting systems. By the end of the 1990s, several management principles originating from the private sector (e.g. management by objectives, the BSC, value-based management, TQM models) had started to develop in Estonian public sector management and governance, including cultural and educational areas.

The International Council of Museums (2010) defines a museum as a non-profit, permanent institution in the service of society and its development, open to the public, which acquires, conserves, researches, communicates and exhibits the tangible and intangible heritage of humanity and its environment for the purposes of education, study and enjoyment. Besides the internal tasks of a museum emphasised in the definition, museums also need to balance their tasks with the interests of external stakeholders and the services of competitors within the leisure and cultural industry in general and in the museum field in particular.

The remainder of the chapter is organised as follows. The second section sets a theoretical framework for analyses, covering the BSC implementation issues in public sector organisations and performance measurement and management framework of the museums. The third section is devoted to a discussion of the methodological issues concerning the empirical study. Subsequently, we discuss the findings of an empirical study analysing the changes in the strategic management framework and the impact of BSC design and implementation on the development of the performance management in the case museum. At the end of the chapter concluding remarks are presented.

16.2 Theoretical framework of the study

16.2.1 Applying the Balanced Scorecard in public sector organisations

The BSC enables organisations to transform organisational strategy into an operating management system. Several authors (Aidemark, 2001; Kaplan, 1999, 2001; Modell, 2004; Neely *et al.*, 2006) have argued that the BSC constitutes a potent performance management tool for the public sector as well as for other not-for-profit organisations. Kaplan and Norton (1992) first proposed the BSC as a strategic performance measurement system, and subsequently pointed out that a complete and effective BSC must have proper key performance measures (Kaplan and Norton, 2001a). According to Niven (2002), performance measures are at the core of the BSC system. The performance measures communicate important messages to all organisational units and their employees.

To exploit the power of performance measures, organisations next integrated their measures into a performance management system, which enables an organisation to align its management processes and focuses within the entire organisation on implementing long-term strategy (Kaplan and Norton, 1996a, Kaplan, 2001b). Performance management is the process by which the organisation integrates its performance with its corporate and functional strategies and objectives (Bititci *et al.*, 1997). Thus the BSC concept, originating from a performance measurement system, came to provide the organising framework for a strategic management system (Kaplan and Norton, 1996a). Mussari (2001) has pointed out that the fostering of 'performance culture' or 'performance orientation' in the public sector has resulted in a growing use of performance management tools. Although the BSC was initially applied to the business sector, Kaplan (1999, p. 3) pointed out that its potential to improve the management of public sector organisations is even greater. The BSC as a performance measurement and management tool has been applied in various public sector organisations, notably in health care (Peters *et al.*, 2007; Qudrat-Ullah, 2007), in higher education (Chen *et al.*, 2006, Lawrence and Sharma, 2002), in the police service (Elefalk, 2001), and in governmental organisations (see Wilson *et al.*, 2003). Gstraunthaler and Piber (2007) suggested using a BSC to address management and control issues in museums too.

Describing the different aspects of a BSC, Chen *et al.*, (2006) have summarised its capabilities as a performance measurement system, a strategic management system and a communication tool. Kaplan (1999) stressed that the start of any performance management exercise must be focused on the strategy of the organisation. By transferring organisational strategy onto a strategy map and a BSC, organisations create a common and understandable basis for each organisational unit and its employees. Kaplan and Norton (2001b, p. 90) defined a strategy map as a logical and comprehensive architecture for describing strategy and specifying critical elements and their links with the organisation's strategy. All BSC projects build a map of strategic objectives first and only afterwards select metrics for each objective (Kaplan, 2009). Besides the financial perspective of measurement and management, which is the essence of the BSC, it also integrates the customer, internal processes and innovation and learning perspectives of an organisation. Kaplan (1999) considered that the financial perspective provides a clear long-term objective for profit-oriented organisations. He goes on to argue that for public sector organisations the financial perspective can mainly play an enabling or constraining role and points out that those organisations must define tangible objectives for their mission, customers and constituencies. Therefore the original sequence of the BSC perspectives can be rearranged, with the customer perspective moving to the top of the scorecard (Kaplan and Norton, 2001b).

In addition, Kaplan (2001) emphasised that within a public service environment, the definition of the customer may envelop a variety of customers and stakeholders. According to Atkinson *et al.* (1997), the stakeholders of public sector organisations can be divided into two groups: process stakeholders (employees and suppliers) and environmental ones (customers, owners and the community). Process stakeholders are concerned with the planning, design, implementation and operation of the organisation to meet the primary objectives or desired result. Environmental stakeholders are interested in getting services for a reasonable amount of money. Kaplan (2001b) distinguished two groups of environmental stakeholders in a non-profit organisation – the donors, providing financial resources, and the constituents, receiving the service. Therefore it is important that organisations place both the donor perspective and the recipient perspective at the top of their BSC.

Concerning the focus and design of the structure of the BSC, there should be a definite connection between organisational and organisational unit (departmental) scorecards. Kaplan (1999) emphasised that when a top-level organisational scorecard has been created, the organisation should deploy the process to its individual departments, and departmental scorecards must reflect the themes and objectives established on the top-level scorecards. From the other side, as was stressed by Kaplan and Norton (1996b), a review of departmental scorecards will generally identify several cross-business issues not initially included in the strategic plans of the organisation. Some studies (Ballantine *et al.*, 1998; Modell, 2004) show that implementation of a BSC at the senior management level of an organisation characterised by a top-down approach leads to a considerable narrowing of the performance aspects, and primarily to the promotion of financial results and efficiency measures oriented towards the senior management level. The senior management responsible for that same top-down approach should also stimulate an interactive dialogue within the organisation. According to Simons (1995, p. 102), it is through that dialogue, the debate and learning which accompany the interactive control process that new strategies emerge. Aidemark (2001) also points out that if the BSC is constructed as a result of a bottom-up approach at department level, then it may be used to communicate the activities of operational services and their corresponding measures to senior management.

In summary, efficient strategy creation, development and implementation need the support and involvement of all management levels. Consequently, in the context of the interactive control system, which according to Kaplan (2009) demands frequent and regular attention from operating managers at all levels of the organisation, the BSC serves as a structure for dialogue, communication and cooperation (Aidemark, 2001) between different organisational units and between different management levels of an organisation. All the abovementioned support the findings of De Geuser *et al.*, (2009), which indicate the positive impact of BSC on the integration of management processes, enabling the greater alignment of various processes, services, competences, and units of an organisation, and also cooperation between different organisational units. Further, Sundin *et al.*, (2010), outline the enabling role of the BSC in balancing organisational strategic goals and objectives, leading to a better understanding of the people on the department level, and how their work is connected to the organisation's strategy implementation. Therefore we can conclude that the BSC serves as a tool enabling integration of different interactive departmental management systems into the holistic performance management system of a public sector organisation.

16.2.2   Performance measurement and management in museums

Thompson (2001), Reussner (2003), Gstraunthaler and Piber (2007) and the International Council of Museums (2010) specify collection and preservation, research, exhibitions and museum education as the main areas of activity of museums. All these areas have to be captured by the museums' performance measurement and management systems. Therefore it would be helpful to distinguish the different management levels that the specific performance measurement system has to support. In museums, Gstraunthaler and Piber (2007) have distinguished three different management levels: ministry (government), board of trustees, and management board levels. At the ministry level, a set of key figures of different museums has been traced. The interest of a board of trustees is to observe the fulfilment of the strategic objectives and follow the relevant performance measures. However, the overall performance of the organisation depends on the activities of the different organisational units of a museum. We propose placing greater emphasis on the internal focus of the organisation's performance, where the real activities take place. Therefore, in order to manage the performance of different departments, it is necessary to measure the performance of the museum as a whole alongside the performance at the level of the operational unit. This would permit creating a tighter link between the units' objectives and the strategic objectives of the organisation. In other words, it allows the whole organisation to shift in the desired direction. The performance measurement at the organisational unit level should evaluate the specific operating activities inherent to the different departments, which allows a more complex performance measurement and interactive management system to be created. This would also support the tighter communication between the different units of the museum.

Leaving the financial measures aside and focusing on budget execution aspects, the common non-financial measures used by museums are the number of exhibitions and the number of visitors to the museum. The latter are easy-to-follow measures and useful for comparison of different museums, but are not satisfactory when assessing the long-term performance and success of museums. The main questions that arise then are: what criteria could be applied to assess how successfully a museum is performing and how well the chosen performance measures can reflect the actual activities and outcomes of the museum. Therefore in the museum management context the performance measurement and management issues are rather complicated. As discussed by Thompson (2001) in terms of the New Zealand accounting reforms for museums, the general notion of non-financial measurement can often fail to evaluate the impacts relating to the performance period and the maintenance and enhancement of the resource base of the museum. Nevertheless, museums (as with other culture related organisations) are in a unique situation, where performance cannot be captured simply in financial terms.

As mentioned previously, for public sector organisations the objectives of the stakeholders and customers serve as the highest-ranking purposes. Hence it seems reasonable to distinguish between different stakeholders and their objectives in the context of museums. Gstraunthaler and Piber (2007) refer to four major stakeholder groups of a museum: politics, the business world, the scientific community and the world of art. For the realm of politics, success has often been translated in terms of the voters' favour. As stated by Schedler and Siegel (2005), strategic planning and strategy selection are political processes in the public sector. Although for the business world the most critical measurement is the capacity to create earnings, the museums' activities in building up, restoring, enlarging or opening collections to the public cannot be measured in simply economic terms. Therefore non-financial performance measures must be used to expand the scope of performance in museums.

Dworkin (1985) has pointed out that each generation has a moral duty to pass its cultural heritage on to the next generation intact. The analysis of museum activities, carried out by Thompson (2001), revealed that the current inputs contribute to the outputs and outcomes of future periods and the previous inputs contribute to the outputs and outcomes of the current period. He specified that objects displayed in an exhibition have often been conserved, restored and archived over many periods prior to the period in which the exhibition is held.

Therefore we can identify specific connections between the different time periods spanned by museum operations, and the operations of the museum departments. Performance measurement and management in museums need to be designed in a manner that provides an opportunity to have both strategic and operative objectives and, in addition, both organisational and departmental performance objectives. Through this chain of activities we can follow the specific value chain of a museum. Bovaird (2009) pinpoints value chain analysis as an important tool for the strategic internal environment analysis of a public organisation. Consequently, we can conclude that the implementation of the BSC at the museum level, as well as at department level, can serve as a tool of performance management that enables better connections and communication between the departments of a museum, and to the museum achieving its strategic goals.

16.3 Case description and research site

There are 235 museums in Estonia. Twenty per cent of them are owned by the State, 50 per cent by local governments, 25 per cent are private and 5 per cent are sub-units of public law organizations. The Museums Act, which regulates the operation of museums in Estonia, also provides a hierarchical categorisation of the museums. Of the total number there are 11 central museums which are governed by the Estonian Ministry of Culture and lead the collection and exhibition activities in different areas. The current case study is based on one of these museums, which we have named the *Central Museum* (CM).

CM was founded in 1909 and is one of the oldest museums in Estonia. It is a museum with a wide range of collections and various responsibilities and competences. The museum is also a cultural tourism and entertainment centre and a well-known research and educational institution. CM organises a variety of events for different stakeholder groups. The strategic approach of CM to performance management is a crucial issue, and is influenced by the planned completion of a new building in 2012. The new facility will increase the space available for exhibitions and museum educational facilities fivefold, and that available to collections fourfold. Thus, it will force managers to concentrate on ensuring that the overall capacity of the museum is utilised as effectively as possible, and that will require the management to pay particular attention to the planning system, and also to performance measurement and management.

The case study is based on primary and secondary sources. These include relevant legislation and regulations, the strategic development plan, annual reports and the museum's performance reports. Regulations and related documents provide a context for the functioning of performance measurement and management. The documental study was supplemented by information obtained through interviews with the director, the financial manager and senior staff members responsible for the main operating units of CM. Interviews were conducted in open-ended and semi-structured formats. The interviews concentrated on stakeholders, internal processes, learning and growth, and financial aspects within the abovementioned operating units. These four aspects help to specify the links between the overall strategic goals of the museum and the objectives of different operating units.

16.4 The main findings and discussion

16.4.1 Strategic management framework change in CM

The organisational structure of CM is based on four operational units (departments) representing the following areas:

- collection and preservation
- scientific research
- exhibitions and events
- museum pedagogy and education

Initially, the performance measurement and management of these operational units was seen by the managers as a mere formality. The main performance measures of the museum were officially the number of exhibitions and the number of visitors. The selection of the performance results of the operational units were regularly summarised, but the general assessment of the performance results and the actual impact on museum performance was poorly recorded. Periodic feedback control took place mainly at an operational unit level, creating problems with the cooperation between operational units. CM activity reporting was available to staff, but joint discussions and meetings about performance were not common in the museum. In general, a clear connection between the objectives and measures of the operational units was missing, and consequently there was no holistic approach to performance management or an appropriate measurement system to reflect the diverse nature and performance of the museum's operational units.

The Estonian Government Decree on the 'Types of Strategic Development Plans and Systems and the procedure of their Compilation, Implementation, Evaluation and Reporting' (adopted in 2005), requires institutions to compile a performance report on their success at meeting objectives and the effectiveness of actions on the implementation of their strategic development plan. The performance report is a basis on which to update the strategic development plan. However, the legislation does not give any methodical advice on planning, budgeting and reporting issues.

Changes in strategic management were prompted by the compilation of the strategic development plan for 2007–2010 in December 2006. The development process started with strengths, weaknesses, opportunities and threats (SWOT) analysis involving employees from all operational units. This was the first strategic development plan of CM, which was arranged by numerous joint discussions and collaboration, and replaced a previous formal annual plan specified under the direction of the Ministry of Culture. The director of the museum commented on this strategy development process:

> All people from all operational units were welcome to our strategic meetings. These meetings were common meetings. Joint discussions created a collective unity and the idea that different opinions are accepted and relevant. This was an impulse for further cooperation.

The strategy development process helped clarify the general mission and the strategic goals of the museum. The mission of CM was defined as follows: 'CM translates, interprets and disseminates Estonian and

Finno-Ugric culture'. The strategic plan defined by the following strategic goals of the museum (strategic development plan, 2006):

- CM will translate, interpret and disseminate Estonian and Finno-Ugric culture through different exhibitions and events;
- CM will be an internationally-acclaimed and trustworthy research centre with the main thrust focused on ethnological research;
- The CM collections will be well-organised; long-term preservation, expansion, systematic development and expedient and streamlined use of collections will be assured;
- CM will be a recognised museum studies centre;
- CM will be a well-functioning organisation.

These strategic goals involve all the main operational units of CM. Moreover, the collection and preservation, research, exhibition and museum education activities represent different stages of the value creation process, and the different operational units cover these stages of the museum's value chain. For example, the collection and preservation department has to conserve, restore and archive the objects displayed in an exhibition for a considerable time prior to the exhibition period. Also, the scientific research department operations have often been conducted before or in parallel with the exhibition period. Therefore the inter-department links (aside from the time connections) play a substantial role in achieving the museum's goals through the operations of the various units.

The development of the BSC started alongside that of the strategic development plan. The elaboration of the BSC proceeded from the mission and strategic goals stipulated in the museum's development plan for 2007–2010 and from the museum strategy map (see Figure 16.1). The strategy map of CM helps to connect the four BSC perspectives and the strategic goals of the museum. The CM scorecard distinguishes the following perspectives: stakeholders, finance, internal processes, and employees and capability of the organisation. The main stakeholder groups include process stakeholders (staff of the different operational units, including research fellows and museum management) and environmental stakeholders (exhibition and events visitors, local and international research community, students and teachers, the Ministry).

The **stakeholder perspective** is differentiated according to the various stakeholder groups and includes the following strategic objectives:

- for research fellows, diverse, broad-based and well-organised collections will be available;

Mission

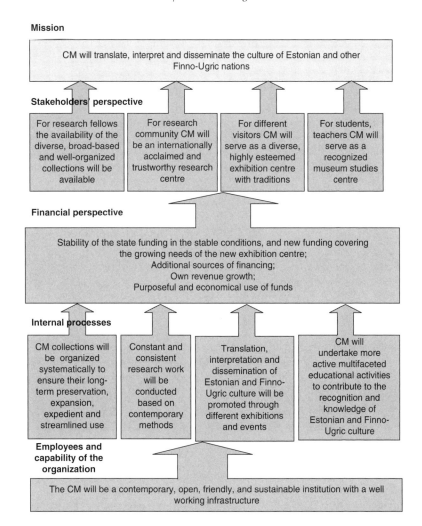

Figure 16.1   Strategic map of CM

- for the research community, CM will serve as an internationally acclaimed and trustworthy research centre;
- for different visitor groups CM will serve as a diverse, highly esteemed exhibition centre with sound traditions;
- for students and teachers, CM will serve as a recognised museum studies centre;

- for the Ministry, operational units, employees and museum management CM will serve as a well-functioning organisation.

CM is financed by the state, and in the main that financing is not dependent on CM achieving specific objectives and performance results. Therefore the most important objective from **the financial perspective** is to receive stable state financing to cover the museum operating and administration costs. The main donor, the Ministry of Culture, has a very important role in enabling stable state financing into CM. On the other hand, CM outputs, measured as the fulfilment of stakeholders' objectives, are important indicators that can serve as a basis for funding from the Ministry. Hence the Ministry has a double role as both a funder and a subscriber to cultural services. If both internal and external stakeholders are satisfied with the performance of CM, it will not lose visitors or alienate other stakeholders and the financial perspective will remain stable.

The **internal process perspective** includes activities which are necessary to meet the stakeholder perspective objectives and also to specify the need for financial resources. As the objectives and measures of the stakeholders' perspective were defined at an operational unit level, internal process targets and measures also had to be defined at the unit level. Proceeding from the strategic development plan of CM, the following objectives for the internal processes of each operational unit were developed:

- CM collections will be organised systematically to ensure their long-term preservation and expansion, and to ensure expedient and streamlined use (collection and preservation unit);
- constant and consistent research work will be conducted based on contemporary methods (research unit);
- translation, interpretation and dissemination of Estonian and Finno-Ugric language and culture will be promoted through different exhibitions and events (exhibitions and events unit);
- the unit will undertake more active, multi-faceted educational activity to contribute to the recognition and knowledge of Estonian and Finno-Ugric culture (museum pedagogy and education unit).

As a result of internal process analysis, the objectives and measures for the internal process perspectives were defined at the level of the four operational units of the museum. The ability of employees and the capability of the organisation serve as the input measure for internal processes and the financial and stakeholders' perspectives. The main aspects include a satisfied and professional staff with a stable turnover rate, professional IT support and a strong and positive organisational culture.

By using the BSC, the museum translated the mission and strategic goals of CM further into specific targets and measures for the lower managerial levels. Hence, the BSC design process first of all concentrated on the operational unit level. The specified targets in each BSC perspective can be linked via cause-and-effect relations into the department strategy maps, which clearly define the connections between targets and strategic objectives. Moreover, these department strategy maps, together with the corresponding performance measures help to examine the strategic achievements of the department.

16.4.2   Balanced scorecard perspectives and measures

In accordance with the discussion in the theoretical section and that above, the analysis revealed that the output and outcome of different operational units are addressed to the different stakeholders and customer groups of the museum. Therefore the stakeholder perspective was moved to the top of the BSC perspectives. Table 16.1 summarises the scorecard concept combining the four aspects of the scorecard and the CM operational units.

The stakeholder and internal processes aspects will be measured by unit-specific operational targets and measures; and the financial and personnel/employees and organisation's capability aspects by common targets and measures allocated to operational units.

In order to achieve the strategic objectives of the museum, different performance targets and measurement indicators were worked out for each operational unit. As mentioned above, the collection and preservation department would be responsible for the availability of the diverse, broad-based and well-organised collections, a responsibility that serves as a basis for the activities of other units.

Below we explain the BSC design, using its application in the collection and preservation unit as an example. Table 16.2 presents the unit-specific targets and corresponding performance measurement indicators used in the unit. The design of the BSC offered a way to combine the financial aspects and non-financial aspects. For instance, one of the stakeholder objectives was defined as enabling access to the museum collections for researchers, to be measured by indicators including the number of borrowed items and photocopies, the number of visiting researchers and readers, and the number of study and training courses based on

Table 16.1 BSC concept of the CM operational units

Operational Units Perspectives	Collection and preservation	Research	Exhibitions and events	Museum pedagogy and education
Stakeholders' perspective	Specific targets and measures	Specific targets and measures	Specific targets and measures	Specific targets and measures
Financial perspective	Common targets and measures allocated to operational units			
Internal processes perspective	Specific targets and measures	Specific targets and measures	Specific targets and measures	Specific targets and measures
Employees and organisation's capability perspective	Common targets and measures allocated to operational units			

the content of the collections. As a consequence of the stakeholders' perspective analysis, the objectives and measures for the stakeholders' aspects were also defined for other operational units.

In general, the financial targets and their corresponding measures were defined as common for the whole museum, not on an operational unit level, although in recent years the amounts of money required to operate the units and to assure the quality of the museum service has been generally established. Therefore the rate variance of the operational unit budget as a percentage of the whole CM budget will be used as a unit performance indicator. In light of the forthcoming new CM building, the implementation of zero-based budgeting methods should be foreseen. At the same time, CM is recognising more activities that offer an additional net contribution to museum financing.

Further, after the analysis of internal processes, targets and indicators were specified for all operational units of the museum, including the targets and performance measurement indicators of the collection and preservation unit (see Table 16.2).

All the targets and indicators were discussed and supported by senior and unit managers. The selected performance indicators help to measure the realisation of the selected targets, in turn helping to communicate the general strategy of the museum.

Based on the various BSC targets and the corresponding measures specified for the major operational units (collection and preservation;

Table 16.2   The BSC of the collection and preservation department in CM

Perspectives	Department targets	Performance measurement indicators
Stakeholders' perspective	Enabling access to the museum collections for researchers	Number of items borrowed and photocopies Number of visiting researchers and readers Number of study and training courses based on the collections
	The safekeeping of items for other museums' or organisations' needs	Number of items deposited Number of depositing institutions
	The supervision of other museums by the collecting and maintaining unit	Number of consultations
	The presentation of information about the collections to various target groups	Number of publications presenting the collections Number of lectures presenting collections
Financial perspective	Stability of central financing	Variance in operating costs Rate variance of department budget as % of CM budget
	Net revenue growth	Net revenue variance
	Efficient use of financing	Fulfilment of cost budget items
Internal processes	The systematic improvement of the collections of artefacts, photos, art, archives, and the library, including organising the annual collection of reference material and images	Number of units received by collections in comparison to the previous year Number of correspondents Number of contributors Number of senders of images Number of images and photos
	The scientific description, storage, preservation and conservation of fieldwork purchased, collected and from donations of articles, photographs and archival materials received	Number of items repaired in the preservation laboratory Number of controlled, ventilated and cleaned items in the collection Number of archived and preserved items Number of researched museum items Percentage of items preserved in the contemporary requirements

(*continued*)

Table 16.2   Continued

Perspectives	Department targets	Performance measurement indicators
	Digitisation of collections and images, insertion onto a database	Number of units associated with the database
	To conduct systematic inventories to maintain an adequate picture of the collections	Number of items in the museum
Employees and capability of the organisation	A satisfied, stable and professional staff	Rate of satisfaction Number of training courses e.g. IT courses attended Rate of employees with professional certification/ qualified/PHD degree
	A strong and positive organisational culture	Percentage of employees aware of the museum's vision and goals Number of interdepartmental cooperation groups/projects Percentage of employees supporting managerial decisions

scientific research; exhibitions and events; museum pedagogy and educational programs), strategy maps were compiled for each unit. The operational unit strategy map defines the connections between stakeholders, financial, internal processes and employees and the capability targets and measures. As an example, the strategy map of the collection and preservation department is reproduced in Figure 16.2.

Targets and corresponding performance measures detailed at an operational unit level as well as at the museum's management level provided an opportunity to develop the performance management system of the museum. The strategy map helps to define the links between different perspectives and to create consensus on the objectives and targets.

The formation of operational unit strategy maps helps to communicate the strategic goals across the organisation and to connect corresponding objectives using the BSC perspectives for each respective operational unit. The specification of corresponding targets and measures requires a

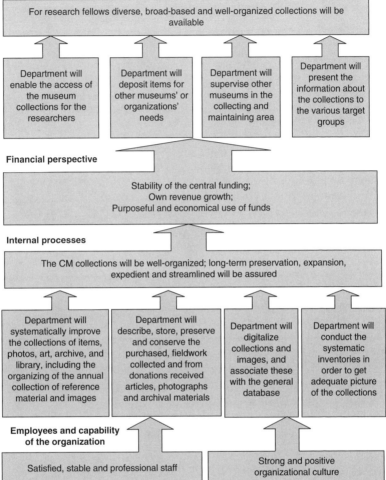

Figure 16.2   Strategic map of the Collection and Preservation department of CM

detailed approach, and is definitely not a simple task, as each operational unit has its own character and activities that shape the museum's overall performance. Nevertheless, setting out the targets and indicators at an operational unit level in a BSC format can serve as a tool that clarifies the relevant cause-and-effect linkages and the deployment of the general mission and strategic goals of the museum.

During the development of the BSC, colleagues from different operational units of the museum pointed out that the process of compiling a strategic development plan and designing the BSC concept made them aware that the BSC serves as a tool for dialogue on and the communication of strategic objectives between different operational units. They felt that consequently the BSC contributed to the creation of efficient value chain activities on a horizontal dimension. As a result, we can add that the BSC also serves as a tool for dialogue and communication between different management levels on the vertical dimension. Therefore our study revealed that the BSC, as an instrument, while contributing to the implementation of performance management in the public sector, also advanced the better understanding of objectives, strategies and success factors at the level of the whole museum as well as the operational unit level, thereby influencing the performance management of the main operating units.

16.5 Conclusion

Several aspects of performance measurement and management have come to be relevant issues in the course of the public reforms in Estonia. The developments in performance measurement and management are related to effective and efficient performance. The BSC, as a performance measurement and management instrument, can contribute to the better understanding of objectives, strategies and success factors on both the museum level and operational unit level. The main performance indicators illustrated the interdependent nature of the various departments and operations which influence the museum management through its range of management levels. Museum professionals found that they could use the BSC as a tool for dialogue and the communication of strategic objectives between different operational units.

The empirical findings revealed that the four perspectives of the BSC formed the frames for discussion and cooperation within and between operational units. Therefore a BSC can serve as a tool to link all stakeholder groups efficiently with each other, and may also provide a museum's senior management with an opportunity to manage those links. In addition, a BSC can contribute a number of connections within an interactive performance management system. Firstly, we identified specific connections between the different time periods affecting museum operations within different operation units or activity areas. Secondly, the main impacts and relations of performance measurement and management can be described by way of a conceptual model, where the value chain principles of the museum are combined with the respective input, output and outcome components. Third, the BSC concept design process serves as a dialogue and communication tool between different activity areas and operational units within the horizontal dimension of management. Fourth, the BSC contributes to level and quality of the communication between operational unit managers, the management board and the Ministry within the vertical dimension of management. Summing up, our study revealed that the BSC contributed to a better understanding of the objectives, strategies and performance indicators at the level of the museum as well as at department level.

Acknowledgement

The research in this chapter has been supported by funding from the Estonian Ministry of Education target funding SF0180037s08 and Estonian Science Foundation under grant agreement no. 7621.

References

Aidemark, L. G. (2001). 'The Meaning of Balanced Scorecard in Health Care Organisations', *Financial Accountability and Management*, 17 (1), 23–40.
Atkinson, A. A. and McCrindell, J. Q. (1997). 'Strategic Performance Measurement in Government, *CMA Magazine*, 20–23 April.
Ballantine, J., Brignall, S. and Modell, S. (1998). 'Performance Measurement and Management in public health services: A Comparison of UK and Swedish Practice, *Management Accounting Research*, 9, 71–94.
Bititci, U., Carrie, A. and McDevitt, L. (1997). 'Integrated Performance Measurement Systems: An Audit and Development Guide, *The TQM Magazine*, 9 (1).
Bovaird, T. in Bovaird, T. and Löffler, E. (eds.) (2009). 'Strategic Management in Public Sector Organisations', *Public Management and Governance*, 2nd edn, London, Routledge.
Chen, S. H., Yang, C. C. and Shiau, J. Y. (2006). 'The Application of Balanced Scorecard in the Performance Evaluation of Higher Education, *The TQM Magazine*, 18 (2), 190–205.
Elefalk, K. (2001). 'The Balanced Scorecard of the Swedish Police Service: 7000 Officers in Total Quality Management Project', *Total Quality Management*, 12 (7/8), 958–66.
De Geuser, F., Mooraj, S. and Oyon, D. (2009). 'Does the Balanced Scorecard Add Value? Empirical Evidence on Its Effect on Performance', *European Accounting Review*, 18 (1), 93–122.
Dworkin, R. (1985). 'Panel Discussion: Art as a Public Good', *Columbia Journal of Art and the Law*, 9, 143–78.
Gstraunthaler, T. and Piber, M. (2007). 'Performance Measurement and Accounting: Museums in Austria', *Museum Management and Curatorship*, 22 (4), 361–75.

Hood, C. (1995). 'Contemporary Public Management: A Global Paradigm?' *Public Policy and Administration*, 10 (2), 21–30.

International Council of Museums (ICOM) (2010). Available at http://icom. museum/.

Johnson, H. and Kaplan, R. (1987). *Relevance Lost: The Rise and Fall of Management Accounting*, Boston, Harvard Business School Press.

Kaplan, R. (1999). *The Balanced Scorecard for Public Sector Organisations*, Balanced scorecard report, Harvard Business School and Balanced Scorecard Collaborative, Cambridge, MA.

Kaplan, R. (2001). *Strategic Performance Measurement and Management in Nonprofit Organisations*, Nonprofit Management and Leadership, 11, 353–370.

Kaplan, R. (2009). 'Conceptual Foundations of the Balanced Scorecard' in Chapman, C. S., Hopwood, A. G. and Shields, M. D., *Handbook of Management Accounting Research*, London, Elsevier.

Kaplan, R. and Norton, D. (1992). 'The Balanced Scorecard – Measures that Drive Performance', Harvard Business Review, January/February, 71–9.

Kaplan, R. and Norton, D. (1996a). *The Balanced Scorecard: Translating Strategy into Actions*, Harvard Business School Press, Cambridge, MA.

Kaplan, R. and Norton, D. (1996b). 'Using the Balanced Scorecard as a Strategic Management System', Harvard Business Review, January/February, 75–85.

Kaplan, R. and Norton, D. (2001a). *The Strategy-focused Organisation: How Balanced Scorecard Companies Thrive in New Business Environment*, Harvard Business School Press, Boston, MA.

Kaplan, R. and Norton, D. (2001b). 'Transforming the Balanced Scorecard from Performance Measurement to Strategic Management: Part I', *Accounting Horizons*, 15 (1), 87–104.

Lawrence, S. and Sharma, U. (2002). 'Commodification of Education and Academic Labour Using the Balanced Scorecard in a University Setting', *Critical Visions on Accounting*, 13, 661–77.

Modell, S. (2004). 'Performance Measurement Myths in the Public Sector: A Research Note', *Financial Accountability and Management*, 20 (1), 39–55.

Mussari, R. (ed.) (2001). *Controllo di Gestione: Best Practices*, Rubettino.

Neely, A., Kennerly, M. and Walters, A. (2006). 'Performance Measurement and Management: Public and Private', Cranfield School of Economics.

Niven, P. R. (2002). *Balanced Scorecard: Step by Step*, John Wiley & Sons, New York, NY.

Peters, D., Noor, A., Singh, l., Kakar, F., Hansen, P. and Burnham, G. (2007). 'A Balanced Scorecard for Health Services in Afghanistan', *Bulletin of the World Health Organization*, 85 (2).

Qudrat-Ullah, H., Chow, C. and Goh, M. (2007). 'Towards A Dynamic Balanced Scorecard Approach: The Case of Changi General Hospital in Singapore', *International Journal of Enterprise Network Management*, 1 (3), 230–7.

Reussner, E. M. (2003). 'Strategic Management for Visitor-oriented Museums', *International Journal of Cultural Policy*, 9 (1) 95–108.

Schedler, K. and Siegel, J. P. (2005). *Strategisches Management in Kommunen*, Düsseldorf, Hans Böckler Stiftung.

Simons, R. (1995). *Levers of Control: How Managers Use Innovative Control Systems to Drive Strategic Renewal*, Harvard Business School Press, Boston, MA.

Sundin, H., Granlund, M. and Brown, D. (2010). 'Balancing Multiple Competing Objectives with Balanced Scorecard', *European Accounting Review*, 19 (2), 203–46.

Thompson, G. (2001). 'The Impact of New Zealand's Public Sector Accounting Reforms on Performance Control in Museums', *Financial Accountability and Management*, 17 (1), 5–21.

Wilson, C., Hagarty, D. and Gauthier, J. (2003). 'Result Using the Balanced Scorecard in the Public Sector', *Journal of Corporate Real Estate*, 6 (1), 53–63.

Index